PROMISE KEEPERS:
Another Trojan Horse

D0167044

Phil Arms

PROMISE KEEPERS:
Another Trojan Horse

Shiloh
Publishers

Promise Keepers: Another Trojan Horse
Copyright © 1997 by Phil Arms. Published by Shiloh
Publishers, Houston, Texas 77083.

Second Priniting, 1997

All rights reserved. No part of this publication may be
reproduced, stored in a retrieval system or transmitted in
any form by any means, electronic, mechanical, photocopy,
recording, or otherwise, without the prior permission of
the publisher, except as provided by USA copyright law.

Except where otherwise indicated, all Scripture quotations
in this book are taken from the *King James Version of the
Bible*.

The Scripture quotations identified NIV are from *the Holy
Bible: New International Version®*. NIV®. Copyright ©
1973, 1978, 1984 by International Bible Society. Used by
permission of Zondervan Publishing House. All rights
reserved.

Printed in the United States of America.

Library of Congress Catalog Card Number 96-071761

ISBN 1-890058-01-7 Paperback
ISBN 1-890058-00-9 Hardcover

Dedication

To the pastors and ministers who grace the pulpits across America and who faithfully carry the burden of the Lord. Many of these great men of God will never be widely known or be heralded in the religious Hall of Fame. Yet, the hearts of these special vessels beat with a love for the Word of God and the God of the Word. It is they who have stayed the impending judgment of God on this nation and who have paid the price to raise His standard high.

I dedicate this book to these pastors whose earthly fame may never reach beyond their own congregants but whose names are known by the dark spirits of the underworld. These prestigious defenders of the faith have far greater riches reserved and waiting just beyond the horizon. For their undying allegiance and personal sacrifices to the cause of Christ, the people of the Kingdom owe them the deepest debt of gratitude.

CONTENTS

Foreward   xi

Acknowledgments   xv

PART I - Makers of Men   17

Introduction   19

Chapter 1   **A Phenomenon**   21
                Carpe Diem

Chapter 2   **Find a Need and Meet It**   29
                Recognizing the Need / Meeting the Need

Chapter 3   **From Wimpy Men and**   35
                Weeping Women to Towers
                of Power - The Lady's Desire
                It is No Accident / Getting Under the Skin

PART II - "Just Little Doctrines That   45
                Do Not Matter Much...Do They?"

Chapter 4   **The Roots of an Idea**   47
                Whose Time Has Come...
                Over, and Over, and Over Again
                But Ugly Stepsisters Keep On Trying /
                It Can Get Heavy / So, What is a Promise
                Keeper? / The Analysis of Paralysis or is
                it the Paralysis of Analysis? / It's Just a
                Horse

Chapter 5   **"That Crazy Bible" and the**   61
                Deceptive Depravity of Sincerity
                The Truth of the Matter / He Didn't Bore
                In, He was Born In / "Put That Bible
                Away" / "But We All Believe the Bible!"/
                Does Promise Keepers Leadership Believe
                the Bible? / "Who Said the Bible is All
                God Has to Say?"

Chapter 6   **The Premise of a Promise**   73
"But Ya' Gotta Believe in You...Don't
Ya'?" / Morality...Counterfeit
Righteousness / Invaded

Chapter 7   **"Time is Now Going to be**   85
                 Extended"
Another Limited View of God / A Biblical
View versus the Limited View - The
Geometry of Eternity / At Issue is the
Character of God

Chapter 8   **They Called This "Revival"**   93
Short Cuts and Dead Ends / "But We Will
Be Like God"

Chapter 9   **What is Wrong With This**   105
                 Picture?
God's Nature versus Man's Nature / The
Limitations of Imitations / Is God
Replicating Himself? / Do You See It?

PART III - The Big Seven   117

Prologue   119

Chapter 10   **Good Versus Evil**   121
                 in the Enchanted Forest
Seven Dwarfs, Seven Promises

Chapter 11   **Promise #1: Sleepy**   129
A Case In Point

Chapter 12   **Promises #2 and #3:**   141
                 Bashful and Grumpy

Chapter 13   **Promises #4 and #5:**   149
                 Doc and Dopey

Chapter 14   **Promises #6 and #7:**   165
                 Happy and Sneezy

Epilogue   181

PART IV - The Terror Within the Trojan Horse 183

Chapter 15   The Evolution of a Revolution   185
*The Failure of Early Warning Systems /
Backup Systems Flash / The Department
of Defense and the Integrationist / Subtle
Seditions / A Breach in the Lines / The
Insufficiency of God's Word / The
Sculpting of Manure*

Chapter 16   The Babble of Babel   205
*"Truth Just Needs a Bit of Tweaking" /
The Promise Keepers' Jesus and the
Phallus*

Chapter 17   It Ain't Necessarily So   217
*You Better Take a Closer Look / Beatles
"Bring Revival" / Promise Keepers
Attempts Damage Control / The Wizards
of Ahs, Oohs and Praise the Lords*

**Chapter 18   The Big Daddy of Promise   243
                Keepers and the Third Wave Wonder**
*The Promise Keepers Tie to the Wimber
Wonder Wave / Spiritual Arsonist and
Strange Fire / Spiritual Barking, Soaking
and Laughing: It's All in the Family*

Chapter 19   Is it the Beauty or the Beast?   257
*Born in the Belly of Deception / The Seed
That Bore This Fruit / Covenantalism and
Kool-Aid*

Chapter 20   Dances With Wolves   271
*"Yeah, But Everybody is Doing It" /
Tolerance, the Betrayer of Truth / The
Lady or the Tramp / Accentuating the
Positive and Eliminating...the Truth*

**Chapter 21   The Baskin "Robbing" Jesus   285
                of Promise Keepers**
*The Promise Keeping Mormons / Promise
Keepers Try Face Lift / "Kissing Papa's
Ring" / Transubstantiation / Homo-Bro's
in the Promise Keepers Family /
Sensitivity Course Softens Promise
Keepers Men*

been personally and privately contacted by this author, as well as by others with equally deep convictions and burdens concerning this horrid deception being perpetrated on the Church. Most of these contacts are referenced within this work and all are thoroughly documented.

While many of these Christian leaders refused to even acknowledge our honest, open and always gentle inquiry, others among them responded to our private requests with either defensive, condescending or contradictory replies. It was this author's intent to include all of these responses in the Appendix of this book until it was pointed out that to publish those letters would be a violation of copyright laws. Had we been able to publicly share these letters, discerning hearts would have unmistakably witnessed the inconsistencies, the blatantly unbiblical reasoning, the tragic display of pragmatism and the new so-called tolerance that grips vast segments of the American Church.

After aggressive, extended and prayer-saturated efforts to fulfill, to the letter as well as to the spirit, the scriptural procedure to deal with those aforementioned persons and their root beliefs, and upon seeing their response or lack thereof to legitimate and scripturally mandated inquiries, the options of what to do next were limited, indeed.

For those whose desire it is to professionally play it safe, to acquiesce to the pressure for political correctness now invading the Church or who seek promotion among men, the contents herein will be taboo. I am certain that to such people the publication of this book was the wrong choice. Regardless of the clarity of the facts and the truthfulness of the present reality, such persons will not be moved or seek to move others away from this growing deception. Fear and deception are as closely related as are Truth and boldness.

The doctrinal revisionism occurring in many spheres of American Christendom over the last four decades has resulted in an almost unconscious transplanting of much of today's Christian ministries' roots into the soils of Jungian-Freudian psychology.

Yet, in all of these variant strains of psychology, there is woven a common thread. It is the principle of "self-preservation," the idea that "I am not to blame for my condition. External forces, over which I have no power or control, have victimized me. Hence, I am not to blame."

There is an overt, as well as covert effort in much of our contemporary Christian literature, ministries and pulpits to exonerate the sinner of any and all guilt. He must be left an "out" so he can "save face." However, men cannot save face and simultaneously seek and find God's face.

The recognition of these truths, combined with an intense investigation into the contemporary Christian men's movement, leaves no doubt about the powerfully deceptive nature of a very real enemy whose strategy is as invasive and as subtle as a serpent.

All the foggy reluctance concerning the pursuit of writing and releasing this book dissipated rapidly in the sunlight of His revealing Word and the discovery of so much confusion rampant among so many concerning the anti-Christian means employed to reach the questionable goals of this new Trojan Horse.

It is too late for trivial semantic jousting and routine doctrinal debate with the clandestine oppressors of Truth and the would-be correctors of the ways of God. Pulpits and Christians with a "finger-in-the-wind theology" will not stand the test now being unleashed on His Church.

With most diligent prayer and the casting aside of unnecessary cautions and illegitimate reluctance, this effort to obey the Pauline admonition "to contend for the faith, once delivered to the saints" is submitted to the Berean heart which is still beating in the Body of Christ. May the truths contained in these pages encourage men and women of God everywhere to "be sober, be vigilant because your adversary, the devil, as a roaring lion, walketh about, seeking whom he may devour." 1 Peter 5:8. Amen and Amen.

To His Glory,
Phil Arms

Acknowledgments

A project of this magnitude demands a considerable commitment of time and energies far beyond the abilities of one person. There are a multitude of individuals who carried much of the ministerial responsibilities that I might stay focused for the time required to complete this book.

My loving, supportive and understanding wife, a major contributor to the redemptive value of this book, made sacrifices above and beyond the call of duty. She graciously tolerated listening to my continuous re-reading of a constantly changing manuscript as it evolved through countless edits and rewrites.

Surely, God has never created a more patient, more virtuous or more brilliant woman than Suzanne. Her rock-solid convictions, her love for God's Word and her unflinching commitment to maintain scriptural integrity in her teaching and lifestyle were and are inspirational and instrumental in the completion of this work.

The staff of Phil Arms Ministries and the membership of Houston Church, where I have pastored for over ten years, can be neither equaled nor surpassed in the encouraging role they have played over these many months of research and writing. Every day I thank God for the privilege to serve with such a magnificently committed people. I have never felt worthy of their love, support and gracious willingness to see beyond the walls of their building to a world desperate for the clearest declaration of God's Truth.

No words can express the gratitude I have for the individual who typed and retyped this ever-changing manuscript. Frank

Introduction

You may well be among the thousands of people who have been touched, blessed, or spiritually inspired by one of the most fascinating phenomena in American church history. In its remarkably short life span of approximately five years, this ministry to men known as Promise Keepers has experienced what can only be called a *"supernatural"* numerical growth to which no other single ministry in modern times can lay claim.

Its ever-increasing influence has swept the nation as a tidal wave of hope. Without doubt, this ministry has been more singularly responsible for tearing down denominational barriers, bringing together diverse ethnic and cultural groups and uniting a *trans*-denominational, *trans*-religious common *"brotherhood"* than any other ministry in America's 300-year church and secular history.

Additionally, without question, the public support from among the nation's highest profile, best-known and highly-respected ministries and ministers has been without precedent and overwhelming. Representing a broad range of diverse denominations and otherwise conflicting philosophies and theologies, these leaders in the field of religion, psychology and relational counseling are promoting Promise Keepers as one of the greatest things to happen to manhood since womanhood.

Network news, the secular press and some in the highest offices in political leadership in America, including the President, have been forthcoming with glowing commentary on the positive influence Promise Keepers is having on the church, society and normally, spiritually unresponsive American men. Ever-increasing numbers of men and women across the nation, both churched and unchurched, religious and non-religious, Christian and non-Christian are praising the sudden and dynamic change in men's lives as a result of this ministry. Equally astounding are the testimonies of its power to touch the soul and psyche of the American male.

When such an obvious historic and unprecedented movement so authoritatively strikes the core need of a people's heart, it must not and cannot go without intense, analytic scrutiny. Such apparent success demands a closer look.

It must be determined why and how Promise Keepers is achieving its goal of producing the fully masculine, spiritual and relationally adjusted man. Historically, men have considered any effort to make them sensitive, spiritually tuned and domestically responsible as an attempt to weaken their manhood. The traditional church's reach toward this same goal has been met with resilient and persistent resistance.

The perception of the church's failure and its obvious lack of numerically successful and clearly focused men's ministries have created a gargantuan and desperate need for a ministry that appeals to the hearts of men. Any church that desires to produce spiritually mature, fully masculine and heroic role models should take notice and throw the full weight of their influence, support and resources into the dynamic ministry of Promise Keepers... shouldn't they?

This book takes a close look at the *"promise"* behind the Promise Keepers. What you see may shock you. Regardless of any opinion, if any, you may hold respecting Promise Keepers, this investigation will move you closer to clear answers on the questions that Promise Keepers' glowing success has raised.

"I have made you an assayer and a tester among my people that you may know and assay their way."

Jeremiah 6:27

CHAPTER 1

A Phenomenon

The biggest shock was that the secular media reported it in the first place. Then came a second shock: the full-page story, complete with color pictures, was not even buried in the sacred folds of the religion section.

Thousands of men, tens of thousands of men, were flocking to a "religious service." Clamoring, enthusiastic, appearing exuberant, these 50,000 men crammed into the University of Colorado's Folsom Stadium with more zeal than that of a Super Bowl crowd, creating an atmosphere of anticipation reminiscent of a boy about to catch his first big fish.

Some had been here the year before. Most in attendance had only heard of the challenging opportunity to combine their masculinity and their manhood with their responsibility and their call as men and to do so with guys just like themselves. All their friends, neighbors, churches and even the local media were lauding and promoting the event.

This, they knew, would be an event to remember.

They could *"feel"* the expectation of a *"happening."*

As they sat in the midst of this massive gathering of men, a menagerie of *"mini-rallies"* across the sea of bodies had already begun.

This was like the pre-game thrill of a major sports contest.

there were no books, then the pages of history, especially contemporary American history, are a resounding, deafening alarm that *"his"* absence at the helm of our society is leading to a national disaster from which we might never recover.

Every segment of society, with the exception of the extreme feminist fringe, long ago recognized the need.

Recognizing the Need

The need for the American male to resist the ever-growing temptation to conform to the comfort of an invertebrate society looms large. Additionally, men in our nation desperately need to realize that flexibility in the area of convictions and ethics, though perhaps good for personal economies, poisons personal spirituality. And last, but truly not least of all, men need to be willing to divest resources once devoted to the temporal and personal pursuits and to invest in their character and families, endeavors that produce virtuous results.

In short, America's families, youth, children and women need men to be *"real men."* Men need men to be *"real men."*

Meeting the Need

The genius of creativity is understanding what pleases and then producing the pleasure. It is becoming the matchmaker of the perceived need to its supply. If the need is to develop *"real men,"* then central to meeting that demand is defining a *"real man"*.

In his book, *"What Makes A Man?"*,[1] Bill McCartney defines his concept of God's ideal *"real man"*. God, according to McCartney's book, wants men to be responsible leaders in the church, the home and the community. He emphasizes that to be transformed from a mere man to a *"real man,"* such a man must commit to what he calls "the three non-negotiables of manhood: integrity, commitment and action."[2]

McCartney drives home his points with a fervor, zeal and infectious excitement about the possibility of men fleshing out this new kind of man. He states, "If you were to take the word integrity and reduce it to its simplest terms, you would conclude that a man of integrity is a promise keeper. He's a guy who, when he says something, can be trusted. When he gives his word, you can take it to the bank. His word is good."[3]

McCartney's pleasant fanaticism and commitment captured the hearts of enough men with imagination and resources to launch the effort that would catapult his vision and cause into the heavens of reality.

Leighton Ford of the Billy Graham Association wrote about listening to McCartney speak of his number one goal in life: "What he said has stuck with me to this day. He said, 'We want to beat Notre Dame and want to be Number One. But my real goal is to use what influences I have to help raise up a generation of promise keepers. I think we need people in our country who will be promise keepers in our family, in our businesses, in our public life, in everything.'"[4]

Obviously, a lot of people felt as though Bill McCartney was echoing their own deeply felt convictions. Otherwise, what has happened since would never have transpired.

Promise Keepers has experienced a phenomenal and unprecedented growth. From the first convention held in Boulder, Colorado, at the Coors Event Center in 1991, it was obvious that a *"raw nerve of need"* had been touched. More than 4,200 men showed up to hear challenges, instruction and motivation on how to become "men of responsibility" in the home, the church and the community. Even the organizers were astounded at the response.[5]

Success propelled the leadership into a deeper commitment and led to an aggressive, intense and well-organized preparation not only for additional coming conventions, but for the founding of a full-time, professional, polished, top-notch staff.

By the time the 1992 convention came around, the crowd grew to well over 22,000 men. The next year's convention attracted 50,000 men.[6]

In 1994, sensing the national readiness for men to be called to arms, the Promise Keepers organization, as it was now known, held seven different conventions in various return." From coast to coast, observers of the nation's religious scene could see the plume of the smoking rockets now poised to boost the Promise Keepers Ministries into the annals of Church history.

Founder Bill McCartney became a mere figurehead in the movement as the administration fell to president of the organization, Randy Phillips, and his staff. The Promise Keepers staff, formed in 1993 with 22 full-time personnel and a budget of $4 million, had grown to 400 full-time employees and an estimated budget of $145 million by 1996.[13]

Much of the secular and religious community in America is aware of the ministries of Promise Keepers' most aggressive supporters, keynote speakers and promoters. Among them are Campus Crusade founder, Bill Bright; president and founder of Focus on the Family, psychologist, Dr. James Dobson; and best-selling author and psychologist, Dr. Gary Smalley. Other well-known names continue to promote Promise Keepers Ministries, calling it "the greatest spiritual awakening the world has known since the birth of the Church at Pentecost." In fact, it is difficult to find anyone of national prominence who has anything but praise for the powerful impact that Promise Keepers is having on American men. It would be tough to find any national move of notoriety in the annals of church or secular world history that has drawn together such mammoth numbers of so many diverse philosophies and religious beliefs while simultaneously drawing so little criticism.

This incredible momentum was due to far more than good public relations. It seemed to most that, at last, legitimate need, through a stroke of perceptive genius and heightened discernment, had been identified and coupled with its supply.

Promise Keepers was not just "off the launching pad"; it was headed into orbit with "all systems go".

"There are some people that if they do not know, you cannot tell them."

—Unknown

CHAPTER 3

From Wimpy Men and Weeping Women to Towers of Power— the Lady's Desire

"A prudent man foreseeth the evil, and hideth himself; but the simple pass on, and are punished."

Proverbs 22:3

Almost every minister, psychologist and marriage counselor says the same thing when asked about our nation's fundamental domestic needs. The *"crying* (no pun intended) *need"* in America, according to women in counseling sessions, is the resurrection of manhood in the home, the church and nation. The obvious and steadily increasing *"absence"* of the American husband and father has been the single most devastating element to work against the American family and society.

The statistics on divorce, single parenting, juvenile crime, drug addiction and pregnancies among minors have skyrocketed in the last two decades. We cannot ignore the correlation frustration level with the American male by American females has "red lined" and is boiling over.

Every social and spiritual indication in society was on its feet with fist in the air 20 years ago demanding "change." Now, with frustration having turned to desperation, women and society have stopped stomping their feet and have fallen to their knees hoping, praying and holding on with their last ounce of inner resilience for the possibility of miraculous change in the spiritual posture and attitude of men in America. The cry went from "We're *not* gonna take it anymore" to "We're too exhausted and *can't* take it anymore." And now, in answer to the secret prayers and deepest desires of millions of women across America, a miracle seems to be happening. Thousands, tens of thousands, hundreds of thousands of men are flocking to conventions across the nation to discover how to become *"real men"* of responsibility, character and integrity. It is almost too good to be true but it does appear that a new, fresh breeze is stirring hearts across the heartland of America.

But why is this happening now? How is it that now, in our most despairing and needy moment, an answer comes that so overwhelmingly meets the needs of so many and can possibly save the home, the family and, ultimately, this nation?

It Is No Accident

President Franklin Roosevelt once said, "In the world of politics, nothing ever happens by accident." That axiom also holds true in the world of spiritual matters. The absolute laws of human tendencies and needs energize sociological cycles that historically repeat themselves.

One of humanity's strongest natural desires repeatedly clashes with another of its strongest natural drives. The desire to follow leadership that exhibits qualities worthy of our acquiescence conflicts with our drive to rebel against authority. Man's (and woman's) natural bent to cast off the restraints and government of an external nature creates a vacuum in the individual and the social soul. The resulting dominating philosophy of most twentieth-century cultures seems to be a resolution that we will be in servitude but we will choose our master. The consequence is often great servitude to horrific masters which ultimately and repeatedly leads to another "revolution" resulting only in a new master.

Between our indentures, we experience that vacuum which cannot long remain empty. The nature of the vacuum creates a vulnerability in both the individual as well as the society. The longer the vacuum exists, the more intensely we search to fill it. Most often, the force that fills such a vacuum of leadership is one that seemingly *"promises"* much, but ultimately delivers little.

History verifies that as this social evolution produces each of our successive masters, each master becomes increasingly worse and more maliciously tyrannical. With the exception of those who discover the Supreme Master, the *"promise"* they progressively believe and follow is more enslaving, dominating and evil than its predecessor. Megalomaniacal personalities and powers prowl the human horizon seeking *"slaves"* who are searching for masters.

History is replete with illustrations but one of the more contemporary is seen in 1930's Germany. After World War I, Germany was a defeated and humiliated nation whose people had been deceived and led into a war to win the glory of world dominance. The nation's government, the Weimar Republic, had led Germany instead to death, destruction and, ultimately, poverty and severe depression. Its national war debt, devastated industrial capabilities and exhausted populace faced a national economy with a 12,000% inflation rate. It became worse, literally, with each passing hour.

Despair ultimately crushed what little semblance of confidence the nation had in its defeated government officials and gave way to a spiritual depression to accompany its economic depression. In this atmosphere of utter hopelessness and emotional and national deprivation, a mustached, third-class artist who had flunked out of school and failed in every human endeavor he had ever attempted, within a few short years, rose from a prison cell to the most powerful dictatorship since the Roman Caesears. His platform and plans for the resurrection of the German people, economy and nation was all too simplistic.

Adolf Hitler faced a nation and a people tired of trying, exhausted from fighting a losing battle and starving for security and a restoration to its former glory. Hitler understood the principle that need demands supply.

Historians, philosophers and political analysts have asked for decades: How did a man like Hitler do it?

Simply put, Hitler made *"promises."* But Hitler's promises, even though some eventually came to pass, were hollow and built upon an ancient Nordic and pagan religion. Even as the populace began to see the fangs of the terrible theo-political monster of Nazism, most, because of the new stability and promises, stood hand-in-hand with their Führer. They were extremely pragmatic.

People desperate for relief and a return to power and plenty were ready accomplices. To every promise Hitler gave, they gave an ear, discounting the root and choosing to lose themselves in the *"sweet taste of the fruit."*

The result: World War II and 60 million people dead.

One philosopher has said, "One thing we never learn from history is that we never learn from history."

Nations indeed, at least externally, seem to have become more politically sophisticated and while still a few remain in power, dictators and despots are not the trend in most parts of the world. However, the human memory is short and it only takes one or two generations for societies to forget the profound necessity for checks and balances in human governments.

The failure in Germany was not the failure of a democratically elected Weimar Republic whose despotic leadership brought Germany to its knees begging for a national and economic savior which ultimately resulted in Hitler's election. The failure in Germany was the spiritual failure of its people long before the appearance of the Weimar Republic. This failure was not due to a lack of theological moorings. Indeed, the world's leading theologians were German. The German populace was for the most part churched. Dominantly Catholic and Lutheran, with smatterings of other smaller Protestant groups, the German people were a "religious people." But when a nation's religion accommodates the governed, it will soon accommodate the government. And religion has yet to produce life, light or a passion for theological and biblical purity.

By and large, with the exception of a few godly men like Dietrich Bonnhoefer, the major theologians of Germany, the Lutheran and Catholic churches and the rest of the religious community welcomed the coronation of the Nazi party and all its atrocities.

People get the government they deserve. When there is a willingness to take moral short cuts to spiritual or fiscal prosperity, the quick fix always leads to false hopes and certain destruction.

God meant men's knees to bend only to Him.

The German people found themselves pleading for relief on bended knee. When their materialistic messiah came with his *"promise"* for prosperity, their bended knees never straightened again. He demanded they maintain the same posture not in prayer to God, but in worship to him. It took a short while, but kneeling knees became the accustomed position of Germans not only in worship of Hitler, but also soon back into prayers for deliverance. They cried for deliverance from *"promises"* Hitler could not or would not keep.

Promises, if they are to bring lasting redemptive change, must be built upon far more than an economic, political, social or even religious foundation. Otherwise, those who follow the *"promise makers"* will sooner or later discover their end is worse than was their beginning.

Getting Under the Skin

The determination born within the soul of a desperate person or nation can produce a willingness to sacrifice what may appear, in such despair, to be non-essentials. This is especially true in a people who are prone to "instant gratification" and immediate relief. The *"Where do I sign?"* syndrome causes a rush to conclusion without the reading of the fine print. And often, ignoring the fine print is not a result of stupidity. We do not want to be encumbered with or hindered by the anxiety caused by knowing what it says.

"Hope deferred maketh the heart sick..." (Proverbs 13:12) is at the root of our desire to hold on to subliminal fantasies as long as possible. In desperate moments, after suffering for so long, when all things we have hoped for finally begin to come into focus and are so close to becoming a reality, we speak to the nay-sayers our warnings to "back off" with their negative observations.

"If I am dreaming, do not wake me up" is the cliché of the day; or, in the words of a popular "Christian" song a few years ago: *"How can it be so wrong when it feels so right?"*

"Sleepwalking" is a dangerous habit. However, a greater danger is "spiritual sleepwalking." Add the catastrophic possibilities of spiritual sleepwalking to the intense ferocity of the one who vehemently demands that no one wakes him and you have the ingredients for total and irreversible disaster.

Internal stresses resulting from external pressures and the desperation created when Christians are deprived of solid doctrinal moorings have left this generation of churches and Christians vulnerable to deception. This vulnerability has been magnified by the fact that, other than the horrific period known as the Dark Ages, people are more biblically illiterate and intellectually and spiritually unmotivated now than they have been during any other moment in history. This generation does not want to be confused with the facts or distracted by the fine print. And yet rejection of spiritual revelation and light ultimately leads to spiritual darkness. Spiritual darkness leads to a reversal in the cognitive powers of scripturally enlightened reasoning. Conclusions and decisions become relative to social trends and personal tastes, desires and opinions.

Pragmatism, which has come to mean doing whatever works best to bring about the desired results, has become the prominent guiding philosophy in the nation's leading evangelical circles. This philosophy, though practiced by many in spiritual leadership in America, is not fundamental to Christian doctrine. It is, rather, a self-contained doctrine that asserts the truth is ascertained by its practical consequences. If one's desired results are the consequences of certain actions, then all such actions are thereby condoned and morally acceptable. Truth is subject to change based upon circumstances and consequences. *Things* are either accepted or rejected on the basis of subjective criteria, not on the premise of *right or wrong*. The line between the extremes of *right and wrong* is blurred to such a degree that there is hardly a line at all. And if there is such a line, surely, the thinking goes, *right* cannot be *that right* nor can *wrong* be *that wrong*. Or perhaps there is something *so right* that the tolerance of *some wrong* is acceptable. To follow such convoluted thinking to its natural conclusion will allow for any *wrong* to ultimately be homogeneous and compatible with any *right*. Makes sense, doesn't it? No, it does not. To those who believe and accept the Bible as absolute Truth, there can be no marriage between the light and the darkness.

But, tragically for many who are too absorbed in this "sleepwalking" to be awakened, pragmatism has become their unspoken philosophy. Few such people host this parasitic way of thinking by design.

Leadership in churches has experienced digressive spiritual evolution. The result has been an incorporation of the DOW Jones mentality into the church. It says, *"Bigger is better and biggest is best."*

It is irrelevant to speak of biblically established facts to those who believe that results, consequences and circumstances moderate or change *"Truth"* once held as immutable. Few conservative, Bible-believing Christians—especially ministers— would admit to such an invasion of relativity into their beliefs and practices. Yet when it comes to taking a closer look at their support of the Trojan Horses that are invading the Church, the attitude of multitudes is, *"Please do not bother me with the facts"* or, if you would, *"What's truth got to do with promise keeping?"*

Asking, *"What does truth have to do with promise keeping?"* is akin to asking, *"What has marital love got to do with sex?"* In both instances, divine design originally meant *"truth and promises"* as well as *"love and sex"* to be intimate, inseparable companions. One divorced from the other is impotent, vulgar and unredemptive.

Has the church in America and its leadership become so

hungry for numerical success and the approval of the masses that Truth has become expendable? Have *"keepers and makers of promises"* become more desired than the standards for Truth? If so, how much Truth are we willing to sacrifice on the altar of success, even spiritual success?

And last, are the sacrifices of Truth, no matter how seemingly small, neutering the victories of our successes? Alas, the missing link is the absence of intense emotional and spiritual energy needed to utilize focused discernment. Thus, the church is vulnerable to deception and a spiritually counterfeited revival that is aborting a legitimate move of God on men and a nation.

PART II

"Just Little Doctrines That Do Not Matter Much...Do They?"

> *"Yea, hath God said...?"*
>
> Genesis 3:1

"Can God-ordained objectives be achieved by the use of man-made means to reach that objective?"

—Phil Arms

CHAPTER 4

The Roots of an Idea Whose Time Has Come... Over, and Over, and Over Again.

"It is hard to fight an enemy who has outposts in your head."

—Kempton

Religionists, philosophers and thinkers (you would think thinkers would *"think"* about legitimate options) have for centuries attempted to figure out the who, why and where questions: "Who am I?" "Why am I here?" and "Where am I going?" They have a hard time answering these questions because they have removed the possibility that God is a God who is personally and intricately involved in the stream of human history. Yet nothing makes much sense if He is not in the equation. Hence, every philosophy, regardless of its sophistication and intellectual attractiveness, is ultimately grouped into one of two rather large stacks of tired old piles of thought.

One of those piles is *"existentialism"* and the other is *"humanism."* The two, of course, are close cousins because they both draw upon man's wisdom and reject God's Truth. It is a strange twist that the promoters of such pagan philosophies classify themselves under the title of *"New Age thinking"*. There is nothing *"new"* about anti-God, man-centered religion. It is as old as the Garden of Eden from whence it all began. So, in the words of some astute and observant individual, *"What is True is not NEW and what is NEW is not TRUE."*

Men attempting to solve their social, domestic and relational problems keep dragging out these tired old *"religions"* to prop up their *"new ideas"* and new approaches to lift humanity upward and onward. Oh, humanity needs help, no doubt. But Band-Aids are useless on a corpse. Man needs more, far more, than therapeutic adjustments, philosophical tuning or a more refined self-image. Today's success and growth formulas, while valuable in a nursery, are worthless in a graveyard. Every effort to improve, remold, redesign or lift man to fulfill His Creator's original intent and design is futile unless and until we confront the Truth of man's condition and dilemmas.

But Ugly Stepsisters Keep On Trying

It is the long-held biblical conviction of Orthodox Christianity that man's sinful nature is his greatest problem. He is cut off from life as a result of his inherent rebellion against a loving God who has gone to great lengths to intervene in humanity's mad rush to destruction.

The Bible clearly defines man's dilemma. The one thing man needs beyond anything else is a relationship with God. Yet that which he needs the most is that which man resists most aggressively.

The Gospel is no *"new thing."* It predates history, and in fact was instituted *"before the foundation of the world."* It is clearly the nature of God to supply the need of man. God's grace presupposed the need that would rapidly develop after the creation. The Divine solution for man's pollution is discovered only when men apply the biblically ordained principles that reintroduce him to his Creator. This reintroduction, or new birth, redeems the whole man, changes his nature, establishes a relationship with a Heavenly Father and empowers him to discover the enlivened Word of God. The individual cost for new birth is no less than death to self, repentance of sin and commitment to the lordship of Jesus Christ.

God's prescription for the living dead, humanity in their sin, is to *know "Him who loved us and gave Himself for us"*. The beginning of such a relationship is accompanied by an invasion of His Person and Life into the very body of the subject.

Clearly, the Bible repeatedly and unmistakably identifies the *"receiver"* as a new creation with a new, redirected focus and an innate power to live supernaturally, in surrender to the indwelling Lord Jesus Christ who now dominates his life. The cost for this emancipating redemption on the human side is total, unconditional surrender in a full turn to Christ.

However, the human tragedy continues because men, and especially religious men, have attempted to assuage the guilt of rebellion and to climb out of their dilemma by their own effort, without God's plan and provision. A spiritual war has raged throughout history as humanity has attempted to justify itself and to promote a way through human effort to pull itself up by his moral bootstraps. Ultimately, man has mixed the *"way of God"* with the *"way of man"* and produced a series of damning efforts in serious conflict with his Creator. On occasion, *"man's new ways"* get a *"face lift,"* a new name and public relations package. But as a rose is a rose, so too, a lie is a lie by any other name.

Historically, man's pride has conceived and birthed one new effort after another in search of this short cut to redemption that would allow him to avoid the way of the Cross and death to his self-life. Our nature vehemently resists the beckoning of the Spirit of God to discover Life through death. His answer has been "religion," multitudes of religions. Yet every religion conceived by devils or men is no more than a Judeo-Christian heresy, liberally sprinkled with mysticism, humanism and often varying degrees of Scripture.

Like the two ugly stepsisters of Cinderella who desperately tried to fit their fattened feet into her beautiful slipper, pride and religion have worked in vain to fit man into abundant living and eternal life. With each successive failure, they tirelessly re-approach the project to try, try again. Therefore, the fundamental flaw with Promise Keepers is not as much in its stated goals as in the organization's man-centered, will-driven and illegitimate approach to the entire Christian faith.

It Can Get Heavy

Have you noticed how much energy and resources it takes to maintain vigilance? It becomes taxing to stand against all those things that are attacking Truth. Many of the defenders of the faith have long since acquiesced to the enemy. To the one who is constantly in the fray of battle, the sheer number, popularity and resources of the enemy seems endless.

Since the second chapter of the New Testament book of Acts and throughout New Testament church history, men and women of God have struggled to maintain biblical integrity and to resist any infusion of tainted doctrine or scriptural compromise. Repeatedly, the Church is warned to be on guard against the invasion of doctrine that is foreign to the doctrine delivered of God. Peter, among every other writer of the New Testament, warned of the imminent danger faced by the church. He wrote, "But there were false prophets also among the people, even as there SHALL BE FALSE TEACHERS AMONG YOU, who [secretly] shall bring in [destructive] heresies, even denying the Lord that bought them, and bring upon themselves swift destruction. And many shall follow their pernicious ways..." (2 Peter 2:1-2).

Not since the days of the Inquisition has the true Church faced such a challenge to its authority, its doctrine or its mission as in this hour of great deception emanating from so many seemingly dynamic, legitimate groups and "Christian" spokespersons. This is an historic period when multitudes of prophecies are coming to fruition. Primarily and specifically, as it relates to our topic, the "religious revival" that is attempting to consolidate all men of faith and faiths of all men into one gigantic army of God to "take this world for Jesus and His Church" is clearly not only Orwellian in its character, but biblical in its prophetic placement on God's timetable.

Many are applauding this new, creative, open-minded, loving and tolerant effort that has found much of its momentum in organizations like the Promise Keepers ministry. However, those who have a grip on church history, who are skilled in handling the Word of God and who can see the prophetic picture borne out in these waning moments of history realize that the phenomenon sweeping as a spiritualistic tidal wave across our land is a clever maneuver on the part of forces with a suspect agenda.

The *"church"* trend in Western Civilization, especially in America, seeks to consolidate all efforts of all Christians, to ignore their differences and to see the big picture of *"impacting our world for God."* (When I italicize the word *"church"*, I am referring to the commonly held contemporary concept that all who belong to a *"church"* are part of the true Church of the Lord Jesus Christ through having experienced new birth. Scripture teaches, to the contrary, that while many may be on the membership rolls, they indeed may not be truly born again and, hence, absent from the true Church's rolls. Christ taught that tares and wheat would grow together and that He would separate the true from the false in the end [Matthew 13:24-30].)

The Promise Keepers' push, as well as that of other ecumenical efforts, is summarized: "It is time for Christians to grow up, quit being petty, join hands, become One with each other, because that is what Jesus prayed... (wasn't it?) and let's just get along and work together to show the world the love of God."

Now that sounds precious. What could be more "Christ-like" than receiving each other without judging or questioning each other's beliefs and convictions? The reasoning continues, if pastors, priests and ministers of all our diverse churches and groups would just quit defending their sacred cows, drop their silly, old, narrow-minded, binding traditions, then a real revival could sweep America and probably the whole world. If we could just join ranks, love each other, worship God together, get to know each other and be tolerant, our unity would release such a manifestation of spiritual revival... wouldn't it?

So say many, if not most, of America's leading evangelical leaders and the "New World Order" para-church ministry of the '90's, the Promise Keepers.

So, What is a Promise Keeper?

According to their statements defining *"What is Promise Keepers?"* the organization's material states, "Promise Keepers is a Christ-centered ministry dedicated to uniting men through vital relationships to become godly influences in their world."[1] On the surface, such a definition appears not only harmless, but laudable, especially in light of the deteriorating spiritual condition of our nation and the condition of our male leadership.

The organization's description of its *"call"* is given in the same publication that defines its ministry philosophy. It says, "We believe that we have a *'God-given mission'* (emphasis mine) to unite Christian men who are separated by race, sectarianism, age, culture and economics...the biblical directive to be 'ambassadors of reconciliation' compels us to breakdown the walls that have divided and polarized the Body of Christ for too long."[2]

Obviously, this "divided and polarized Body of Christ," according to Promise Keepers, is the real spoiler in all efforts to accomplish the Christian commissions, efforts, desires and designs. And not just division, but it is the division among Christian *men* that is at the heart of this spiritual paralysis. The clearly stated solution, according to Promise Keepers' agenda, is to bring men together on the basis of a common cause that is so vital that it precludes the importance of any distinctions among the men that brought about a division and separation to begin with.

The Analysis of Paralysis
or is it the
Paralysis of Analysis?

It is clear that Promise Keepers' leadership has a heart that longs for a "worldwide community" of Christian men who, under the umbrella of their organization, would allow nothing to keep them apart as it relates to the spiritual objectives and goals of Promise Keepers. Clearly, as Promise Keepers' statements and position papers indicate, the organization has analyzed the profound and complex needs in the nation, the church and worldwide Christendom and have concluded that "Christian" men, regardless of their denominational and religious background or of their current spiritual and moral condition, must consolidate their spiritual efforts and *"be one."* Their analysis of the church's and the nation's spiritual paralysis resulted in the conclusion that, as the Statement of Faith says, they are compelled to "…break down the walls that have divided and polarized the Body of Christ for too long."[3]

I will deal most thoroughly with this stated position and appeal of Promise Keepers a bit further along. For now, suffice it to say that I believe the "walls that divided and polarized the Body for too long" are those that have, almost entirely, been erected by the very Word of God. These walls, in fact, are not restricting in the slightest the sovereign movement of the Holy Spirit in the affairs of men and the Church.

A major premise for Promise Keepers' birth and perpetuation is flawed to its very foundation. That premise is an erroneous diagnosis of our national and domestic problems and what will cure them. We must understand that *"walls,"* hedges and covering are not innately evil, nor are they a hindrance to God. In fact, the same philosophy has raised its head in the Church on every occasion that the immutability, finality and inerrancy of the Scriptures has been questioned. In order for man to re-approach the human dilemma with a new and improved version of solutions to man's pollutions, he must put forth a renewed effort to set aside God's Truths. Each successive generation seems to produce its own set of would-be philosophers who are willing to assault the Scriptures and to raise their own new standard.

Fulfilling Promise Keepers' dream of unity among what they call "Christian men" necessitates a neutering of the repeated scriptural mandates for Believers to "have no fellowship" with (much less be in covenant with) anyone whose belief system is out of harmony with the Word of God's clear directives. We shall shortly examine the insidious, diabolical nature of the *"unity movement"* now being promoted by Promise Keepers, but such extra-biblical theology sounds so, well, so spiritual, generous and yes, *tolerant.*

The hallmark on this generation of many of America's "Christian leaders" seems to be an attitude that a loving, generous, and *tolerant* God has such a desire for a *"bigger, more inclusive and numerically encompassing tent"* that the word *"NO"* is no longer part of His vocabulary. Has God truly changed His mind concerning His admonition that believers should be *"contending for the faith that was once for all delivered to the saints"* (Jude 3)? Is the twentieth-century church to drop doctrinal convictions defining what constitutes being a Christian and how one becomes *"born again"?* Are we to cease defining God and defending the relevance and uniqueness of His written Word? Even momentarily considering such tyrannical ideas is ludicrous and diametrically opposed to everything God's Word teaches respecting biblical integrity, doctrinal purity, spiritual growth and true revival.

The concept that we, regardless of our religious and doctrinal background and beliefs about what the Bible teaches on critical matters, should just "forget all that stuff and be one for Christ" is appalling to scripturally rooted and grounded believers. In fact, it should appall anyone who understands the eternal and all-encompassing importance of holding intact our deep commitments to the full revelation of God in the Scriptures. It indeed was God who put a *wall*, with the words *"DO NOT EAT,"* around the tree in the Garden of Eden. His admonition to "stay away" and respect the established *"wall"* was clearly for humanity's great and everlasting benefit.

Contrary to much popular theology, God still uses the words *"do not."* He has called all believers to respect the walls He has established. Misguided zeal, driven by false spirituality, attempts to ignore God-ordained boundaries. Walls may represent a divisive polarization to Promise Keepers' leadership and others who desire that we come together on the basis of a common experience, but the Word of God demands *separation: separation* from the world and from its polluting influences (2 Corinthians 6:17). It calls for *separation* from concepts foreign to biblical instruction on spiritual growth (Galatians 6:7). It commands *separation* from religious sounding, but false theologies (Colossians 2:8). It requires *separation* from those who even insinuate that there is any other *"way"* to God but through the atoning and finished work of Christ (Galatians 1:8-9).

The Promise Keepers' goal, simply put, is to tear down each of these walls of "separation." Their confusion on this matter has led them to cuddle up in the bedroom of religious perversion with some wicked, cultic and hedonistic beliefs and groups. Later in the book we will look closely at some of the *"diverse"* and perverse belief systems that Promise Keepers welcomes into their fellowship.

Promise Keepers ignores the scriptural requirement to remain separate from those who have a "form of godliness but deny the power of it" (2 Timothy 3:1-6). They have snubbed the Scriptures' call for *separation* from those who reject the Word of God as the final revelation of God (2 Timothy 4:1-5). Promise Keepers' disregard for the biblical call to maintain *separation* from ministers of darkness appearing as angels of light is flagrant (2 Corinthians 11:13-15). Scripture's appeal for *separation* from those who teach that spiritual growth and power are to be found in the strength of fleshly efforts and *"promises"* rather than in the sufficiency of Christ is another wall ignored by Promise Keepers (Colossians 2:18-19). The Bible repeatedly reminds us that *separation* is one of the major components of spiritual victory and moral and doctrinal purity necessary to perpetuate the mission of God's Church. The walls established by the very laws of the Word of God, historically adhered to and maintained by those with discerning hearts, must never be assaulted, no matter how appealing, seductive and high-tech that appeal may be.

The walls that God's people must militantly assault are the walls within our hearts and lives that resist His dominance in us. The walls we must tear down are those that keep us from "counting all things that are gain to me...as dung, that I might win Christ...and be found in Him" (Philippians 3:8-9). The walls that hinder our love affair with the Word of God, our intimacy with Christ and our ministry to and through the Body of Christ in which God's Spirit has planted us are the walls we must destroy. These walls are the true hindrances to revival and renewal. The walls that God's men, skilled in the Scriptures and who, with profound discernment, have recognized as divinely constructed to keep out destructive heresies, doctrines of devils and contamination of biblical integrity, are those same walls that Promise Keepers is attempting to breach and destroy.

The audacious and publicized intentions of any group to assault "the walls that have kept the Body of Christ apart for too long" should set alarm bells loudly ringing in the heart of every Spirit-controlled Christian in America. These kinds of buzz words attempting to sanctify with their "spiritual" spin on an age-old philosophy whose design it is to water down God's Truth are phraseologies familiar to the more seasoned veterans in the ongoing battle for the Bible. This terminology and its goal calling for *"unity"* are not unique to the popular Promise Keepers ministry, as we will shortly discover.

Many of the walls that separate what religious, ignorant and deceived people perceive as the *"the Body of Christ"* are built by the heart, mind and Word of God. We should approach *"walls"* with the greatest of discernment and with an understanding that much of the ground around such walls is holy ground. It is dangerous, indeed, to touch that which God has set aside and to assault a fortress that God Himself has erected. And yet, the *hiss* of the serpent echoing his *"Hath God said..."* is increasing in volume in these last days, days full of deception.

It's Just A Horse

In its promotional material, Promise Keepers says, "We adhere to historical truths of biblical orthodoxy and identify our Statement of Faith as our foundation."[4] That statement in itself should identify the Promise Keeper ministry as a spiritual Trojan Horse.

Troy, you remember, was the most famous city of all Greek legends. The philosopher, Homer, wrote of the celebrated Trojan War in his poetry. The Greek legend tells us how Greece, even after a 10-year siege, was unable to capture the fortified and well-defended city of Troy. Therefore, the Greeks developed a strategy of deception to conquer the city. They built a gigantic, hollow, wooden horse, which they filled with many of their armed warriors. Soon, the remainder, and what seemed to be all, of the Greek army boarded their ships and sailed away, giving the appearance of having given up the fight.

In a short time, a Greek spy named Sinon, whom the city of Troy had befriended, persuaded the Trojans to bring the horse left by the Greeks into the city. They had been convinced that there was a mystical quality to the horse and that if they would bring it within the city gates, it would make them invulnerable.

When night fell, Sinon released the armed troops within the horse. The warriors then killed the guards, opened the city gates and let the returning Greeks in. The city was then captured and destroyed.

How clever of the Greeks, yet how curious of the Trojans. How much like contemporary Christianity. Troy had sought, after a 10-year success, to add to an invulnerability that was already possessed.

The Church in general is much given today to seeking that which we already have. Even more tragic in its consequences is the fact that the Church, through various unnecessary additives, has historically subjected itself to the spiritual poisons of those pretended friends with, knowingly or unknowingly, darkened motives.

The Church has been infected by adapting philosophies,

trends and goals that are alien to its God-given commission. The lack of discernment, coupled with the "new mysticism" so active in America's Christendom, has seduced the masses. The *"keepers of the gates"* have been either silenced or their warnings unheeded. And amazingly, as in ancient Troy, which slept on in a self-induced false sense of security while the enemy poured into its bulwark, so the Church slumbers on, unwilling to hear the warning of the *"keepers of the gates."*

Promise Keepers has the seductive allure necessary to attract the attention of a slumbering American church. Much of the church that is not asleep seems to either be anesthetized or mesmerized. The anesthetic has been liberally applied to our spiritual discernment while leaving carnal judgment fully sensitive and cognitive. To such a "sleeping spirit," success is primarily measured by marketability, "number of noses" and size of budgets. Few ministers, pastors, evangelists and church leaders escape this lust for visible, physically measurable success. Thus, the massive majority of America's leading clergy are mesmerized by the unprecedented, explosive growth, the phenomenal number of men in attendance, and the high profile of so many popular preachers and speakers who are affiliated with Promise Keepers.

Also contributing to the American church's infatuation with Promise Keepers is the fact that a great number of our churches are spiritually dead or on *"life-support"* with few men of true, spiritual depth at the helm of their leadership. Suddenly, a ministry has appeared that motivates men to get off the pew and make new and seemingly dynamic promises to become *"real men."* What pastor in his right mind would look at those men who have in the past demonstrated, at best, only flickers of life but are now bubbling with excitement over their new-found ministries provided through Promise Keepers and tell them, "Men, we perhaps ought to stop a minute, pray, biblically re-evaluate and test the spirits before we plunge ahead"?

As stated earlier, men, particularly in America today, could be considered, at least based upon statistics reflecting diminishing family commitments, to be spiritual invertebrates. Going into the ministry, rather than adding backbone, only exacerbates the problem of weak-principled men. Strong spines, however, are not standard equipment given those entering the ministry. To have spiritual backbone necessitates the ministry going into the man.

"Thy word have I hidden in mine heart, that I might not sin against thee."

Psalms 119:11

CHAPTER 5

"That Crazy Bible"and The Deceptive Depravity of Sincerity

"Wherewithal shall a young man cleanse his way? By taking heed thereto according to thy word."

Psalms 119:9

An irate viewer of one of our television programs in which we examined Promise Keepers' ministry from a biblical perspective had just about exhausted all of his defense of the various attributes of Promise Keepers. In an exasperated, last-ditch effort to qualify his favorite men's ministry and justify his zealous promotion of it, he said, almost to himself, "But, listen, they are so sincere....We cannot let a little doctrine that does not matter that much, anyway, keep us divided."

I will deal with the false concept of the need for the full *"unity"* later, but my heart does go out to so many who for a long time have searched for a meaningful relationship with a church or ministry that sparks enthusiasm, excitement, and revival in their hearts. I have no doubt that my detractor on the phone was also sincere. However, sincerity cannot be the gauge by which we measure legitimate moves of God or approve the validity of a ministry. That standard is already established.

Many of us have wide-ranging views on a great number of issues, from eschatological outlooks to Greek or Hebrew epistemological translations. Time alone will tell who is right and who is wrong on some of these more complex matters. But matters central to the current "doctrinal destruction Derby" are the fundamental tenets of the Christian faith, not *"little-doctrines-that-do-not-matter-much-anyway"*. These, more than pillars holding up the Christian faith, are the foundational underpinnings and central in determining how one becomes a Christian, and what he or she does do to attain spiritual development and maturity. They are, essentially, the entire issue.

These "little doctrines" that we are told "should not keep us apart," which are now being sacrificed on the altar of neo-evangelism's marriage to neo-ecumenicalism, are not inconsequential to the Christian Church's foundation. These great doctrines of the faith such as new birth, God's commands for Christians, the believer's ministry in the local church, and qualifications for leadership in the church, the doctrines of grace, God, Christ and the Holy Spirit are only a few of the vital, doctrinal footings upon which the true Church of Jesus Christ is built. These are not just "little doctrines." These are the heart and soul of the entire Christian faith. If they are treated casually, or as nonessentials to any ministry, then that group removes itself from the qualifications necessary to act as an authoritative agent of God's Church and His fully revealed Word.

A casual glance at the scriptural convictions of the major proponents of the unity movement which is Promise Keepers' primary objective is telling indeed. Those who do not hold the Word of God sacred, the Truths of God final and absolute find it comfortable to affiliate with these groups because these great Bible doctrines have never been essentials for their *"faith."* Those calling for a divorce of Christianity from the integrity of these doctrinal distinctions of Scripture, frankly, have nothing to lose and much to gain.

The Truth of the Matter

Those who have supported ministries like Promise Keepers may not find it palatable to learn that the issue is not primarily about doctrine at all. Not that any trade-off or concession of vital biblical truths for the sake of unity is right, but the issue strikes deeper, much deeper, at the heart and soul, even to the very existence of the spiritual life and vitality of the Church of the Living God. It would be tragic enough if doctrine was all that is being sacrificed in this unification of all *"Christian men everywhere by the breaking down of walls... that have kept the Body of Christ apart for too long."*[1] However, not just "little doctrines," but the very integrity and soul of the Word of God itself is under assault. If it were possible for this assault to achieve its fundamental goal, it would destroy the foundational beliefs system of the Church, render impotent Her message and cause local churches to collapse as a house of cards. Thankfully, God has a remnant that will insure not only the Church's viability, but Her ultimate victory. Yet this war over the Word of God's validity has raged for millennia, and in fulfillment of its own prophecy, the challenge to its infallibility and inspiration is intensifying as we draw closer to the end of this century and the beginning of the next.

Students of contemporary biblical history know that this assault on the Bible's inerrancy began in earnest almost a century ago. Theologians promoting "higher criticism" and liberals discounting the supernatural recorded in Scripture attacked from the theological left.

He Didn't Bore In, He was Born In

The most damaging, covert and insidious assault on the Bible's integrity has been, like the egg of the worm planted in the budding apple, smuggled into the Church to do its damage from within. The worm cleverly plants its young eggs to incubate in the tender, young and growing apple blossoms. Upon its maturing, the apple, red, shining, and delicious, from all external appearances seems healthy and edible. But deep within the core is a "growing spoiler" feeding on the apple's hidden life. The apple is contributing to the growth and health of the parasite within. Ultimately, with the exterior of the apple mostly intact and the interior mostly eaten away or rotten, the little worm pops out and crawls away to mate. The poor old apple, host and provider of all Mr. Worm's needs, is left to finish decaying. When we see a hole in an otherwise beautiful apple, we usually think, *"Hey, a worm has bored his way into this apple."* But in reality, the worm was placed in the apple long before it even became a fruit and it has now bored its way out into the world as a fat and happy worm.

So it is with the current assault on that which all discerning and mature Christians hold dear and that which is the very foundation of our faith, the Word of God. This subtle, covert spiritual terrorism against the Truth of God is being perpetrated by those most visible in the leadership of the current movement that have focused on unifying all God's people on the basis of common experiences and goals. Promise Keepers' philosophy, so clearly defined in its promotional literature, exposes an over-emphasis on legitimate-sounding goals and eager acceptance of experience-oriented Christianity, seasoned with its de-emphasis on the vital doctrines established by the Word of God.

This philosophy treats the Scriptures as subjective information relative to interpretation. And the desire of leadership in Promise Keepers is to prove without doubt, as we shall see, that the clear, basic, orthodox Truths articulated in the Scriptures are "not worth fighting for," nor are they important enough to the organization's objectives to be concerned with. In fact, such concerns hinder their objectives. Such "trivial" facts, precepts, principles and doctrines once held precious to the heart of the Church, and for which hundreds of thousands of martyrs were tortured and slaughtered, are now considered only minor *"walls"* that *"have kept the Body apart for too long."*[2]

These are critical and monumental walls established by the Word of God and maintained by men and women of God down through Church history for the purpose of setting certain identifiable, diabolical groups and philosophies at a distance from the true and living Church of God. They are the walls that Satan has struggled for years to bring down in order to debilitate and infiltrate the Church. Only the sheer grace of God working through dedicated reformers and church leaders who adhered to strict vigilance decade after decade secured and preserved the Light of Truth, tragically, often at the expense of their own blood. But now, we are told by the new evangelicals who are walking in step with their new bride, the ecumenicalists, that it is narrow, legalistic and arrogant to guard the gates and stay on the wall to protect it.

"Put That Bible Away"

Recently, a devotee of Promise Keepers and of the Vineyard Movement now sweeping our nation told me that he hears God's voice speak directly and audibly on frequent occasions. Jesus appears to him regularly and physically for little visits. After I asked him to show me any place in the Word of God that could qualify his experience as a legitimate, scriptural phenomenon which had occurred in the presence of reliable witnesses since the end of the first century, he incredulously replied, *"You and your crazy Bible. You need to put that Bible away and get in one of our prayer groups. Start learning how to experience God. God is not limited to that Bible of yours."*

Once again, I heard that subtle hiss of the serpentine devil whispering as he did to Eve in the Garden, *"Yea, hath God said ? Surely it's not true. You are really missing out Mrs. Eve, by being bound up by the Word of God. Go ahead, take the fruit... it's a real experience. It's okay. You and your crazy Word of God. Eat it, Eve!"*

And so she did.

"But We All Believe The Bible!"

What does it mean when a church, a ministry, or anyone says, *"But we believe the Bible"*?

Those in the ministry repeatedly hear such statements by individuals, groups, cults and various errant denominations and movements. This assertion seems to be the great qualifier for any and all who want the "Good Lord's Stamp of Biblical Approval" on their mission.

Often the reason so many claim to believe the Bible is simply because they have little or no grasp on what the Bible teaches. And while many claim (and in many cases, blame) the Bible, such a statement does not give the true Church sufficient reason to condone or approve of those making that claim. In fact, the discerning minister must seek the answers to several questions before considering any organization, movement, or ministry as a legitimate, Bible-centered entity.

Those questions include:

Does the organization/ministry believe and adhere to the Bible as the infallible, inspired and inerrant Word of God?

Does the organization/ministry believe the Bible in addition to other authoritative sources?

Does the organization/ministry believe that the Word of God, the Bible, is complete, without need of any additional word of revelation?

Is the Bible the organization or ministry's sole rule and source of information?

Does Promise Keepers Leadership Believe The Bible?

The introduction of Promise Keepers' Statement of Faith states, "We adhere to the historical truths of biblical orthodoxy and identify our Statement of Faith as our foundation."[3]

What does that mean?

Only those in the organization who penned this statement could explain the meaning and intent of the chosen phraseology. Promise Keepers' wording in that sentence could mean many different things or it could mean nothing at all. A growing number of organizations and ministries generalize their purpose and belief system so that no one interested in joining their mission can find anything with which to disagree. Many such statements and position papers are intentionally kept "broad" enough to attract almost anyone anywhere.

We must determine what Promise Keepers' leadership means by their adherence to "historical truths of biblical orthodoxy,"[4] a claim of almost every known Christian and quasi-Christian group as well as of most sects and cults that have separated themselves from the true Christian Church over its 2,000-year history.

Is Promise Keepers being ambiguous by design or default?

Any number of so-called Christian denominations, as well as numerous cults, agree with the Promise Keepers' statement that they "adhere to the historical truths of biblical orthodoxy." A few that can comfortably *"fit"* their theology and doctrine into such a statement are:

The Holy Roman Catholic Church
The Church of the Latter Days Saints (Mormons)
Metropolitan Community Church (catering to
    homosexuals)
Unity Church
Church of Christian Science
Rev. Sun Myung Moon's Unification Church

Incidentally, my research has yet to reveal any such group that is not welcomed by the organization. In fact, these groups are aggressively encouraged to participate in all facets of Promise Keepers ministries. Obviously, by its own admission, Promise Keepers accepts the validity of almost any claiming to believe in the Bible regardless of what else they believe, and considers them to be part of the Christian church.

Many other so-called Christian churches and denominations claim that they, too, "adhere to the historical truths of biblical orthodoxy," while in reality they do not subscribe to that statement's true intent. One such organization is the United Pentecostal Church, which believes there is no salvation for anyone who is not water baptized in the *"Name of Jesus only"* and which does not manifest baptism in the Holy Spirit with the evidence of speaking in tongues. Another such group is the United Church of Christ, which believes and teaches that it is exclusively the True Church and that members of other denominations are damned until they repent. Repentance, according to them, will be followed by water baptism in a Church of Christ only and then, one is *"saved."*

So, again, Promise Keepers' confession of adherence to the historical Truths of biblical orthodoxy is a barren, empty and baseless claim that should clearly sound alarms in the spirit of any credible, godly, discerning individual.

But it does not, does it?

The majority of the founding, current leadership of Promise Keepers is involved in churches, ministries and organizations which are wholeheartedly and publicly convinced that the Bible, indeed, is not a closed canon and that the Word of God is not sufficient to meet the needs of God's people. Additives, extra-biblical expression and manifestations are fully operative, necessary, laudable and preferable.

For those with no sense of biblical Church history, and who are not rooted and grounded in the Scriptures, such a charge is minor and irrelevant. To them, the charge has no bearing on whether or not any group is sanctioned of God. But to open the possibility that God is giving more divine revelation through spiritualistic experiences is to shut out the possibility of knowing Him and victoriously walking with the True and Living God. A world of demonic spiritism wraps its tentacles around those who have such a demented theological grip on God's Word and, without fail, births unimaginable deception and darkness into their lives.

So, the question is, do all Promise Keepers leaders believe the Bible? We could probably answer, yes, they believe the Bible *to the degree that they accept it as complete.* These men believe that God is still *"revealing"* additional *"words"* to the Scriptures. Therefore, most of them not only believe the Bible, but they also believe much more.

"And Jesus said, be sure that the light within you is not darkness or how great is that darkness" (Matthew 6:23).

"Who Said The Bible Is All God Has To Say?"

How precious it is when a believer discovers the sufficiency of Christ and the glorious fullness expressed in the Word of God. Such intimate, indescribable moments of cascading joy, peace and sweetness are available to those who discipline their minds and hearts to mine the gold and the glory on the pages of their Bible.

God has signed, sealed and delivered His absolute and total revelation to man in the Scriptures. Writing on the Isle of Patmos, the Apostle John received the closing words of the Word of God. In that moment, the Holy Spirit promised not only special blessings upon those who seriously read the book of Revelation, but He also promised to visit great curses upon anyone audacious enough to add to or take away from the Revelation of God.

The Apostle, inspired by the Spirit of God, wrote: "For I testify unto every man that heareth the words of the prophecy of this book, If any man shall add unto these things, God shall add unto him the plagues that are written in this book: And if any man shall take away from the words of the book of this prophecy, God shall take away his part out of the book of life, and out of the holy city, and from the things which are written in this book" (Revelation 22:18-19).

The historical pattern of the Old Testament being finished and sealed after the prophetic ministries of Ezra and Nehemiah was followed at the closure of the New Testament. From the moment of the last prophetic utterance of these Old Testament men of God, the voice of God, through any legitimate persons recognized as those with the seal of God's authority, was silent. This silence lasted for 400 years. At the end of that period, John the Baptist, the last great Old Testament prophet of God, burst upon the scene to begin speaking to the New Testament era.

According to Scripture, after Pentecost, the Holy Spirit began to move upon men to write down the events of Christ's life, the beginning of the Church, and New Testament doctrine. The last of these New Testament books written was The Revelation and with its finish, the canon of Scripture was closed. The 66 books of the Bible that we recognize today as the Word of God were complete and assimilated by earth's godliest living men of the church by the early second century.

Then, by the fourth century, church councils had executed an intense and difficult test of legitimacy in order to verify and confirm these 66 books as the final Word of God. There is no other Word from God. The Bible is complete without any need whatsoever for an additional *"Thus saith the Lord."* There has never been, since the New Testament closure, a recognized, legitimate, new word from God that the Church as a whole has stamped as authoritative.

Today, organizations operating outside the context, commission, call and covenant of a Holy God to His people, are generating the most horrendous, unimaginable, and unprecedented flood of heresy into and through the Church in history. Out of this heresy we are witnessing the birth of a tolerance and acceptance of neo-paganism, ritualism, Satanism and humanism by the Church. Such is, no doubt, a set-up for the apostasy of the false religious systems of the last days so clearly prophesied throughout God's Holy Word.

It is an overwhelming burden to many that an organization such as Promise Keepers Ministries, with its roots deeply imbedded in a movement that treats the Word of God with flippant irreverence and mindless disregard, cannot only survive, but that it can even prosper. Perhaps more of a burden lies in the fact that the few who are willing to "cry out and spare not" are becoming the laughingstock of the Church and are being branded with such titles as "divisive", "mean-spirited", "legalistic" and "heresy hunters." But to some believers, the clarity of the overwhelming and deep-rooted conflict between Promise Keepers' stated positions and the written Word of God is so stark that these godly, discerning few are traumatized with spiritual shock over the casual acquiescence and cooperation of so many high-profile Christian leaders involved in this slaughter of biblical Truths.

Hosea, recording the burden of the Lord, wrote... *"My people are destroyed for lack of knowledge, because thou hast rejected knowledge... "* (Hosea 4:6).

What a revealing truth that people, even God's people,

rarely receive and act on the Truth of God. Historically, the people of God have suffered great deprivation, severe chastening and loss of magnificent benefits when they have rejected the Truths of God. And yet, truth is always the first casualty in every spiritual and cultural war. But such rejection of revelation provokes into action the principle of replacement.

When men willingly compromise truth, they soon become the prisoners of *"tolerance."*

Christianity begins with "repentance."
Promise Keepers begins with "I promise to..."
—Phil Arms

CHAPTER 6

The Premise of a Promise

"For other foundation can no man lay than that which is laid which is Jesus Christ."
1 Corinthians 3:11

The first man to approach me about Promise Keepers' ministry was so excited. He said, "You gotta take a look at this fantastic men's ministry, the Promise Keepers. I am so excited. I have found a place where Christian brothers can join together and learn to open up to each other and to God." I found it difficult to interrupt his zealous and impassioned appeal for me to approvingly look at the material he had gathered that promoted Promise Keepers' ministry. He continued, "And look at these seven promises. It is the whole bottom line of everything God's people are all about." Then he read them to me.

We will look at all seven of the promises that Promise Keepers ask men to make in light of a true biblical analysis. But first allow me to point out the obvious. The name, "Promise Keepers", goes far beyond a mere implication of its theological foundation. It defines it. The name fully promotes the concept that men can, by the making and keeping of basic promises, experience spiritual growth as Christians and thereby achieve God's purposes in their lives. Repeatedly, the position of Promise Keepers' material states that the attributes of *"Christlikeness"* will be born in the life of those willing to make and keep *"promises."*

The seven promises that men are asked to make sound honorable, biblical and commendable. Promise Keepers' leadership—more specifically, its president, Randy Phillips— has written that these seven promises "emerged out of an intense time of prayer and discussion among our staff and board of directors."[1] Very few men, even ministers, have found fault in the "Seven Promises of a Promise Keeper". However, the first question to ask is not, "Are the promises laudable or even biblical?" but, "Is the premise of making promises God's designated pattern for Christian men to grow in Christ and to fulfill His call on their lives?" Phillips writes in the book, *Seven Promises of a Promise Keeper*, that men hold the keys to national revival, a spiritual awakening and a true move of God in the American home, the church and nation.

He writes, "Promise Keepers believes it starts by making some promises...promises intended to be kept."[2] He then explains *how* men are to keep these promises. Those rooted and grounded in the Scriptures find it obvious that the principles and goals innate within the promises are redundant to the already biblically defined manifestations of Spirit-controlled living. The objectives expressed in these seven promises are the natural fruits produced by men who live Christ-centered lives. Promise Keepers' attempt to focus on these attributes and the effort necessary to accomplish them is like a chicken attending barnyard group sessions to learn how to grow feathers. Attending such sessions is unnecessary to *"chicken-hood."* Feathers, by God's design, grow on chickens. By the same token, Christian men following the biblical prescription will, by the nature of their new birth, manifest the characteristics of men of God. Christian men do not require *"barnyard"* group sessions to produce godliness, especially sessions where *"fowl"* of other species attend, pretending to be chickens. Of course, the purpose of a man's local church is to facilitate the growth, disciplines, ministries and fellowship necessary to insure that he develops into what Promise Keepers attests are many of their goals for all men to accomplish, if they are to be "real men". As we shall see, Promise Keepers assumes a mantel and an authority that God has exclusively relegated to the Body of Christ. There are great dangers and severe consequences for such scriptural breaches.

Successful Christian living is not predicated upon a believer seeking or honing a particular character facet or attribute of the Lord Jesus Christ. Not one attribute, any more than any particular gift of the Spirit, is to be idolized or sought. The key to living a victorious Christian life that transforms the believer as well as the world around him is his constant preoccupation with the Lord Jesus Himself. The victorious Christian seeks an intimate fellowship with Christ and discovers a deeper knowledge and sweeter relationship with Him in worship and in His Word. Losing one's self-centeredness, self-confidence and self-focus, and allowing the heart, mind, body and soul to be increasingly absorbed by the life of Christ within is God's biblically prescribed process of spiritual development and maturity. True spiritual growth is learning to choose against "my" ability to improve "me". The "me" must die to self for Christ to manifest His Life through my life.

The road to world revival is not the same road one travels when, by an exercise of will power, promises are made to enhance one's conduct and efforts are made to emulate Christ-likeness. As honorable, spiritual and even logical as that may sound, that is not Christianity; rather, it is a fundamental tenet of *humanism*. Christian living is not realized by our imitating the life of Christ or attempting to be like Jesus. Paul said, "For me to live *is* Christ" (Philippians 1:21). He is not saying, "You are looking at a pretty fair reflection of Him" but rather, *"It is Jesus being Jesus in and through me."* Someone once said "no one can be Jesus quite like Jesus can be Jesus". Paul defines with clarity the all-consuming *"Christ life"* of the Christian life. He writes, "I am crucified with Christ: nevertheless I live; yet not I, but Christ liveth in me;

and the life which I now live in the flesh I live by the faith of the Son of God, who loved me and gave Himself for me" (Galatians 2:20). All the feeble promises of the flesh in the universe, regardless of how noble sounding, cannot attain the goals or desires that God has for those who belong to Him— even if such promises are kept.

An obvious, forgotten truth is found in the words of Isaiah the prophet: "...We are all as an unclean thing and all our *righteousness* is as filthy rags..." (Isaiah 64:6).

Man is left in his fallen state without the capacity to change his corrupt, unrighteous nature or to will, through renewed effort or promises, a reproduction of the nature of a holy and righteous God. In brief, my old *"me"* will not get any better, any more righteous, or any holier if given more time, more focus or more effort. My *"me"* has always been my problem, not my solution. A *"me"* who makes seven newer, improved promises or even 7,000 promises can never reach God's standard.

"But Ya' Gotta Believe in You...Don't Ya'?"

The key to changing our world is allowing God to change us by the power of His resurrection, not by earnestly making promises that reinforce human goodness or even godly virtues based on human effort. Every Christian must understand that in the very seed of man-made attempts to accomplish God-given objectives is seen a micro-cosmic view of the fall of the human race.

It does not matter how many *"promises,"* oaths, vows or covenants men make to their churches, wives, children or each other to change their conduct. Conduct is not the fundamental problem with man. What we *are*, not what we *do*, is humanity's fundamental problem. It does not matter what we *do* unless we change what we *are*. And only the power of God, through the redemptive process, changes what we *are*. That process, as a growing Christian discovers, is not perpetuated by the struggling little train philosophy of *"I think I can, I think I can, I think I can."* To the contrary, it is achieved by realizing *"I know I can't, I know He can."* The Word of God repeatedly emphasizes that God, in His loving grace, initiates and perpetuates the manifestations of Christ in every believer. Paul wrote, "For it is God who worketh in you to *will* and to *do* of His good pleasure" (Philippians 2:13).

In spite of this clarity in the Scriptures, men long to create and attempt to sanctify new and improved ways to finish the work that Christ has started. In fact, this is often the objective of many of the world's cults that focus on some new leader who claims to have "come to finish the work that Jesus left undone." We are reminded of the false prophets who claim this Messianic mission to be their call, men such as Rev. Sun Myung Moon of the Unification Church, Louis Farrakhan, leader of the Black Muslim movement, Joseph Smith, founder of the Church of Jesus Christ of Latter-day Saints (Mormons) and, more recently, David Koresh of the Waco, Texas, "Branch Davidians." Frankly, we are not equipped to be God, though there is that within our fallen nature which causes us to "think more highly of ourselves than we ought" (Romans 12:3).

My five-year-old son, now that his 16-year-old-sister has begun to drive, insists that he be allowed to drive as well. Clearly, with his 60-month-old motor skills, eye and hand coordination, 46-inch height and stubby little legs, he is hardly prepared for the event. (Let me rephrase that: *He* is quite ready for the event; *I* however, am not.) Likewise, God the Father knows the limitations of our humanity and spiritual skills. We are not now, nor will we ever be, prepared to *"vow"* ourselves into holiness, righteousness or godly conduct.

Man can achieve *moralistic* goals through the sheer power of his fallen will and determination. But such achievements are non-redemptive because, again, man's basic problem is not that he is simply immoral. Man's debilitating problem is that he is *dead* in trespasses and sin. He needs no reformation; he needs regeneration. Man does not need to get better, try harder, or grit his teeth and try, try, again. Every step man takes to redouble *his* efforts through rededicated promises to raise his quality of conduct to the standards of a Holy God is doomed from its inception. It is difficult for man in his darkened and deadened spiritual reasoning to conceive that what got him in trouble to begin with, his effort to be as God, is precisely the trap Satan is using to perpetuate fallen man's hopeless condition. Satan's ploy appeals to human ego to exercise the power of the man's will. The man, keeping his promises, will supposedly become like God. This is not Christianity!

The seemingly high standard to which a man can pull himself up by the moral bootstraps of his unbiblical *"promises"* appear to others of his fallen race in their fallen condition to be a high plateau of great spiritual achievement. This trait within the rebellious heart of man seeks atonement in his effort to be as God without God. This philosophy of religion affords man the perceived luxury of being a spiritually self-made man, without the incumbency of God imposing demands on his life that he die to himself. Fallen man would rather work to improve himself. This is an antiquated approach used by men who desire to anesthetize the conscience and relieve the conviction that is a symptom of their alienation from God.

This ever-increasingly popular approach to spiritual growth appeals to man in his unregenerate state and carnal reasoning. The power of this appeal helps explain the numerical success of Promise Keepers.

Hence, apostate Christianity, *not* atheism, will be the ultimate New World Order's last religion.

Morality... Counterfeit Righteousness

And yet, the diabolical plan from day one has never been, again, to make man bad, but to make him moral and acceptable in his own eyes. Tragically, morality is a cheap, satanic counterfeit for the righteousness of God which He so longs to manifest in our lives.

The Apostle Paul fought the inrush into the local churches of his day of various false doctrines, such as gnosticism, the Galatian heresies and a multitude of other man-made additives to the Gospel. Two thousand years ago, the prophetic pen of the Apostle called the church at Colosse to challenge the

THE PREMISE OF A PROMISE ■ 79

"new" ministries and false teachers that were, like parasites, attaching themselves and their man-made, will-based heresies to the people of God. The Church no doubt was being assaulted by teachers who were, as many are today, attempting to rewrite the plan of God. Corrupted hearts will never cease to refocus man's efforts on fallen flesh to finish what men cannot even begin without Divine intervention or complete without God supernaturally perpetuating the process. Paul, after warning this church of the deception of false, but seductive and persuasive teachers, admonishes them in the most severe terms to reject these heretical ministries. He writes a clear, passionate appeal, "As ye have, therefore, received Christ Jesus the Lord, so walk ye in him, rooted and built up in him, and [established] in the faith, as ye have been taught, abounding with thanksgiving. Beware lest any man spoil you through philosophy and vain deceit, after the tradition of men, after the rudiments of the world, and not after Christ. For in Him dwelleth all the fullness of the Godhead bodily. *And ye are complete in Him,* Who is the head of all principality and power" (Emphasis mine) (Colossians 2:6-10).

Throughout history, very little has changed other than the names of the old serpent's attacks on the Truth. Clearly then, as now, men were coming up with "better ways" more attractive and accommodating to their fleshly pride than the way of the Cross and death to self.

How desperately the Church in our nation, especially as we face the appeal of ministries like Promise Keepers and so many other popular groups, needs this Pauline word from Colossians. American Christianity has lost its vitality. It hungers for additives that will rekindle the fire of its message and ministries. But the watered-down philosophies of humanism and secularism that quenched the church's flames in the past are the same spiritually waterlogged beliefs that contemporary and deluded Christians are now drawing from, believing them to be fuel to pour upon the flickering flames. But the more there is of *man* in the life of the church, the less there is of God.

God has expressed a singular desire of man. The exclusive effort He requires of those who respond to His call is to *"present their bodies as a living sacrifice"* to God (Romans 12:1). With this "corpse", God is able to manifest the extension and expression of His life to and through humanity.

The fallen nature of man dies hard and so desires to make up for the spiritual deficit resultant of his rebellion. Yet the essence of the Christian faith is that Christ has done it *all* and in Him is *all* and every believer has *all* of Him in *all* of them. He is sufficient without feeble promises on man's part. This *"all-ness"* that we have in Him is truly the great luxury of the Cross in which every believer can relax and find completeness. The *"rest"* reserved for those who cease from the dead works of repeatedly rededicating, recommitting and promising to do better and try harder is a *"rest"* that, once attained, is sweet indeed. *"There remaineth, therefore, a rest to the people of God"* (Hebrews 4:9).

As many of us have already discovered, we can only *"try to be"* a Christian for so long. Attempting to do what God never intended for us to do is frustrating. Yet, the battle between the flesh and spirit rages. Forever, flesh looks and lusts against the Spirit and says, *"Hey, I can do that."* But try as it may, flesh cannot, even if assisted by and encouraged by promises to try harder. The joy abiding in the believer at *rest* in Christ's finished work is sufficient evidence that promises and oaths to perform better are unnecessary, and insult what Christ has already accomplished for us.

Ministries that promote reaching God's objectives through man's achievements will continue to flourish and grow because of the fallen concept that implies surely somehow man can reach out and climb up to the pleasure of God without divine intervention. How much more precious it is to relax in His finished product and to discover the glory residing in His Word, which releases His Life *in* our life.

The secret of the successful Christian is only a secret because so few in the ecclesiastical chain of command have been willing to expose popular, but deadly and contagious germs of deceit. That is why the Truth so shocks the religious system. It is almost a foreign concept that upon salvation and the receiving of Jesus Christ as Lord and Savior, we receive all of God and He is sufficient.

Paul, in writing of this doctrine of "dying to the old" and "living to the new" spent much time explaining the fullness of this Truth and the central focus that every Christian is to maintain on Jesus and off of *"self."* He wrote:

> "Giving thanks unto the Father, who hath made us [fit] to be partakers of the inheritance of the saints in light; who hath delivered us from the power of darkness, and hath translated us into the kingdom of his dear Son; in whom we have redemption through his blood, even the forgiveness of sins; who is the image of the invisible God, the first-born of [all creation]; for by Him were all things created, that are in heaven, and that are in earth, visible and invisible, whether they be thrones, or dominions, or principalities, or powers: all things were created by Him, and for Him; and He is before all things, and by Him all things consist. And He is the head of the body, the church; who is the beginning, the first-born from the dead, that in all things He might have the pre-eminence. For it pleased the Father that in Him should all fullness dwell" (Colossians 1:12-19).

What a relief this should be to men who feel that their performance has been the key to their spiritual success or failure. All any Christian needs is to yield to Jesus and to simply trust and obey Him.

Spiritual-sounding smooth talkers without a rooting and grounding in the Word of God will continue to plague the Church. They are accepted because of biblical illiteracy on the part of the vast majority of Western Christianity and they have been thrust into a nation's limelight as "spiritual leaders" in spite of their sheer, audacious tenacity in corrupting the Scripture. That is the recent history of American Christendom.

Invaded

The Promise Keepers organization, from its stated goals and objectives to its methods and techniques to its invitation to those involved in deviant beliefs, demonstrates an intrusive and invasive nature.

Paul was fully discerning of the coming invasion of the church by bold, blatant and seemingly "spiritual" but false, heretical teachers. Hence he wrote: "Let no one defraud you by acting as an umpire and declaring you unworthy and disqualifying you for the prize, insisting on self-abasement and worship of angels, taking his stand on visions [he claims] he has seen, vainly puffed up by his sensuous notions and inflated by his unspiritual thoughts and fleshly conceit, and not holding fast to the Head, from Whom the entire body, supplied and knit together by means of its joints and ligaments, grows with a growth that is from God. If then you have died with Christ to material ways of looking at things and have escaped from the world's crude and elemental notions and teachings of externalism, why do you live as if you still belong to the world? Why do you submit to rules and regulations [such as], do not handle [this], do not taste [that], do not even touch [them], referring to things all of which perish with being used? To do this is to follow human precepts and doctrines. Such [practices] have indeed the outward appearance [that popularly passes] for wisdom, in promoting self-imposed rigor of devotion and delight in self-humiliation and severity of discipline of the body, but they are of no value in checking the indulgence of the flesh—the lower nature. [Instead, they do not honor God] but serve only to indulge the flesh" (Colossians 2:18-23)(Amplified Version).

Note that Paul stipulated these people "neglected" the body, the local church, and had come up with a better way than that plan God gave to His Church (*more on this later*).

Observe how descript Paul is of ministries that encourage Christians to bring themselves into the spiritual bondage of self-imposed commitments that are not commanded or honored by the Father. Promise Keepers insists that the seven promises, rigorously followed and truly kept, produce liberating revival. However, God's Word teaches that these kinds of self-imposed promises produce pride and bondage. These practices appear to pass for profound spirituality. But promoting these self-imposed commitments—even if and when such *"promises"* are kept—does not honor God but rather it only encourages and indulges our flesh. We get so proud of *"us."* Perhaps changing the name from "Promise Keepers" to "The Promise Keeper" would allow hearts to refocus onto the One True Keeper of His Word, the Lord Jesus Christ.

But then, perhaps He does not really keep His Word. For men who speak so highly of a Promise Keeping God and His faithfulness to be true to His Word, is it not strange, indeed, that these same men insist that this same God is not exclusively bound by His Word? Why else would they deem it necessary to add so very much to that Word through false teaching? Our problem is not with a God who keeps His Word to men. Our problem is men who will not obey the Word of God.

"Redeeming the time, because the days are evil."

Ephesians 5:16
The Apostle Paul

CHAPTER 7

"Time is Now Going to be Extended"

"I alone know the end from the beginning."

Isaiah 46:9-10

God is sovereign and has predetermined, as well as predestined, His prophetic order, clearly articulated His scenario of coming events and set the clock on its irreversible countdown. However, through an interesting use of the Greek word *"kairos"*, Promise Keepers president Randy Phillips suggests in a book he helped write that God is going to hold off on fulfilling prophetic events in order to give "His sons" the opportunity "to seize the moment" presented by the seven promises of Promise Keepers Ministries.[1]

Phillips states: "We believe the Lord is now extending His *kairos* an opportunity to make a difference. But His sons must respond and make the commitments that *we* believe will seize the moment: the seven promises of a Promise Keeper."[2] (Emphasis mine)

Kairos means "a fixed time frame or period of time specifically set aside by God for the happening of the event it is referencing".[3] It is referring to a time slot set aside by God for the unfolding of a particular event or events. It also indicates a time frame marked at its beginning, its life span and its closure by those clearly defined God-initiated events. It is quite different from another Greek word *"chronos."*,[4] used in the Scriptures, which describes a generic measure of time that is used in such instances where there is not specificity of events or occasion. For example, Paul, in his description of the waning moments of Earth's history, wrote young Timothy, "This know also, that in the last days perilous times (kairos) shall come" (2 Timothy 3:1). It must be understood that under the Holy Spirit's direction, the Apostle used the word *kairos* rather than *chronos* to emphatically and forthrightly speak of a duration of measurable time marked at its beginning, its transpiration, and its ending by defined features.

So *kairos*, by its biblical definition, is not a flexible, expandable or "capable of being extended" time frame. By choosing the word *"kairos"*, Phillips seems to suggest that the Promise Keepers phenomenon is so necessary to the plan and the desires of God that God has decided to give the world time to get in on the Promise Keepers revival; therefore, God must rewrite His plan to allow us more time.

This assertion is biblically errant. In no way does Scripture indicate the possibility that God is capable of being taken by surprise because He "forgot" to factor in sufficient time for human and Church history to be played out according to His own sovereign council. Every opportunity for full redemption, victory for believers and His Church has been placed within God's time-frame of the historic and prophetic equation. He does not, will not, need not, amend His schedule or extend this dispensation because He feels that "just this one more ministry needs to develop so humanity and the world will have one last chance 'to seize the moment'."

We are having our "last chance". God is the eternal NOW.

Another Limited View of God

The tragedy of much contemporary theology, such as that

reflected in the *"kairos"* statement is that it is divorced from a purely biblical base. Unfortunately, a great number of ministers in the public eye have an errant scriptural perspective. God's "plumb line" has, to many, become relative. Almost all doctrinal issues have developed wide and varied meanings among different parts of the Body. Yet we are warned by Paul to rightly divide the Word so that "no Scripture is given for any private interpretation" (2 Peter 1:20). In other words, the Bible means what it says and stands on its own authority, without any flexibility to man's opinion or preference.

The most popular contemporary approach to theology among modern-day western Christendom is illustrated daily on much of so-called Christian television. Many of America's most visible media ministries, as did the humanists of old, tend to reduce God to a sensual, logical and often, even physical manifestation. Millions of "Christians" are attempting to create a God who is compatible with their shallow living and carnal thinking and they are simply dancing to the tune of their favorite television preachers. They now measure God's presence by His physical manifestation and their emotional expression. They have, alas, created a god of their "imagination" and secured a false sense of knowing Him through sensual experience instead of through disciplined commitment to Him and obedience to His Word.

When an organization, whether it is Promise Keepers or one of a multitude of other like-minded, pseudo-Christian ministries—refuses to adhere to biblical guidelines and begins to define truth based upon cognitive experiences and biblically baseless teachings, then anything goes. The unfortunate results are that a menagerie of groups and spokespersons, all to the scripturally illiterate and/or less vigilant of "Bereans," become authoritative and credible.

The "walls that have separated the Body of Christ for too long," described in Promise Keepers' Statement of Faith have indeed already started crumbling. The result is the most confused, ungrounded, "blown about by every wind of doctrine," population of church members since Acts 2.

The limited commitment to "study to show thyself approved unto God, a workmen that needeth not to be ashamed"

(2 Timothy 2:15) and the unwillingness to tenaciously hold preachers and ministries accountable to God's Word has birthed a limited view and understanding of a Holy God.

And the breakdown of doctrinal purity among what were once Bible-believing groups is growing ever worse. That is why some men and groups can make outlandish and bizarre statements with only a few, even in the ministry of traditional Bible-believing denominations, even raising an eyebrow of concern.

This limited view of God engenders statements such as Phillips' "kairos" assertion and insures that Promise Keepers' vision of "revival can be realized as 'His sons' seize the moment" and join millions of others to make the seven promises of a Promise Keeper.

A Biblical View vs. the Limited View
The Geometry of Eternity

When men are loosed from a biblical anchor, they begin the drift toward dangerous concepts and jaded doctrines. To say that God will "extend *kairos*'" is clear evidence that those who conceive that such is possible have rejected the biblical view of not only the nature of God but of the nature of *"time"*. Such a conclusion is made by man when he mistakenly uses non-spiritual and linear concepts to explain spiritual and non-linear truths. In other words, most people, especially those exposed to prophecy teachers attempting to lay out a visual aid for the prophetic scenario, understand time as a "time line". On such a time line, the extreme left typically represents the beginning of human history and the far right represents the culmination of human history as man has known it, climaxing with the Second Coming of Christ and the beginning of a New Age.

Teacher, author and prophecy scholar Chuck Missler often discusses this mistaken concept popularized by man's limited view of God. He echoes many related truths on "time" that are now confirmed by science and physics as well as the Scriptures.

Phillips' misunderstanding of the nature of both time and God is a common mistake. In fact, most people do perceive God to be One who has a lot of time. Although that is rhetorically true, this kind of thinking is not only bad theology, it is bad physics. Science has now conclusively proven, what serious students of scriptural prophecies have long known, that time is a physical property.

Even Einstein understood a created and ordered universe and the necessity of chronological events that transpire in a precisely measured frame work of time. Einstein knew that if the universal system was to remain stable and not rapidly deteriorate into chaos, time had to follow its created pattern and purpose.

In his Theory of Relativity, Einstein reveals that we live in at least a four-dimensional universe, made up of height, depth, width and time.

Interestingly, science is rather late in discovering what the Bible has clearly taught on this matter for millennia. Paul, under the inspiration of the Holy Spirit, penned: "That ye may be able to comprehend with all saints what is the breadth, and length, and depth and height and to know the love of Christ" (Ephesians 3:18). The four dimensions described by Paul are not spoken of figuratively. The Holy Spirit, in stark contrast to many in leadership of contemporary Americanized Christianity, is not flippant or irresponsible in His use of words. In fact, He is perfectly precise and descript. These four dimensions that Paul mentions; height, width, length and depth refer to the Omniscient and Omnipresent God intricately woven into and orchestrating the existence, the structure and movement of the entire universe as an expression of His all-consuming power, purpose and plan.

Paul's emphatic repetition in explaining God's all-consuming sovereignty was to enforce the truth that God is far above those things which He has created and that He has calculated into His creation any and all eventualities. Paul said to the Ephesians, "The eyes of your understanding being enlightened; that ye may know what is the hope of His calling, and what the riches of the glory of His inheritance in the saints" (Ephesians 1:18). God is a God who has predetermined and preset His schedule and Promise Keepers is only one of many who clearly has a contoured view of this biblical Truth.

In fact, one of the most interesting facets of the Bible is that no other religious book in history perceives or presents our universe in any more than three dimensions which God transcends and within which He operates. This, again, is because of the limited view of God held by those who refuse to understand the sacred and sole authority of God's Word.

Without the benefit of modern calculus, physics or science, Maimonides, a Jewish scholar of the12th century, concluded that time and space, as well as mass and energy, had their beginning in Genesis 1:1. He also theorized that the Earth has 10 dimensions. He believed that four of these dimensions are knowable and that the other six are unknowable. This is not 12th century mysticism. Today, particle physicists are discovering that our physical universe has at least 10 dimensions, and that four are knowable while the other six are, according to complex calculus, inferred and "curled" beyond the limits of current technology's ability to measure them directly. Maimonides, observed these basic facts by studying Genesis more than 800 years before our scientific community, after spending billions of dollars to dissuade themselves of a created and ordered universal system, finally concurred with the ancient Bible scholar.

Why is all this important?

The answer is that men at the helm of many of America's largest ministries are teaching heresies and error that not only defy basic and increasingly forgotten Truths of Scripture, but they are also teaching things that have no credibility in commonly known, universal, absolute realities. For the most part, not only are most major pulpits silent about the routine teaching of such errors, but they have, in fact, joined the march into the jaws of demonic doctrine and extra-biblical teachings simply because of intellectual laziness and ignorance of the Scriptures. Such silence on the part of these pulpits who could redirect the hearts of their flocks are tantamount to spiritual high treason. Acquiescence to error by spiritual leaders only confirms the error as truth and perpetuates the flood of heresy.

Why does God need not reschedule events which He has

preordained in order to fit Promise Keepers' agenda into His universal plan? Simply because God, as Creator, is not subject to the creation nor is He at its mercy. Time is, as is the earth, a created physical property and as a physical property, it is changed by mass, acceleration and gravity. In other words, physical consequences are imposed upon it as a result of the ever-changing motion of the physical entities around it. A sovereign God pre-fixed the entities according to His Omniscient foreknowledge.

Readily available resources confirm what the Scriptures have already stated, that time, unlike God, does change. If you have a clock and move it to a weaker gravitational field, it will run faster. Scientists tell us that nearer the surface of the Earth, the frequency of a clock's movement will increase by about 1:10 to the 16th per meter. In other words, if you move a clock 100 yards, it will change in increments so small that without sensitive measuring devices, it is unnoticeable, but it does change. Missler illustrates such truths with the example of a clock that is physically moved rapidly to a different directional location. A clock carried on an airplane will move slightly more slowly than a clock sitting at home on a bed stand. A clock on an airplane carried West will vary because of the gravitational influence upon it.

At Issue is the Character of God

Reading the statement that "God would extend *kairos*" to accommodate the Promise Keepers' agenda and goals so that humanity can finally experience revival forces one to question the *eternal, omniscient* and *sovereign* character of God.

The Scriptures clearly teach that God is *eternal*, that His existence has no beginning and no ending. He is unchanging and self-existent. Isaiah 57:15 says, "...It is He who inhabits eternity." The same prophet of old wrote as God spoke in Isaiah 46:9-10, "I alone know the end from the beginning." He not only exists from eternity, but He exists from Himself. The New Testament book of James says, "Every good and perfect gift cometh down from the Father of lights with whom there is no variableness nor shadow of turning" (James 1:17). Because God knows the beginnings and endings, yes, even about the Promise Keepers phenomenon, it is not necessary for Him to reconsider His eternal plan to accommodate that ministry. The Spirit of God uttered to the prophet Samuel, "And also the strength of Israel will not lie nor repent, for He is not a man, that He should repent" (1 Samuel 15:29).

The *omniscience* of God testifies that His knowledge of events past, present and future is total and complete. The psalmist declared, "Great is the Lord and of great power, His understanding is infinite" (Psalm 147:5). The plan of the Ages and each man's part in it has been known to God from all eternity. God has no such things as an "afterthought". Paul wrote to Rome, saying, "Oh, the depth of the riches both of the wisdom and knowledge of God! How unsearchable are His judgments and His ways past finding out" (Romans 11:33).

If God was going to extend *kairos*, or time, it would throw into question His sovereignty. Such a statement makes God subject to that which He, according to Scripture, has created.

Is God subject to mass, to gravity, or to time? Clearly, the answer is "NO". God is outside the "time line" altogether. Does not the Word of God teach that Jesus was "crucified before the foundations of the world" (Revelation 13:8)? In the measurement of time used to place the events of human history, had the crucifixion taken place prior to the life of Christ? No. Not in a historic sense. Yet, because God has predestined every event in human history, He, in His foreknowledge, declared what *was not* as though it *was* because, in Truth, it *was* indeed.

Every human attempt to impose man's zealous but erroneous concepts into the closed, divine Word and plan is futile and will always result in a blatant refutation of God's Truth. Neither man nor time exists to complete or confirm God. He does not exist because we exist. We are, because He is.

"He who has truth on his side is a fool as well as a coward if he is afraid to own it because of other men's opinions."

—Defoe

CHAPTER 8

They Called This "Revival"

"There is a way which seemeth right unto a man, but the ends thereof are the ways of death."

Proverbs 14:12

It was in the late 80s. The birth of Promise Keepers was years away and yet the spiritual and sociological factors, along with the increasing biblical illiteracy necessary for its success, were evident all across America's spiritual horizon. Many of us witnessed the slow spiritual decline in the demand for doctrinal purity and heard the crescendo in the call for a more loving, tolerant and gentle Christianity.

I witnessed this prophesied rise in popularity of the *"unity"* movement, and for a while was both intrigued by it and uneasy about it. The ministries of men like Francis Schaeffer, Dave Hunt and Dr. John MacArthur, coupled with a consecrated personal commitment to study the Word of God and to seek His heart, prompted the pieces of this puzzling move of *"the Spirit"* to fall in place for me. I began to see where it was all leading. The following experience was embryonic to my fuller understanding of the character of this ever-increasing call for "tolerance and unity," which is the purpose of ministries such as Promise Keepers.

Some time ago, I went through a two or three-year period during which I was frequently a special guest on Trinity Broadcast Network, one of America's largest Christian television networks. Paul and Jan Crouch of the network had always been kind and courteous hosts. (Incidentally, our television program, whose coverage still straddles the North American continent, was at that time purchasing weekly air time on TBN.)

On what was to be my last occasion to appear on *"Praise The Lord,"* I was caught somewhat off-guard when I walked into the Green Room and met, face-to-face, Earl Paulk, pastor of the Chapel Hill Harvester Church in Atlanta, Georgia. He calls himself a bishop and accordingly wears a white collar. Although I found Mr. Paulk to be a pleasant and cordial man, I did, however, (and still do) have great concerns with not only his theology, but with his philosophy of ministry as well because of my extensive research into the doctrinal positions held by him and his followers. He was well aware of my personal convictions since he was, he said, a regular viewer of our program.

When the special guest host for that night's program entered the room just minutes before we went on the air, I asked to speak to him privately. Off to the side, I told him I had some deep and profound misgivings about the beliefs system and ministry of Mr. Paulk, and asked him to excuse me since I could not sit silently on live television and, by my silence, condone what Earl Paulk represents.

The host, taken aback, responded by saying, *"Oh come on, we don't muzzle anyone here. If you want to say something, say it. We're all big boys. We can all take it."*

Within minutes, I had taken my place on the set with host Richard Hogue. Earl Paulk was sitting a few yards in front of me, just behind the camera line, on the first row of the studio audience.

After the initial formalities, Mr. Hogue began to discuss the revival that he said was sweeping America. He then asked what I thought about this "great revival."

My reply obviously stunned him as well as many of the listeners.

In summary, I said that I did not believe we were in a spiritual revival in America. Historically, when revival has come to various societies, it has always been accompanied by certain "birthmarks" such as holy living, a collective consciousness and repentance of national and individual sin, as well as a spiritual healing and cleansing in the land. I continued in this vein saying that this so-called "revival," if it was a revival, was the first one in Church history to leave in its wake an unprecedented number of abortions, an acceptance and applauding of perverse lifestyles such as homosexuality, a pandemic spread of venereal diseases and a national plague of AIDS. I pointed out that homes were falling apart across America with a 50 percent-plus divorce rate, to say nothing of the steadily increasing number of violent, teenage gangs, an alarming increase in every category of crime and an ever-growing racial hatred bringing strife and division to our cities. I pressed the point that this was not true revival, but rather a revival of a *"last days"* satanic spirit that the prophets foretold would accompany this last generation.

The host then asked why so many pastors, preachers and leading Christian spokesmen had been insisting that revival was sweeping our nation.

The tenor of my response to this was that such statements by these people could be attributed to an abysmal lack of true spiritual discernment. I then referred to Mr. Paulk, his next guest, as being very much a part of the problem. I was, after reading a number of Earl Paulk's writings, familiar with his theology on the call of the Church and Christian living, as well as with his beliefs on communicating with the dead and a number of other teachings. His beliefs concerning "last days" prophecies and his "Kingdom Dominionist theology" are in deep conflict with the Word of God. Yet Mr. Paulk was being heralded and promoted by not only that evening's TBN host, but also by a number of other high-profile TBN personalities, including Paul and Jan Crouch, as one of America's great spiritual leaders.

As the live interview continued, I alluded to some of the less-known positions of Earl Paulk as opposed to some of his more unusual beliefs, in deference to kindness. That is when things got interesting. Mr. Paulk, who was still sitting in the studio watching and waiting his turn was, I was later informed, obviously upset. The host then attempted to discredit my understanding of historical Church positions concerning eschatological matters in order to defend the credibility of Mr. Paulk. I attempted to maintain a Christ-like attitude throughout the segment as I contended for the obvious Truth that was being discussed.

After the dialogue had continued along these lines for some time, the host decided that it was time for a singer to do a number. He quickly thanked me for coming and rushed me off the set. After the song came to an end, Earl Paulk had taken his place on the set.

As this interview began, among the first words out of Earl Paulk's mouth were, "And I wonder where Rev. Phil Arms stands on the issue of tongues?" I assume that he meant to expose through such a question how very "unspiritual" I am because he was fully aware that I do not speak in tongues. He wanted to assure all the viewers of a charismatic-Pentecostal and Full Gospel doctrinal persuasion that he, because he does speak in tongues and shares their "common experience," was clearly far more spiritual, thus should be considered a more credible theologian than myself. Mr. Paulk laboriously attempted to imply that "speaking in tongues" is the "litmus test" for correct doctrine and the qualifier of all Truth. Clearly, the inference was "you cannot trust people who do not speak in tongues." Such confused conclusions of course, would disqualify the majority of Christian history's most dynamic men and women of God, including the Son of the Living God, the Lord Jesus Christ.

The "common experience" shared by the founders and directors of Promise Keepers as well as their home churches and spiritual fathers is the identical experience that Earl Paulk attempted to use in his effort to intimidate and polarize this author. The issue of speaking in tongues, rather than being the Comforter's sign gift for the early church, has been used by so many contemporary Christians and ministries to bring great discomfort to the Body of Christ. Certainly not all of those who believe in and practice "speaking in tongues" use the issue, as did Paulk, to elevate themselves and to negate others. Those who do demonstrate such an arrogance over their "superior spirituality" are neither filled with the Holy Spirit nor exercising legitimate spiritual gifts.

Several months later, according to public court records, sexual scandals and allegations broke out in mammoth proportions at the Chapel Hill Harvester Church in Atlanta, Georgia where Paulk was the Senior Pastor. This nationally publicized sex scandal involved dozens of women who were charging not only Earl Paulk, but others on his staff as well, with sexual misconduct and sexual abuse.

Below is one of the many articles that appeared across America exposing not only these heartbreaking moral failures, but also Paulk's biblically fraudulent defense of his conduct. The leading charismatic magazine in America, *Charisma,* published the following article:

"Women Charge Minister with Abuse"
Chapel Hill Harvester Church
Decatur, Georgia

"A group of women, former members of the Decatur, GA. Chapel Hill Harvester Church-now called Cathedral of the Holy Spirit-publicly accused church founder Earl Paulk, Jr., and other leaders of sexual misconduct and of attempting to cover up a pattern of widespread immoral behavior.

Tricia Weeks, 44, a former church spokeswoman and ghostwriter for several of Earl Paulk's books, said she was sexually involved with him from 1986 to 1988. She said that in spite of her Christian upbringing, she was convinced after working closely with Paulk that a sexual relationship with him would not threaten her salvation or her marriage vows. 'I heard repeatedly—both privately and publicly as a doctrine woven into his preaching—that, on the contrary, such bonding relationships were used by God to bring confidence and power to one's spiritual calling. It is important for people to realize the powerful biblical justification that Mr. Paulk uses for his perverted thinking.'

Weeks and other women said they had been indoctrinated to believe that Christians who are spiritually mature can handle sex outside of marriage. This so-called 'kingdom relationship' teaching, the women said, was an off-shoot of Paulk's focus on 'Kingdom Now' theology.

Rationale:

Paulk has written, 'I lived years of my life in complete adherence to a rigid morality which was devoid of any expressions of compassion or tenderness. Only years later...did I begin to comprehend that God's desires in Christian relationships are demonstrated in the example of Jesus Christ...he was touchable and physically expressive... Jesus deliberately broke moral codes of his day to love and minister to certain people.'"[1]

This justification by Earl Paulk of his well-publicized moral failures grieves the hearts of Christians with scriptural convictions. But when anyone starts down the road of compromising biblically sound, doctrinal distinctions, as I believe Promise Keepers would have all Christendom do for the sake of unity, they will, without fail, experience compromise in areas of their personal lives.

These events concerning Earl Paulk were widely covered by both the Christian and secular media. I would not have mentioned them unless Paulk had not so forcefully inferred that he had attained a higher level of credibility and spiritual evolution as a result of a "spiritual gift" that he possessed, but which is lacking in the majority of the Church.

The unity sought by Promise Keepers and many of America's most high-profile Christian ministries requires a surrender of theological positions traditionally held by doctrinally balanced believers. It does not, however, require such from the ministries who are calling for ecumenical unity, as most of them have never been doctrinally balanced. These who seek to make us all "one" do not hold dear the great doctrines and tenets of the Christian faith; hence, they have little to lose and little to surrender but much to gain.

It must also be pointed out that no perceived "gift of the Spirit" qualifies an individual to elevate his or her personal beliefs and actions to be more sacred and vital than the precious, immutable Word of God. Nor does any level of perceived spiritual achievement, possession of spiritual gifts, or rank in the hierarchy of the Church guarantee that one will live a pure life, free of sexual impurity and moral failures.

A word of caution against pride for those who are not part of what is commonly called the *"Pentecostal, Full Gospel or Charismatic"* persuasion. To these I say, neither is there special guaranteed exemption from failure of any fleshly temptation for you. Every Christian must have a daily disciplined walk with God in order to maintain moral purity. Our guarantee for moral purity is not reliance upon our spiritual achievements or *"gifts"* or even "believing sound doctrine." Our assurance for such victory is stated in Galatians 5:16, "This I say then, walk in the Spirit, and ye shall not fulfill the lusts of the flesh." Triumph over the lust of the flesh is secured and maintained on a daily basis as the believer applies the sound doctrine he professes. In short, he must be possessed and obsessed by not only the True doctrine of God, but the True God of the doctrine.

Learning the great doctrines of the Faith and applying these precious Truths through regular disciplined Bible study are vital to living a Spirit-filled, purpose-driven Christian life. Promise Keepers' focus on breaking down these doctrinal pillars of the Faith will produce disastrous results for those who follow such ill-conceived theology.

It does matter what we believe about God, about the Bible, and about what constitutes spiritual growth. Such doctrine dictates how we conduct and live our public and private lives. If our beliefs on these matters are not solely focused and founded on Scripture without the infusion of human wisdom, carnal compromise, extra-biblical spiritual experiences, and unscriptural demand for physical manifestations, then, ultimately, our hidden life will openly manifest spiritual failures. We will not be able to maintain a holy or consistently godly tenor in our lifestyle and our witness. We will not experience spiritual growth as expeditiously as we otherwise might, nor will we remember our frail humanity, its tendency to fail and to never "think more highly of ourselves than we ought." We are again reminded, *"let him who stands take heed, lest he fall"* (1 Corinthians 10:12).

Those who choose to receive Jesus Christ as Lord and Savior must therefore maintain a vigilant effort to grow in "the grace and knowledge of the Lord Jesus Christ" through God's biblically prescribed techniques. To approach spiritual growth and/or renewal on any other premise is fraudulent and will always result in spiritual disaster. Paul told the church at Colosse, "As you have received Christ Jesus the Lord, so walk ye in Him, rooted and built up in Him and established in the faith" (Colossians 2:6-7).

The imperative upon each believer, especially in these waning days of history as Satan intensifies his efforts to derail Christians, is to challenge the clear assaults upon God's Truth. It is never comfortable when we are forced to lovingly, but firmly *"contend for the faith"*. And, certainly, there will be few who applaud such efforts.

Those who are corrected will most often resort to the psychological sleight of hand to refocus attention away from their error and onto their concept of truth and the perceived failures of others. Flesh has adopted the old warrior's tactic that "the best defense is a good offense." Hence, God's Word admonishes that "they comparing themselves among themselves are not wise" (2 Corinthians 10:12).

Tragically, many men in spiritual leadership and pulpits across this great nation still refuse to speak out against the popular trends that they suspect or even know contradict biblical Truths. The unity movement has thrown its deceptive net and drawn in multitudes of men in and out of pulpits who are too intimidated to take a bold, scriptural stand on issues. Great Truths have become "expendable" for the sake of presenting a "united Christian community" resulting in a wholesale slaughter and sacrifice of the basic essentials to the Christian faith.

Pragmatism is the order of the day for a growing number of churches and their leadership. Their "altars" are full of "truths" that have been sacrificed, leaving little room for the corpse of our "self-centered, ego-driven, flesh-powered ministries." So, instead of paying the price to experience a legitimate, dynamic move of the Spirit in true revival, we have redefined His message, rejected His methods and poisoned our ministries. The resulting madness is a delusion that has hypnotized and paralyzed many church leaders and laity with a lust for numerical success and hassle-free, comfortable ministries that maintain the "status quo." When such men are then able to create an atmosphere with spiritualistic theatrics passed off as "miracles" to convince the scripturally illiterate masses that *"God is with us"* and call it revival, so much the better for their charade.

This spiritual atmosphere into which the phenomenal ministry of Promise Keepers was born is the Americanized *"church."* The majority of this church's leadership, after decades of compromising, accommodating, and emulating the worldly system that they were commissioned to change, has been assimilated by that system. Thus, that which appears to secular society to be "the Church" has not only taken on the world's spiritual blindness, but has become infected with the spiritual equivalent of its most deadly disease, AIDS. In short, the American church has lost its ability to resist those infections that threaten its very existence. This is a primary reason for the overwhelming and unprecedented success and growth of Promise Keepers, whose spiritually infectious tentacles are now embracing every Christian denomination in America and calling it "revival."

Short Cuts and Dead Ends

The Promise Keepers' plan contradicts the plan of God for spiritual growth and true revival. The Old Testament repeatedly illustrates God's specific, divine plan laid out for men who desire to interact with Him. The Levitical priests were under stringent demands and requirements about how to approach God and how to maintain His pleasure and presence, and under no circumstances were these God-ordained approaches to be breached. No *"short cuts"* in worship, in Temple activity or in blood sacrifices were tolerated. Everything had to be done precisely God's way without the slightest variation or the results were disastrous and often deadly.

In the New Testament, God has with great detail established precisely how and on what conditions man can approach and develop a relationship with Him. It is a narrow way and yet it is most inclusive. Anyone can enter relationship with God if he or she is willing to enter through the door of His Son and His atoning blood by grace through faith. Regardless of who says otherwise, God has not given another way for the redemptive process to work. By the same token, God has a clearly established plan for our fellowship with Him and for our consistent spiritual growth and maturing.

So, why is it that in ever-increasing numbers, people are succumbing to the spiritual seduction of ministries such as Promise Keepers that promote short cuts, new options and improved methods for believers to achieve God's goals? Can it be that the answer to this question is that the curse of the fall has wedded man's heart to the mistaken idea that, indeed, "sacrifice is better than obedience?"

"But We Will Be Like God"

> *"And the serpent said unto the woman, ye shall not surely die; For God doth know that in the day ye eat thereof, then your eyes shall be opened, and ye shall be as [God], knowing good and evil."* Genesis 3:4-5

It is apparently the conviction of Promise Keepers that spiritual revival and renewal will spring out of men whose lives have been changed because they made a series of promises and kept them. In fact, this is the basis upon which, according to promotional material, the Promise Keepers ministries was founded.

The organization's president, Randy Phillips, writes "Promise Keepers believes it starts by making some promises... promises we intend to keep." Then he states how through "prayer and discussion, the staff and board of directors" came to this conclusion.[2]

This plan revolves around the *"promise"* idea, which asserts that man is capable of pleasing and being most like God by exercising the power of his will to "perform" the tasks defined in their seven promises.

Clearly, God as the Father desires that each of His children be an extension and an exhibition of the life of Christ. As previously stated, the goal for the believer is to demonstrate Christ's power, life, love and choices not through the flagellation of the flesh, the external disciplines of expression and conduct or through self-imposed restraints, but rather by a "death to self." But man's fallen nature desires to be far more than *like* God; it wants *to be* God. This serpentine obsession still slithers among the people of the Creator. It persists in the suggestion *"wouldn't you like to be as gods?"* just as it did to Eve on that infamous day recorded in Genesis 3:5.

Humanity, since hearing that satanic invitation, desires to attain the throne and tends to listen to the seducing hiss. And the nature of seduction is subtle, so subtle because it works in league with man's fallen nature and its tendency to self-justification. Many spiritual leaders across America have "sanctified" their acceptance of the demonic invitation to compromise truth by falling into the ancient snare that "surely, laudable ends justify sometimes dubious means."

The willingness on the part of many Christian lay people, as well as leaders, to accept the subtle satanic seduction to participate in and support Promise Keepers simply because, as most will tell you, *"it does so much good and helps so many men and families,"* indicates a spiritual shallowness and intellectual laziness in American Christianity.

This new approach to creating *"real men,"* to supposedly be quickly followed by *"real revival,"* though wrapped in pious talk, is still no more and no less than the same old wrong road, built to reach a God-given goal in a God-forbidden way.

"...Truth is perished, and is cut off from their mouth."
Jeremiah 7:28

CHAPTER 9

What is Wrong With This Picture?

"The devil... is perfectly content to see you becoming chaste and brave and self-controlled provided, all the time, he is setting up in you the dictatorship of pride."[1]

—C.S. Lewis

"Man-invented" ways to appease God and achieve His pleasure are based upon the erroneous concept that there is some kind of equality between the nature of God and the nature of man. Contemporary thought in much of our church leadership presupposes that we are on the same "spiritual plane" as God and, therefore, we have an innate capacity to "act like God." Taken far enough, this embryo of error evolves into *"not only can we act like God"* but we can *"become God."* One final step remains, and millions of people in our society have taken that final step: believing, in fact, that they *"are God."*

New Age Christianity attempts to combine that concept with the biblical teaching of New Birth. The result is the creation of the concept that man has an innate divine potential, which, once developed through his human efforts, releases "the god" or "the Christ" within. But our salvation in no way qualifies us to begin acting as though we are co-redeemers, sovereigns or smaller images of God. To the contrary, every believer is made *"new"* in Christ Jesus and it is His life we are to live, not our life elevated, improved or sanctified by self-induced efforts that produce a new and improved old nature equipped with an evolutionary capacity to *"grow"* into gods.

Many cults, such as Mormons, do teach that we are all evolving into "little gods." This skewed theology, or more precisely, doctrine of devils, has worked its way into today's Christendom through popular media teachers, preachers, authors and Christian personalities. It is little wonder that a ministry like Promise Keepers can experience such unprecedented growth in the presence of our nation's current theological and doctrinal chaos and biblical illiteracy. When allegiance to visible results and measurable success runs far deeper than allegiance to God's Word, it produces an *"anything goes"* theological free-for-all atmosphere resulting in the birth of Promise Keepers-style ministries with amazingly little resistance from a once-vigilant Christian community.

God's Nature versus Man's Nature

> "God is not a man, that he should lie; neither the son of man, that he should repent. Hath he said, and shall he not do it? Or hath he spoken, and shall he not make it good?"
> Numbers 23:19

God indeed is a God of His Word. The essence of His character is holiness. Unfortunately, this generation of Christians has been taught that the fundamental character facet of God is love, but focusing on this trait of God without viewing the full biblical portrait of God's nature leads to heretical beliefs. Some who do not understand the nature of God's love in the context of His full character erroneously use His love as an escape clause. They believe that God's love causes Him to overlook man's sinful, damned condition and to simply forgive and unconditionally accept man in his unrepentant state. To accept this faulty concept of God's love, one must divorce the scriptural teachings on God's love from the Truth that God is far more complex and has a multitude of other corresponding divine attributes. Such flawed biblical interpretation has caused massive numbers of people to create a new reality complete with an imagined loophole allowing them to, in their thinking, escape their accountability to a Holy God for their sinful condition. The Bible teaches that God is primarily and supremely Holy. Without holiness as the foundational character facet of God, every other character facet, even His love, would be flawed and subject to failure. Hence, every divine aspect of God's sovereign nature acts in concert with the others in a perfectly balanced harmony. His holiness demanded "the shedding of blood without which there is no remission of sin" (Hebrews 9:22). God's love made provision for the death penalty due as a result of man's sin to be paid by His Son. Love and holiness were perfectly balanced in His redemptive promise and process for man's redemption.

The Bible is full of God's promises relative to man's relationship and fellowship with Him. God says, *"If you will... then, I will."* This also applies to our covenantal relationship and interaction with God.

God initiates the "hunt" for those willing to hear His promises. It is God who, by His Spirit, quickens the heart of man to act upon His promises. He delights in performing His Word for His beloved if only we will respond to His call. No one who knows God through a relationship with Jesus Christ would argue with the fact that God is a promise-keeping God. But the concept of God's graces being contingent upon the promises of man to Him are foreign, as we shall see, to the Scripture.

The Limitations of Imitations

The conflicts that Promise Keepers' philosophy of ministry has with the written Word of God are rudimentary and can be traced back to a *"contemporary-modernistic"* theology that, in finding no biblical definition for its ever-growing doctrinal network, has set out to define itself. This has resulted in a neo-Christianity that considers doctrine a secondary priority to its most important objective. That objective is the unification of all Christians to, as Promise Keepers' sixth promise says, "demonstrate the power of biblical unity."[2]

Historically, at least in the American Church, this assault on doctrinal integrity began with a group who was, in its beginning, called *"modernists."* This group's desire was to make the church more "hip", "cool" and "relevant" by de-emphasizing dogma. The darkest days of his ministry, according to Charles Haddon Spurgeon, the renowned pastor of London's Metropolitan Tabernacle and eighteenth-century defender of the Faith, fell during his ongoing battle against these pioneer pragmatists in his own time and nation. Their goal to unify all Christians regardless of doctrine had an opposite effect. For instance, to use the words *"Full Gospel"* or *"Spirit-filled"* in today's Christian circles implies that there exists a group of Christians which has "more of Jesus" or a fuller, more complete revelation than the average Christian. Such an approach to defining ourselves often leads dividing the spiritual *"haves"* from the *"have nots."* Dichotomizing the body and developing "groups" whom we consider to have "more of God" than others because of physical manifestations of spiritual experiences derived from external and extra-biblical sources always leads to additional error and divisiveness.

The semantics and terminology used by Promise Keepers lays the foundation for theology that is foreign to the Scriptures. Such semantic and phraseological license is illustrated in the Promise Keepers' statements that God is a "model" or "cast" into which we are to pour ourselves. If God is our model, as Promise Keepers' material states, then it naturally follows that we should attempt to reflect that model by behaving in a way that models the prototype.

It helps the student of Scripture to understand the all-encompassing, Christ-centered nature of true salvation. Promise Keepers' theology minimizes the central role played by the indwelling Spirit of God in manifesting through believers the person of Jesus Christ. The theology simultaneously maximizes the role that the power of man's fleshly will and natural abilities are to play in the Christian life. This theology is wrong; God is not our model. His goal for humanity has never been for man to imitate Him, but rather, to allow His dominance to manifest Christ through us as believers. Otherwise, we face a futile feat. We are not to reflect His image. We are not to be mirrors. We are to be as rivers flowing with the life of Christ. Jesus, in referring to the abundant life resident in Him, said, "...and rivers of living water shall flow from your innermost being" (John 7:38).

This *"flow"* from within the believer is not the believer pumping or working up a stream of water via his efforts and promises to do good. This river is as an artesian well springing forth from the believer who abides in Christ.

The Promise Keepers' concept of how men can become dynamic Christians fulfilling their call is flawed. The theology that bases itself on *"imitating"* divine character and attempting, through human efforts, to reflect the nature of God has a diabolical root. Throughout history, many other religious systems and various denominations have been built upon the *"imitate Christ"* theology. Such are fond of using verses such as 1 Corinthians 11:1, which reads in one or two contemporary translations: "Be imitators of me just as I am of Christ." The King James Version, as well as a number of other translations, uses the word "followers" instead of "imitators" in this verse.

One of the wonderful things about living in our age is that we have inexhaustible libraries to assist our Old or New Testament study of the Scriptures. Any student can easily look up Greek or Hebrew words or passages and then cross-reference them to insure their contextual integrity and doctrinal purity. Almost any respectable expository dictionary reveals the true meaning and intent of 1 Corinthians 11:1. The Greek noun Paul uses that some translators have rendered "imitate" is *"mimetes."* In the setting of this passage and the sister passages of 1 Corinthians 4:16 and Ephesians 5:1, this is literally the word "follow." Paul is admonishing the Corinthians, and subsequently all believers, to follow the pattern he has set in allowing Jesus Christ to be himself through Paul's life.

Some may argue that Paul later stipulated that we should

"work out our salvation..." (Philippians 2:12). Surely there
is, as the argument goes, something we can do. A brief look
in a good expository dictionary of the New Testament will
clear up any confusion. Paul here uses the Greek word
"katergazomai," translated into English as the word "work."
Paul uses the Greek word "soteria" to describe a specific
facet of the believer's salvation. In each of the instances, the
verb tenses surrounding it determine which aspect of salvation.
Philippians 2:12 refers to that part of our salvation wherein
there is "peace and fellowship" with those who share the
same "soteria" or "salvation."[3]

The context of Philippians 2:12 regards conduct among
Christians at Philippi. Paul states emphatically that the church
at Philippi must obey God by being of the same mind, united
in spirit, thereby insuring no fleshly retaliation toward offending
fellow believers. Paul does not tell them to laboriously work
to "imitate" the Lord Jesus Christ. On the contrary, "Christ
in you" is ever his theme. Christ is the source, the originator
and the force that motivates and energizes them to "live out"
the "live-in-Christ." He literally bends over backwards to
emphasize the futility of Christians who attempt to model
their self-life after Jesus. Reinforcing the believer's need to
depend exclusively on God's indwelling Spirit to manifest
Christ, Paul wrote, "For it is God who worketh in you both
to will and to do of His good pleasure" (Philippians 2:13).

Reading this epistle of the New Testament is like reading
an admonition concerning the current-day doctrinal crisis
promoted by Promise Keepers, who, like so many in the early
church, is sowing error and "trashing" the entire message of
the Gospel.

Correcting the "wrong" doctrine in Galatia—typified by
that of Promise Keepers—certainly prompted Paul to pen this
letter. We must read his masterful polemic to be guarded
against deceptive error as well. He writes of the superiority
of "the gospel of Christ." You see, it was not that these
foolish Galatians directly denied the Gospel, but their minds
were becoming inoculated with legalistic and ritualistic ideas
which destroyed its vital doctrine. The Apostle profoundly
states, "It is all of Christ!" "I am crucified with Christ:

nevertheless I live; yet not I, but Christ liveth in me; and the life which I now live in the flesh I live by the faith of the Son of God, who loved me and gave Himself for me" (Galatians 2:20).

To reiterate the fact that Christ is living through him, he rejects yet again the notion that his fleshly efforts "to be like Jesus" have anything at all to do with true Christianity. He defies that idea in 'Galatians 2:21: "I do not [make void] the grace of God; for if righteousness comes by the law, then Christ is dead in vain."

Promises solicited from Christian men in order to manifest Divine desires and character are unadulterated legalism and have absolutely nothing to do with spiritual maturing.

Paul wanted to insure there would be no doctrinal leakage concerning our need to allow the indwelling Christ to live His Life through us. He writes in Philippians 1:20-21, "According to my earnest expectation and my hope, that in nothing I shall be ashamed, but that with all boldness, as always, so now also Christ shall be magnified in my body, whether it be by life or by death. *For to me to live is Christ, and to die is gain.*"

We do not grow spiritually, as Paul clearly states, by grunting and groaning or by following rules. We grow by consistently yielding to the life of Christ within. Paul boasts of nothing that he could produce to contribute to this perpetual work of the grace of God.

In this exchanged life, Paul discovered intimacy with Christ. This precious intimacy is the fruit produced in the life of a Christian who moment by moment goes against self-effort and self-focus. The opposing theology that teaches Christians are to strive to be like Jesus and work to honor promises that will improve Christian *performance* is not to be found in the Scriptures. Paul had already fought that battle and reported on its tragic results in Romans 7. The condemnation resulting from such fleshly empowered pursuits left Paul saying, "Oh, wretched man that I am! Who shall deliver me from the body of this death?" This "body of death," resident in every member of the human race, could not, even through Paul's most persistent and sincere efforts, produce the quality of life that was discovered as he "ceased from his own works."

Paul proclaims his passion to "Be found in Him, not having mine own *righteousness, which is of the law, but that which is through the faith of Christ, the righteousness* which is <u>of</u> <u>God</u> by faith" (Philippians 3:9). He reports that God's power provokes our move toward God. The Holy Spirit's presence and power produce the manifestation of Christ-life. God causes us to experience positional and practical righteousness. His power in the Person of the Indwelling Christ prompts the heart, wooing it to do His will and way.

What is the believer's role in this salvation? The believer's role is to participate with the Holy Spirit, so that "for me to live is Christ." Note, again, the believer is not to strive through fleshly efforts to imitate or follow the *"cookie cutter"* Christian mold; rather, he should yield to His dominating Person within. Paul was emphatic on this point though always excited about the wonder and the glory of its manifestation in and through the believer. He reflected on this in writing to the church at Colosse, "Even the mystery which hath been hidden from ages and from generations, but now is made manifest to his saints, to whom God would make known what is the riches of the glory of this mystery among the Gentiles, which is Christ in you, the hope of glory" (Colossians 1:26-27). To most, the glory of relaxing in the luxury of God's finished work at the cross is still a mystery.

So the believer, as mentioned earlier, is to opt for death to all such efforts to imitate the character and nature of God. Christianity is Christ, which is the essence of Paul's statement in Philippians 1:21, "For me to live is Christ." It was not the desire of this Apostle to *"act out"* God's likeness. His history as a Pharisee proved the futility of such idolatry of the flesh.

A misunderstanding of the victorious Christian life is apparent in Promise Keepers' concept that man can, through promises, emulate Christ and thereby produce the results and desires of God. The organization promotes the view that God, because He has made promises, expects man to achieve His desires for man by man reciprocating with promises. This is a flawed and heretical view of the nature of God as well as the nature of salvation. Scripture does not demand that men respond to God on the basis of promises that are anything remotely related to those seven promises of Promise Keepers. Such theology, if true, would negate the necessity of the Cross.

Much like the statement by the president of Promise Keepers that God would extend time, the concept that promises on man's part can fulfill the will of God and accomplish His ends is a serious breach of the Scriptures. Such human efforts do not in even the most remote way reflect the true nature of God's plan for our sanctification. That plan is clearly laid out in the Word of God. In a coming chapter, we will see that plan as the Scriptures define it.

Is God Replicating Himself?

Promise Keepers' previously stated basis of its ministry and its philosophy is summarized in its material, which states: "God is our model. Consequently, a Promise Keeper chooses to reflect the trustworthy nature of His Lord. This character is summed up in the word integrity."[4] This unscriptural concept of man emulating the *"model,"* God, is the foundation of Promise Keepers' philosophy of ministry, which teaches men to reflect God's nature by keeping their promises to act like Christians.

Once more, I emphasize the New Testament Christian Pauline position defining the Christian life as one that does not attempt to fulfill promises to be more like God but rather, it is Christ's life within the twice-born believer. Paul clearly articulates this in Galatians 2:20, *"I am crucified* with Christ: nevertheless I live; *yet not I, but Christ* liveth in me; and the life which *I now live* in the flesh *I LIVE BY THE FAITH OF THE SON OF GOD*, who loved me and gave himself for me" (Emphasis mine). Believers are not reduced to the use of their own "faith," much less reliance on their own will power to keep feeble promises as a way to manifest a likeness of God. Paul clearly attributes even the *"faith"* to believe and to move God, to the indwelling life of Christ.

These are not small matters, nor are they semantic nit-picking. This matter of "Christ in you" versus "human effort" to create His likeness through following His model is the basic issue at the root of Promise Keepers' legitimacy or illegitimacy. Yes, we can see the sincerity of many brothers in Christ who condone Promise Keepers' efforts to activate God's plan, but sincerity is a powerful deceiver.

Do You See It?

The Promise Keepers' statement, after saying, "God is our model" and that we are to try to "reflect His trustworthy nature," adds, "This character is summed up in the word, integrity."[5] The definition of integrity is "a firm adherence to a code of moral values."[6]

Whoa!

Even a casual look at Promise Keepers' material reveals that the organization's doctrinal view advocates keeping promises that create a "firm adherence to a code of moral values" and thereby, equates it with being a "Christian." Such reasoning must conclude that any man—born of the Spirit of God or not, regenerate or unregenerate—has the capacity to "reflect His nature" by adhering to a "moral code" in order to achieve this sought-after integrity. Perhaps this helps us more fully understand why Promise Keepers is so flexible with various groups whose doctrine of salvation is antithetical to the Word of God. Promise Keepers' material suggests that any man so inclined is capable of making promises to enhance conduct and character, whether he is Roman Catholic, homosexual, or Mormon—all of whom are encouraged to participate in Promise Keepers ministries

This openness by Promise Keepers' leadership to the various concepts of what constitutes a true doctrine of salvation is not incidental to the fact that men are discouraged from confronting other participants who hold unscriptural views of the new birth.

But, the question remains, is integrity truly the nature of God?

In short, *it is not.* No more than God is subject to *time* is He subject to being measured by moral codes or human character traits such as integrity. Integrity can only exist in the framework of the possibility of the absence of integrity. Integrity is a result of making correct moral decisions. God is not struggling and has never struggled with such human conflict as that of being forced to choose between right or wrong. That is why God is not capable of simply telling the truth. *He* is the *Truth*. He supersedes all human yard sticks of moral measurement. Promise Keepers' summation of God's character with the word "integrity"[7] is demeaning and blasphemous. It is another concept born in a carnal, limited view of God with absolutely no basis in the Word of God. You do not spell Christianity, **I-N-T-E-G-R-I-T-Y**. Forever and always, *Christianity* is spelled, **J-E-S-U-S**.

"In Him dwelleth all the fullness of the Godhead bodily" (Colossians 2:9).

We must scratch our heads in awe when reading Promise Keepers positions, statements of faith, and beliefs. They certainly cause one to ask how men, especially men in responsible positions of Christian leadership or casual students of Scripture, can find compatibility or common ground between true Christianity and this very obviously camouflaged but easily spotted man-made attempt to yet again invade the sacred walls of the Body of Truth under the guise of an alliance.

Men who believe they have the power to vow or promise themselves into a state of righteousness via a list of godly actions do not comprehend the depth of human depravity.

This Promise Keepers-taught concept may ultimately produce men successful in their performance but, in truth, they will fail to live redemptive lives that drive others to Christ. Such self-sufficient men will sense no need of the cross, the resurrection, or the Spirit of God. They are self-contained men who only need to become more resolved and resolute.

Is the *"power of God unto salvation"* no longer innate within the Gospel alone, as Paul declared in Romans 1:16? In reading Promise Keepers' material, we cannot escape the fact that central to their belief system is the conviction, and perhaps to them a subliminal one, that the *"power of God unto salvation"* is now in their seven promises.

Man's reach, once again, exceeds his grasp.

PART III

The Big Seven

> *"For through the law I died to the law that I might live to God."*
>
> Galatians 2:19

Prologue

The seven promises of a Promise Keeper can be broken down into two categories. The first set of promises is redundant to the Christian faith and inherent to man's covenant of salvation. It is indeed a vain repetition as well as an indication of one's shallow understanding of the Christian faith to attempt to "lay these foundations" again, reflecting a return to dead works. To do so is to ignore the fullness of the relationship that the believer has already established with the Lord Jesus Christ and to assume that it is incomplete. The second category of these promises falls under the umbrella of non-essential additives to a God-accomplished salvation. These have been *"attached"* to the package of our *"new life"* by Promise Keepers as addendums with no intrinsic or spiritual value whatsoever to one's walk with God. They are *"weights"* which, if committed to, add unnecessary and unscriptural burdens to the believer. Rather than bringing liberty to the child of God, they bring new bondage.

Although the Promise Keepers' demands appear to be spiritual, they are, rather, evidence of the undying love affair between the fallen nature of man and his deceived heart that yearns to enjoin an illicit effort to do something for God. However, the very essence of the Christian experience is that which God has done and is doing *for*, *through* and *in* His people. Jesus taught, in word and with His life, the futility of attempting to "do something" for the Father without the Father. He only acted in concert with the heart and mind of God. He said, "...The Son can do nothing of Himself, but what He sees the Father do" (John 5:19). Jesus spoke and acted when spoken and acted through by the Father. We see, for our instruction in this behavior, Spirit responding to Spirit. God is pleased with those actions, prayers, thoughts, deeds, and ministries that He initiates. However, the Promise Keepers agenda is based upon man promising performance for, rather than his participation with, the Father.

Efforts born in the soul of man's religious drive to achieve goals that appear godly and good always end in futility and frustration. Man's old nature yearns for the flesh to do something for which it can take credit.

The writer of Hebrews admonishes, "...let us lay aside every weight, and the sin which doth so easily beset us...looking unto Jesus, the author and finisher of our faith" (Hebrews 12:1-2). Everything of divine design that is going on in the life of the believer is of divine origin and ultimately is to be accomplished exclusively by divine energies.

Serious Bible students familiar with the diverse heresies that frequently sprouted up in the early church will witness their seeds being sown yet again in the seven promises of Promise Keepers. The seven misguided but sincere little helpers discussed in the following chapters will expose the vanity of these promises. Any levity is not intended to dilute the serious nature of the issue, but the necessary gravity finds comfort in the balance that, "A merry heart does good like a medicine" (Proverbs 17:22).

"Heigh Ho, Heigh Ho, It's off to work we go..."
from Snow White and
the Seven Dwarfs

CHAPTER 10

Good Versus Evil in the Enchanted Forest

"Take heed, therefore, that the light which is in thee be not darkness."
Luke 11:35

Society programs us from the time we are children to think of God in terms of the "good" in our world and Satan in terms of "evil". This fairy-tale theology has grown up in the hearts and minds of this generation and its acceptance is being promoted by such popular, man-centered ministries as Promise Keepers.

The fairy tale so popular among children around the world, "Snow White and the Seven Dwarfs", features some vivid illustrations contrasting evil with good. As most of these children's stories of old, "Snow White" is loaded with spells, magic and other expressions of the occult, and like many contemporary ministries, it attempts to erase the curse of "black magic" with the use of "white magic". Those who are sensitive to the between-the-lines messages in such stories can easily correlate them to the contemporary dilemmas that we, as spiritual warriors, face on a day-to-day basis.

The ancient belief that evil can be overcome by good is the thesis of not only this beloved fairy tale, but of many in Christian ministry today.

However, the source of "black magic" is identical to that of so-called "white magic". Neither is capable of overcoming the other, nor is there an effort on the part of either to do so because the two are not at odds. They have an identical purpose: deception. Attempting to overcome evil by man's goodness or sincerity creates a conflict of interest. Accordingly, expecting the evil within man to be conquered by his innate "bit of good" fails to satisfy the Divine standard. Human morality cannot overcome human immorality. Man, within himself, cannot—regardless of well-intentioned promises—struggle against the evil resident within his own nature (see also Romans 6-7).

For example, Paul repeatedly described the condition of man that leaves him impotent in any struggle against the internal and external evil he faces. He wrote, "As it is written, there is none righteous, no not one: there is none that understandeth, there is none that seeketh after God. They are all gone out of the way, they are together become unprofitable; there is none that doeth good, no, not one" (Romans 3:10-12). The Apostle Paul explains this dilemma as being a symptom of the fact that men, without God's intervention, are "dead in trespasses and sin" and are "by nature the children of wrath" (Ephesians 2:1-3).

The prophets of the Old Testament wrote, "We are all as an unclean thing and all our righteousnesses are as filthy rags" (Isaiah 64:6) and that "The heart is deceitful above all things, and desperately wicked, who can know it?" (Jeremiah 17:9). But man does not really know that. He is deceived and he cannot moralize away evil. Actually, such moralizing is in league with evil. Both are striving to achieve the same goal. Evil is repulsed only by holiness.

Man's morality simply attempts to emulate the nature of God in order to facilitate evil's repulsion of Him. If only man can, so the convoluted reasoning goes, *"raise"* himself to a standard that nullifies his need for God, then evil's desire has been accomplished and man can thus be his own god. The truth is, man's *"goodness"* can never qualify him for acceptance in the spiritual economy of a Holy God.

Seven Dwarfs, Seven Promises

Snow White's happily-ever-after ending that finds her galloping off into the sunset with her Prince Charming falls short in dealing with the fact that *witchcraft* created Snow White's exile to the forest and her subsequent "soul-sleeping coma" induced by the wicked step-mother's "poisoned apple." The story falls short because it pretends to overcome an *"enemy"* with the *"enemy."* I am radically committed to the well-established scriptural truth that all such *"little stories"* are part and parcel of the satanic propaganda born in Eden. Although I am not convinced that all authors of such tales intentionally participate in this deception, I believe they play a major role in facilitating erroneous concepts of the nature of God versus the nature of evil at a critical point in the development of our young children.

Familiar to all who know the story, the Prince eventually appears and, falling in love with the "comatose" Snow White, kisses away the curse of the "wicked apple." They ride the steed into their future to the cheers of the helpful, kind, and once again, lonely Seven Dwarfs. It is an integral part of the story to understand how, in spite of the great efforts expended by the seven little fellows, the dark personality of the jealous stepmother would soon find a way to destroy Snow White.

Of course, all such tales of this era contained a villain, a hero or heroine, a victim and usually a few *"side kicks."* Each of these characters are designed to play a part in the heart of the reader that personifies the drama of life and the supposed universal struggle between good and evil.

It is difficult for many of us who are given to teaching, writing or the ministry not to think out categories and applications when reading tales such as "Snow White" to our children. But in analyzing the seven promises of Promise Keepers, I could not escape this correlation between the <u>seven dwarfs</u> of the popular fairy tale and the <u>seven promises</u> of

Promise Keepers. A bit of characterization is inevitable when attempting to make a point, but the art of teaching certainly includes repeatedly pointing out the obvious with the liberal use of illustrations.

Snow White aptly illustrates humanity, the focus of evil intentions. Satan's malicious desire, born of his jealousy, is to seek out and destroy that which is lovable and pure. Down to the very disguise of a harmless, poor old woman that the wicked stepmother assumes for the purpose of deception, the similarity of her character with that of Satan stands true. He is extremely adept at creating illusions and putting on the face of innocence to hide his ugly, devious and deadly intentions.

As the story continues, after being warned of the evil conspiracy against her, Snow White escapes into the forest where she is left at the mercy of the wilderness, without hope, and despairing over her dilemma. She is, as is humanity, now a victim of her condition. For her, it was her beauty, for humanity, it is his sin. The raging jealousy of a wicked stepmother separated Snow White from all the luxury of her inheritance in her father's kingdom; in a comparative sense, man's sin has separated him from the glory of a relationship with his Creator and all that the Father God longs to do for, in and through him.

Ah, but alas, Snow White meets the seven wonders of the woods. They love her, they take her in and provide a shelter from the elements that oppress her. Snow White, with a new sense of purpose and camaraderie is now happy, comfortable and, it appears, safe from the evil that has been stalking her. And those warm, cuddly, little guys lift her spirits and calm her anxieties. They work hard to provide for and to please Snow White, the new-found object of their affections. So much like _false_ hopes, _false_ commitments, _false_ protection and _failing_ promises are these seven _"wee ones."_ They initially offer what they cannot ultimately deliver. But, at least a short reprieve to Snow White's fear is forthcoming. So what if she just _thinks_ she is safe? So what if the seven dwarfs are only miniature mirages of a true and lasting deliverance from the murderess who haunts her? So what, indeed!

Imagine the unrestrained joy in the song of the seven

sincere sidekicks as they *toil on* to provide for their lovely guest. Indeed, the hills (and the forest) come alive with the sound of their music, *"Heigh Ho, Heigh Ho, it's off to work we go."*

And Snow White has found a home where she too, works— she cleans and cooks while she enjoys the fellowship of these seven special friends.

But, the best laid plans of dwarfs and girl fail to protect this precious one from the wicked one. The cunning stepmother slips into the docile, domestic setting like a wolf in sheep's clothing to finish what she has begun. The seven little helpers, now absent, at best had only delayed the inevitable "apple of death's" delivery to its unsuspecting victim. Now, with Snow White no longer alert to the stalker's evil intent and at ease in the false security provided by the seven dwarfs, the enemy does her deceptive deed and Snow White falls to her fate.

Like the seven promises of the Promise Keepers ministry, the seven dwarfs in truth, though lovable, though sincere and though offering temporary sanctuary for the tired, worn-out flesh of Snow White, can in no way stay the sentence of death hanging as the "Sword of Damocles" over the head of humanity.

You may be inclined to say, *"But it is only a little fairy tale."* To which I respond by reminding you, while it may well be just a fairy tale, it is also a most apt illustration of the theology of millions of church "members" in America as well as the central theological focus of ministries like Promise Keepers. Man's goodness, no matter how well-intentioned, noble or sanctified with religious dribble, will never be able to overcome evil.

The fundamental tenet of the religion of Satanism is not exclusive belief in the "doctrine of darkness"; rather, it is a combination of darkness with light. Evil creates a world of "grays and shadows." In fact, it is no coincidence that the high priest and author of *The Satanic Bible* has titled his lurid work from the pit, *The Book of Shadows.*[1] Shadows are created when any object interrupts the flow of light to the object it is meant to illuminate.

There is a shadowy Christianity today as the power of promising to *"do good"* is being promoted for the purpose of overcoming evil. But the truth of Scripture demands a change in this darkened reasoning. Accordingly, the Apostle Paul addressed the church at Corinth as he rhetorically asked, "…for what fellowship hath righteousness with unrighteousness? And what communion hath light with darkness?" (2 Corinthians 6:14).

The stark difference between the belief system couched in fairy tales such as "Snow White" and the belief system inherent in Promise Keepers is that life is no fairy tale. Unlike Snow White, who was in a coma, men today are spiritually dead. Humanity looking to himself is, therefore, without the hope of "living happily ever after." Romanticizing the concept that good can overcome evil by writing a religious code that fantasizes that "all will be well if we will only try harder" does not change the Truth or the man. The fact that man is attempting to reduce the scope of a universal spiritual warfare to a simple matter of personal choices to be more vigilant in his inner struggle against evil is advertising the fact that evil has already won that struggle through its deception of the warrior. Man's protection from evil and the provision for deliverance from it will never be discovered in seven dwarfed commitments and promises to try to do better. The temporary sanctuary offered by these seven promises as was offered by the seven dwarfs may serve to give hope, aid and comfort to the weary. Women tired of their spiritually unmotivated husbands, and nagged-at, preached-to, guilt-ridden laymen as well as "tired-of-trying-to-motivate-'em" pastors are all looking for a way out of their spiritual woods and deserts. And suddenly, as the cavalry charging over the hill at the last desperate moment, along come these seven sincere supporters with their promises of sustenance and security. But they are seven promises that fail to produce more than a false security that disarms and deceives. Death can only respond to death with more death. Death only yields in the presence of life, as darkness must yield to the presence of light.

The carrot ever dangles in front of the donkey with the promise that the next step will give reward to the seeker. The human race is committed to his works-oriented religion and, after all these years, is much like the advertised Eveready

Battery Rabbit: *"still going... still going... still going."* And much like the seven dwarfs, Promise Keepers participants will perpetuate their spiritual journeys as they, instead of resting in the finished work of the cross of the Lord Jesus Christ, trudge on in the power of their flesh, chanting....
"Heigh Ho, Heigh Ho, It's off to WORK we go..."

"Pride can often be used to beat down the simpler vices."[1]

—C.S. Lewis

CHAPTER 11

"...If by grace, then is it no more of works; otherwise grace is no more grace. But if it be of works, then is it no more grace..."

Romans 11:6a

Sleepy

Promise #1
Sleepy

1. "A Promise Keeper is committed to honor Jesus Christ through worship, prayer and obedience to God's Word through the power of the Holy Spirit."[2]

On the surface, this is a fairly decent description of the practitioners of the Christian faith. Such a commitment looks harmless, perhaps commendable, and yet, an honest analysis of this first "promise" demands that its content be kept in the context of the character revealed in the Promise Keepers' whole ministerial philosophy. When this sound interpretive procedure is applied to investigating the entire root system of

Promise Keepers, the searing reality that keeps surfacing is that we live in an age during which words do not mean what they used to mean. Terminology, even that used among many Christian ministries, especially Promise Keepers, has become extremely subjective. I have named this promise *"Sleepy"* because I am convinced that any believer who casually accepts the Promise Keepers' proposal and commits to the first promise must be spiritually asleep to its implications. Only a vigilantly sober, fully cognitive and spiritually engaged individual with an aggressive *"Berean"* attitude would be, at first glance, discerning enough to see the vague deception contained in this promise.

Promise Keepers extracts from the Christian a "promise" to reinvent the wheel, to do what the natural process and empowering of their regenerated nature is to be accomplishing. This promise implies that there is more than one kind of Christianity: the kind demanded and provided by God, and yet another demanded by Promise Keepers.

A Christian honors Jesus Christ, worships, prays and moves to obey God's Word. A Christian's new nature in Christ practices every requirement of promise number one and does so through the power of the Holy Spirit.

Is Promise Keepers attempting to develop a brand of Christianity that is superior to biblical Christianity?

This first promise clearly implies a distinction between Christians who do what Christians do and are what Christians are and those so-called "Christians" who do not honor Jesus Christ, do not worship Him, do not pray and do not obey the Word of God.

This first demand facilitates the popular but unscriptural concept that one can claim to be a Christian without producing the life, light, fruit or evidence of that Christianity. Yes, Christians can sin, fail and go through periods of spiritual darkness. However, Paul assured the Philippians, "Being confident of this very thing, that he who hath begun a good work in you will perform it until the day of Jesus Christ" (Philippians 1:6). We can rest assured that God never abandons a child of His to the darkness from which He saved him, nor does He allow that true believer to live an entire lifetime without producing clear evidence that he belongs to God. A believer receives constant assurance through the indwelling Holy Spirit that he is not his own, "but that he has been bought with a price." As a believer makes decisions and choices, God is an ever-present reality who woos, corrects or chastens him back into fellowship.

The believer is a believer because at new birth he receives the call of the Spirit of God to honor Jesus Christ, to worship and love Him. Upon his surrender to that call, the Holy Spirit enters into that believer and births a new creation. The believer is driven to pray and he hungers for the Word of God and its application to his life through the power of the Holy Spirit.

This is a Christian.

Tragically, the Promise Keepers' concept of a Christian is synonymous with what I call the *Christian-humanist*. The Christian-humanist feels that if he subscribes to the Christian ethic, confesses to believe the Bible, lives a good life and is on the roll of a local church, then surely he is a Christian. To accommodate this unbiblical view of Christianity, our society has developed churches and ministries that teach while one may indeed be a Christian, it is possible to be a perpetually worldly or "untransformed" Christian. This "Christian", according to such thinking, lives a self-centered, self-focused life with no time, resources and or thought for a Holy God. This "Christian" has not committed to obey even the most basic and elementary call of the Christian faith. He lives in a state of self-absorbed callousness toward the church, the things of God and the people of God. He is unrepentant, but religious. When such a clearly unregenerate person reads or hears this first promise, it makes sense. He knows that committing to "honor Jesus Christ through worship, prayer and obedience to God's Word through the power of the Holy Spirit" is something that he has never truly done. So he is convinced that this is something new and unique to be added to his *"Christianity,"* which in reality was not Christianity at all.

In stark contrast, true Christianity drives its possessor toward the Lord of that relationship. While there are certainly levels of spiritual growth and development, the Bible knows not of a believer who demonstrates no spiritual growth or development. Even those believers who stray outside the will of God or fall into sin experience the real and quick presence of God through His chastening hand.

God moves on the disobedient Christian. The writer of Hebrews penned, "For whom the Lord loveth he chasteneth, and scourgeth every son whom he receiveth. If ye endure chastening, God dealeth with you as with sons; for what son is he whom the father chasteneth not? But if ye be without chastistement, of which all are partakers, then are ye bastards, and not sons" (Hebrews 12:6-8).

Upon reading this very first promise, the scripturally literate are curious as to why Promise Keepers demands that Christian men promise to do what has already become a reality in their life as a Christian. Again, such an erroneous approach to the Promise Keepers plan to make men *"real men"* is born of *"supplemental theology."* Characteristic of the doctrine of the Promise Keepers' leadership is the doctrine that Christianity is incomplete without additives. Consequently, they regularly add to the Word of God via new and often contradictory public prophecies, along with what they believe to be "words of knowledge" and their so-called "visions" (see also Chapter 17). They invent and seek out new experiences that are extra-biblical in nature and they legislate new demands and requirements for the believer to shoulder.

But Promise Keepers' addition to the demands of the Gospel does not stop with the call for participants to become spiritual pack mules to carry the heavy burden of ill-conceived doctrines. Promise Keepers is telling their followers that to become "real men" and true "promise keepers", they must enhance their covenant with God by also vowing to other men that they will behave and act Christian.

To require a believer to act like a believer is much like asking a goldfish to act like a goldfish. The nature of the goldfish insures he will pursue those natural tendencies that distinguish him as a goldfish and that he will act accordingly. To propose that a Christian must promise to act like a Christian and to *"perform"* as a Christian indicates that those extracting such a promise do not understand what it takes to become a

Christian. This fundamental chink in Promise Keepers' theological armor exposes many erroneous beliefs, not only of Promise Keepers' leadership, but of their authors, materials and a number of the speakers at their regional rallies.

One need not read much of Promise Keepers' materials to realize that Jesus Christ, the Word of God and even the Holy Spirit that it promotes are not always synonymous with what true, orthodox, Bible-believing Christians have believed concerning these issues since the birth of the Church and the closing of the Canon. Investigating Promise Keepers' *"promises"* uncovers a theology full of heretical holes. Promise Keepers' unorthodox interpretation of God's Word and redefinition of its intent and context neuters the uniqueness of Christianity and compromises the exclusivity of the Faith.

Any believer who is examining the legitimacy of Promise Keepers must do so aggressively. The Apostle Paul admonished the church at Thessalonica to *"Prove all things"* (1 Thessalonians 5:21). He impressed upon them the need to leave no facet of an issue contested against the Truths of God. As the obedient believer applies the "testing of the Spirit" principles to the first promise, he is arrested by caution and prompted to dig a little deeper. Just such prompting led this author to peel back the thin veneer of the first promise's rhetoric and examine Promise Keepers' expanded explanation of its seven promises in the booklet, *"The Seven Promises of a Promise Keeper."*

The insights gleaned from my investigation are worthy of a brief but revealing commentary about the irreverent attitude toward definitive Christianity and Bible doctrine that promise one, Promise Keepers and its supporting cast demonstrate.

A Case In Point

Pastor Jack Hayford, a supporter of Promise Keepers, responded to my inquiry as to how he could possibly back the organization considering its disregard of sound doctrine. But had I read his statements in the book, *"The Seven Promises of a Promise Keeper"* before I had written him, my questions would have been answered.

Anyone who has ever heard Pastor Jack Hayford speak has heard a caring, tender and gentle-spirited man. I have always considered him to be gracious and warm and I would never question the sincerity of his heart or unkindly question his motives. Yet Pastor Hayford's article in the book illustrates a belief which conflicts with spiritual realities and the Word of God.

Pastor Hayford, under the section of the publication titled *"Redeeming Worship"*, states, "Redeeming worship centers on the Lord's table. Whether your tradition celebrates it as communion, the Eucharist, the Mass or the Lord's Supper, we are all called to this centerpiece of Christian worship."[3]

That statement crosses the line separating the absolute Truths clearly articulated in the Word of God from the damnable heresies that Scripture repeatedly warns us of. The assertion violates Scripture and defies the very concept of our salvation's relationship to the atoning blood of the Lord Jesus Christ. I know of no one who is irrevocably committed to the infallibility of God's Word who would agree with any part of Pastor Hayford's statement. The biblical purpose of the Lord's Supper overwhelmingly conflicts with the purpose of the Mass and Eucharist. Since the Reformation, during which tens of thousands of godly Christians were slaughtered and tortured for rejecting the Mass, true Bible-believing people have known the Mass to be a profane, apostate deformity of biblical truth.

How is it possible for a man to "honor Christ and be obedient to His Word" as Promise Keepers instructs and simultaneously accept Hayford's statement as truth? Although Pastor Hayford would not, I believe, intend it to be so, his statement aligns him with those diabolical religious zealots whose hands are dripping with the blood of the martyrs of the Reformation. Those godly saints, whose lives were sacrificed on the altar of the defense of the Word of God, were cruelly snuffed out by those who subscribe to the heresies promoted by such a statement. How is it that educated *"men of the cloth"* can ignore and condone the horror of a system as overtly antichrist as Catholicism?

No one can remain ignorant, except by design of the wicked one, to the vile and inhumane acts that are a part of the

Roman Catholic Church's history. A masterful theolog and author, and, in my opinion, one of this century's "last days" reformists, Dave Hunt, has written a bestseller long overdue. In his book, *A Woman Rides the Beast,*[4] he quotes renowned historian Will Durant, who in his book, *The Story of Civilization,*[5] wrote of that era when every citizen in Rome was required to be a Roman Catholic or be considered a traitor and face the sentence of death. The paganized religion of perverted Christianity was forced upon the entire society. It is said that no religious system in human history, including the ancient bloody Jihads of Islam, could match the ferocity, torture and terror perpetrated by the Roman Catholic Church. Will Durant writes:

> "Compared with the persecution of heresy in Europe from 1277 to 1492 AD, the persecution of Christians by the Romans in the first three centuries after Christ was a mild, humane procedure.

> Making every allowance required by a historian, and permitted to the Christian, we must rank the Inquisition, along with the wars and persecutions of our time, as among the darkest blots on the record of mankind, revealing the ferocity unknown in any beast."[6]

The Catholic system that spawned the bloody Inquisition used, as one of its many excuses to charge people with heresy, their denial of the efficacy of the Mass.

And though Jack Hayford believes and teaches that the Eucharist and the Mass are synonymous with the Lord's Supper, certainly the Catholic Church would be among the first to disagree. It, in fact, takes issue with such statements and demands that the Eucharist is part and parcel of the "works" system that qualifies participating Catholics for salvation.

Thanks to Dave Hunt's willingness to research and write this book—and risk great persecution because of his willingness to do so—we have ready access to Catholic history in general and its exploitation of the Catholic-invented Eucharist in particular.

Vatican II's affirmation of traditional Catholic positions on this states:

> There should be no doubt in anyone's mind that all the faithful ought to show to this most holy sacrament (wafer which allegedly has been transformed into Christ's body) the worship which is due to the true God, as has always been the custom of the Catholic Church, nor is it adored any less because it was instituted by Christ to be eaten.

> (quoting Trent)...He is to be adored there because He is substantially (physically) present there...Whole and entire God and man...permanently...through that conversion of bread and wine which, as the Council of Trent tells us, is most aptly named transubstantiation...in the Eucharist, we become partakers of the body and blood of God's only Son...(and) the partaking of the body and blood of Christ has no less an effect than to change us into what we have received.[7]

This absurd claim that the Catholic priest possesses the power to bring the Body of Christ, through the physical properties of a wafer and wine into those ingesting it, insults the Christian faith. To adopt Catholic doctrine as one's own necessitates not only a full rejection of biblical claims, but the creation and acceptance of whole, new, (actually they are as ancient as man's fall) doctrines that have no claim to scriptural legitimacy.

Promise number one, in light of Promise Keepers' receptivity of and encouragement to the Catholic Church to participate, is an empty, meaningless commitment without value or integrity when analyzed in light of Promise Keepers' concept of Christianity. The Jesus Christ that true believers honor and worship, and whose Word they obey, is not the same Jesus as the one taught by, adhered to or believed by the Roman Catholic Church.

Understanding that the Catholic Church takes such an absolutely unyielding stand on the Eucharist and the central role it plays to the Catholic's salvation makes it very difficult, if not impossible, to accept the fact that God wants true Christians to be unified and in fellowship with them as is Promise Keepers' stated agenda. And how can Jack Hayford, Promise Keepers' leaders or any other true Christian condone a religious system which believes that the sacrifice for sin is in the Mass? Jesus' words from the cross as He "gave up His spirit" were, "It is finished" (John 19:30). But according to Catholic priests, who alone are allowed to perform the Mass, they continue to sacrifice day in and day out, the body of Christ.

Another quote from Vatican II and the New Universal Catechism reveals the Catholic belief that forgiveness, atonement and salvation are contained within the Eucharist and Mass. It states, "Each time Mass is offered, the sacrifice of Christ is repeated. A new sacrifice is not offered, but by divine power, one and the same sacrifice is repeated ...In the Mass, Christ continues to offer Himself to the Father as He did on the Cross." But in an "unbloody manner, under the appearance of bread and wine."[8]

Are we willing to trade "ye must be born again" for the Roman Catholic sacrament of eating a wafer and drinking the wine in order to receive Christ? Are we willing to sacrifice the work of the Spirit at new birth for a work of the flesh? This heartbreaking and disgusting perversion of redemption in the Catholic Church's belief in transubstantiation is nothing less than blasphemous.

The spiritual pollution innate within the call of promise number one is the subjective nature of the *"Jesus"* that Promise Keepers desire Christian men to honor. This *"Jesus"* is not exclusive in nature as is the Lord Jesus Christ of Scripture or the call of Promise Keepers for men to perform the requests in the first promise would not include those who worship in and through the Roman Catholic system of idolatry nor a number of other religious cults which Promise Keepers receives as legitimate. We expose these in a coming chapter.

True Christians should feel a righteous indignation when they hear a teacher who is as widely known as Pastor Hayford say that there is no difference between the table of our Lord and the demon-driven, satanically-inspired activity of the

Catholic Church's Eucharist. When one contemplates the abysmal amount of antichrist, anti-biblical, and anti-intellectual doctrines of salvation historically perpetrated by the Roman Catholic Church, it defies the imagination to think that any Christian minister would have the audacity to lend even a hint of credibility to the godless religious system of the Catholic Church.

To add insult to injury, Promise Keepers demonstrates a greater audacity in its appeal for Christian men to violate the Scriptures by fellowshiping with priests and others in the perverted religious belief system represented by Catholic dogma.

The Catholic Church, while publicly tipping their cones and habits to Protestants who receive and accept them into their sphere of influence, is continuing to preach that they alone are the exclusive, universal and singular avenue to God and heaven. According to this sordid, religiously seductive and deceiving system, those who are not Catholics are damned to hell. However, the Bible teaches, in spite of Promise Keepers' open-arms policy to Catholics and their antichrist doctrine, that if men look to such for salvation, it will lead to their spiritual destruction. Shall we trust the catechism or God's Holy Word? Promise Keepers' policy gives them equal credence.

A distraught Catholic who appeared desirous to know Christ, after my counseling session with him, stated, "I'm so confused. They tell me your Bible is wrong and you tell me our Catholic priests are wrong. I'm damned if I do and damned if I don't." Such is the perceived dilemma of millions of Catholics who hear the true Gospel. They pay a heavy price when choosing Christ over their Catholic heritage, tradition and, often, their Catholic family's wishes.

Pastor Hayford's statements identifying the Lord's Supper as meaning the same thing as the Mass and Eucharist are deceptive beyond belief. Perhaps one would choose to believe that his bizarre comparison is simply the result of a shallow understanding of the Scriptures or ignorance of Catholic doctrine. Whatever the reason for such an outlandish violation of the Word of God, it clearly promotes and condones another Gospel. What a tragedy, considering the multitudes of Catholic men and women who find comfort and security in Hayford's commentary on the Eucharist and are driven yet further away from true salvation through the atoning blood of Jesus Christ and the finished work of the cross.

In this first of seven promises required of Promise Keepers, we are afforded a mere introduction to the vain, repetitious and unnecessary nature of the remaining six propositions. The most redemptive quality, if there is one, of this promise, is that it provokes cautious believers to investigate further, to look beneath the pious-sounding rhetoric to discover the true nature of the **beast**. This discovery of Promise Keepers' well-hidden but dubious nature should serve as a wake-up call to the spiritual somnolence of Christians who have been caught dozing when they should be discerning.

This overview of promise one, in light of Promise Keepers' true and, more or less, camouflaged agenda, only slightly begins to bring into focus the full Promise Keepers objectives. A bigger picture concerning Promise Keepers begins to develop as we put promise one in perspective with the promises that follow it. The true meaning of promise one begins to come to light.

I have discovered however, that many of those already committed to Promise Keepers frankly do not care to be confused with absolute biblical fact; they desire to simply *"sleep"* on.

"Self-made men ultimately end up worshipping their creator."

—Clapp

Chapter 12

"Thus saith the Lord; cursed be the man that trusteth in man."

Jeremiah 17:5

Bashful and Grumpy

Promise #2
Bashful

"A Promise Keeper is committed to pursue vital relationships with a few other men; understanding he needs brothers to help him keep his promises."[1]

Meet the second of the seven dwarfed efforts. Because promise number two is custom-made to appeal to the more timid soul, we have named this promise after the lovable dwarf, "Bashful". The bashful Christian, fearful and unable to stand alone in the power of grace and glory of God, will definitely need to rely upon someone else to help him do the right thing. Obviously, God's promise to sustain him, to grant overcoming power, and if and when necessary, to raise up brothers within the body of his local church are insufficient to meet Bashful's needs.

Promise number two neuters the confidence of the man of God in Paul's admonition to *"stand firm"* (Ephesians 6:13). Stand *alone* if and when necessary, as is often the case if one is a man of conviction, but stand. This is yet another representation of the numerous extra-biblical additives that Promise Keepers is so given to promoting. At least they did not attempt to place an out-of-context Scripture reference with it. And for good reason. The premise for this promise is not found in or hinted at anywhere in the Word of God. It is a concept born of social psychology and is more applicable to an ant farm than to the believer. Spiritual victories are not achieved by employing the principles of the "buddy system" that "partners" the believer into a "fellowship" with those outside their Bible-believing local church and, in Promise Keepers' case, very possibly outside the realm of sound doctrine and even the Christian faith. No Christian is instructed by Scripture to depend upon any external power or persons beyond the Lord Jesus Christ and those within the church to minister to his spiritual needs.

For every Christian, there is, in the body of the scripturally sound local church, a viable, living, supportive family, a fully functional supportive network that is wholly autonomous and independent of any other ministry. This anatomically illustrated Bride of Christ is self-contained within that church's spiritual structure where the Holy Spirit gifts, equips and edifies its members who have been knit together in a unique spiritual union to Christ and to each other by the Holy Spirit.

Promise Keepers is an *organization* created by men. The church is a living *organism* born of the Spirit of the Living God. There is no legitimate basis to even compare the intricate intimacies that God's Spirit harmonizes among His people in the church with an independent para-church organization such as Promise Keepers that is a scripturally illegitimate compilation of Christians, cultists, moral perverts and spiritualistic nomads. Forgive my clarity, but few will understand nothing less than a clear, bold and "no holds barred" appraisal of these kinds of issues, especially if they are already emotionally committed to that particular group. The Word of God forever teaches that the support system for the believer is the local church. "Oh, but" someone may say, "since the church has **failed** to activate and produce godly men, it is now the responsibility of Promise Keepers to pick up where the church has **failed** and get the job done."

Wrong, wrong, wrong!

The church has never failed and never shall fail: *"The gates of hell shall not prevail against the church"* (Matthew 16:18). A lot of our leaders, preachers, denominational bureaucracies and church members have failed but the Church is very much alive and about the work of the Kingdom of God.

The question we must ask when reading this promise is, "Does a believer really need another person to insure that he keeps his promises and commitments?"

Promise Keepers says a true Promise Keeper is committed to seeking out and developing "relationships" with a "few other men." Why would this be a necessary and vital commitment for men who want to walk with God to make? This demand, placing on men the need to be with men in an "accountability" group is surely a scriptural mandate, isn't it?

No, it certainly is **NOT**.

Outside the fellowship, discipleship and ministry within the local church, God has demanded no such interaction nor has He commanded men to "pursue vital relationships" with other men. To the contrary, God's Word repeatedly demands that **no spiritual fellowship** be pursued with anyone outside the beliefs system of the Bible-based, New Testament church. Fellowshipping with other believers who are not in one's local church but whose faith is rooted and grounded in the Word of God is not going to put Christians *"at risk."* However, the sought-after system of Promise Keepers, which forces men with different doctrines and often even totally different *"religions"* into a spiritual setting for ministry, clearly and absolutely violates the Word of God (see also 2 Corinthians 6:11-17).

The Christian is not instructed to adopt the isolationist theology of the monk; but rather, he is commanded to go into the world and share the Gospel, to invade society as *"salt and light."* But the pressure that Promise Keepers' places on men leads them to falsely believe that in order to spiritually succeed and grow, they must have **more** than faith in God and submission to His Word. Other men, Promise Keepers teaches, must be there and hold that Promise Keeper participant "accountable" to his word—otherwise, he will be assured of spiritual failure. This, too, is a subtle but obvious satanic deception concerning the sufficiency, the sovereignty and the retaining power of God. It proves how empty is yet another "promise" of Promise Keepers that encourages men to honor their pastor and church.

The Bible does place upon each believer the personal responsibility of maintaining a Christian testimony that is a clear witness of his love for Christ. God has authorized that, in certain circumstances, the "church" may, after an exhaustive, biblically prescribed procedure appealing to the heart of any church member persisting in an ungodly lifestyle, exercise church discipline. An illustration of this is found in 1 Corinthians 5, where a certain man was steeped in a lifestyle that contradicted his testimony as a believer. The steps taken by that church authority ultimately brought the rebellious *"saint"* to repentance.

The accountability that all believers are to recognize and submit to is exclusively that which Scripture imposes upon them. True accountability must have the option to excise a penalty for failure, otherwise there are no teeth in the *accounting*. The police hold the citizen *accountable* to obey the speed limit. If the citizen refuses to be *accountable* then the police officer is to *ticket* for penalty, the lawbreaker. The speed laws have *teeth*.

My three children are accountable to their parents. If they ignore that accountability and conduct themselves in a way that shuns our parental authority, they are held "accountable." My wife and I believe and practice the biblical concepts of raising children to honor Christ and the necessary disciplines that we must use to enforce our parental authority and our children's understanding of accountability. However, I have no authority to hold my neighbor's children accountable to me. Correspondingly, Promise Keepers has no authority to impose a responsibility of accountability upon any man, Christian or otherwise.

Once again, Promise Keepers' leadership arrogantly assumes the authority that God has granted solely to the local church.

Additionally, the Word of God is full of stories of men, women, boys and girls who, because of their deep love for God, were forced to stand alone upon their convictions. There was no one to *mentor* them, to hold their feet to the fire and to insure they walked with God. What kind of Christianity does Promise Keepers conceptualize that would call for a man of God to have a group of men to *keep an eye on* the believer and to be certain that he keeps his word? Some Christianity this must be, and some promise, too, that is only credible when he who makes the promise is intimidated or pressured by extra-biblical accountability to other **men**. Obviously, such a man is not trustworthy when out of touch with his group. One's commitments are no more trustworthy than his willingness to keep them, whether or not the appointed *"watch dogs"* are on guard.

What we do when no one is looking and when we feel no one will find out is a decent measure of how real God is to us and the depth of our walk with Him. Our love for God, our absolute commitment to Him and His ever-flowing grace to us insures our obedience, secures our love, consumes our passion and provokes our forsaking of the world. Unreliable human relationships, especially if those humans have *suspect* beliefs, can never secure a person's yieldedness to Christ or prompt the supernatural obedience necessary to walk in harmony with the will and Word of God.

To quote a credible source... *"Thus saith the Lord, cursed be the man that trusteth in man, and maketh flesh his arm"* (Jeremiah 17:5).

Promise #3
Grumpy

"A Promise Keeper is committed to practice spiritual, moral, ethical and sexual purity."[2]

I am sorry, but I do not think I can do that. In fact, I know I cannot do that. I tried to do that for 23 years before I discovered the Life of Christ. It was a lot of work. Besides, it was boring and frustrating and it filled me with horrible guilt because I just could not do it.

Promise number three is a set-up for a spiritual ambush and disheartening failure. Those who try to do it will sink into the despair that ultimately follows trying and failing, trying and failing, over and over again. This promise is obviously created for our little buddy in Snow White named "Grumpy." People who are constantly displeased with their own short-comings, experienced when trusting "self" to maintain lofty expectations in the power of fleshly promises, can be downright "grumpy."

Paul the Apostle also tried to make promise three work. He wrote of it to Rome, saying, "For I know that in me (my flesh) dwells no good thing, for to *will* is present but how to perform [it] I find not" (Romans 7:18). This Apostle would not have been a very good Promise Keeper. He stated that while he did possess the power of his *will* and could "promise to do good," he always ended up failing to keep his promise. No matter how much he promised and willed it so, he could not be *"righteous."* He attributes his constant failure to "measure up" to the spiritual, moral and ethical demand of God's law to another law that was within him that worked against the desires of God.

Who among the family of God has escaped Paul's frustration which he shares in Romans? "For the good that I would, I do not; but the evil which I would not, that I do. Now if I do that I would not, it is no more I that do it, but sin that dwelleth in me. I find then a law, that, when I would do good, evil is present with me. For I delight in the law of God after the inward man; but I see another law in my members, warring against the law of my mind, and bringing me into captivity to the law of sin which is in my members" (Romans 7:19-23).

Honest men (and women) identify with his despair as he cries out, "Oh wretched man that I am, who shall deliver me from the body of this death?" (Romans 7:24). Indeed, millions of Christians who desire to go on with God in consistent growth and spiritual victory have found themselves *parked* here. Contrary to Promise Keepers' philosophy, the believer's answer to Paul's question on "who shall deliver me" from the perpetual tendency of the old nature to sin is not found in a fleshly promise to try harder to achieve consistent victory. Such Promise Keepers-promoted techniques have been tried and tested and have been proven to fail by some of the greatest men in the Bible, among them, Paul.

Tired of failing, at the end of his rope and in despair after realizing the futility of attempting to be a promise keeper only to, with each new effort, be a promise breaker, he then becomes a God-seeker. He immediately points to the victory he discovered in *"death to self"* and of *"living to Christ."* *"I thank God,"* he proclaims, my deliverance from all that I am not is *"through Jesus Christ"* (Romans 7:25).

Promises to keep *law* will always guarantee failure, followed swiftly by self-incrimination and condemnation. No matter how many guards we may appoint to keep an eye on us, without forsaking self-effort, self-improvement and self-helps, we are destined to fail and to live under self-condemnation. But, "There is therefore now no condemnation to them who are in Christ Jesus, who walk not after the flesh but after the Spirit" (Romans 8:1).

The key to freedom from the guilt of failure that always follows our promises to *"be good,"* and to the liberty that frees our hearts from the spirit of "Grumpy" is not found in our promises to Him, but in His promise to us. It is the heart's desire of the Father that His people grasp the glory of resting in the luxury afforded by the truth of His Word, "whereby **are given to us all** exceedingly great and precious **promises, that by these** ye might be partakers of the divine nature, having escaped the corruption that is in the world through lust" (2 Peter 1:4).

Promise Keepers' focus on men promising God a better performance is so far from practical Christianity that it is indeed mind-boggling that such massive numbers of Christian men and church leaders have "bought into" such a system. But, again, it is the desire of our fallen nature to attempt to crawl out of our dark spiritual holes via our own efforts and then, while patting ourselves on the back, we suddenly discover we are yet, in a hole. Many such holes are indeed spiritual graves and only a resurrected life delivers from the darkness of that seemingly inescapable pit.

Peter points men to promises that work. These are God's commitments to men. They are indeed, "exceedingly great and precious promises." God gives His men these promises so that they might be "partakers of His nature," not participants with their human nature improved. These promises guarantee man's escape from the "corruption that is in the world" that feeds and nourishes men's lust. God's promises never fail to secure deliverance, power, joy and total freedom. God does not rely upon man's feeble promises, but He expects the believer to fully trust His. Of course, we may attempt to exercise the option to keep on trying in the power of our flesh. But if we do, stay out of our way because we are "grumpy" until God's promised victory becomes our own reality.

*"A pig ate his fill under an oak tree and then started
to root around the tree. A crow remarked, "You
shouldn't do that. If you do dig up the roots the tree
will die". "Who cares?", answered the pig, "As long
as there are acorns".*

—Author Unknown

Chapter 13

*"Seest thou a man wise in his own conceit? There is
more hope of a fool than of him".*

Proverbs 26:12

Doc and Dopey

Promise #4
Doc

*4. "A Promise Keeper is committed to build strong
marriages and families through love, protection and
biblical values."*[1]

This promise can surely bring healing and revival, one would
think, to the home and nation. In this promise we find yet
another futile effort to attain the lofty goals that promise
healing to America's wounded and hurting families. Surely
one would suppose that this promise contains the seeds of
healing for America's families. Hence, we have nicknamed

the fourth promise after Snow White's dwarfed and chubby little sidekick, "Doc".

Promise number four loses its credibility, in part, because it, like the other six promises of Promise Keepers, focuses on what Scripture teaches will be the by-product and fruit of the life focused on the Lordship of Christ. Promise Keepers' mutated use and its subjective application of the term "biblical values" render this promise as an irrelevant and scripturally neutered commitment. As one is introduced to the high-sounding "Christian" terminology that characterizes Promise Keepers' events and materials, unless he is discerning and/or aware of the many catch phrases and pivotal wordings that mock the true intent of their meaning in a scriptural context, then he can be easily deceived and *"led away captive"* (Colossians 2:8).

Promise four illustrates the cunning nature of Promise Keepers' entire doctrine, a hybrid doctrine with only intermittent conformity with the Word of God. The so-called "biblical values" alluded to in promise four and expanded on throughout Promise Keepers' materials are a mixture of poisonous principles found in anti-biblical contemporary psychology, theories born in the imaginations of its biblically illiterate leadership and a spattering of mysticism along with some Scripture. Once a breach compromises the *"dam of diligence"* that holds in check *"destructive heresies"* that piggyback into the church via ministries like Promise Keepers, a flood of sordid concepts will inundate that Body. Ultimately, these heresies will take their toll on that church unless remedial action is taken to arrest it.

The only way to attack this spiritual cancer of *"tolerance of the leaven"* is to perform radical surgery with the sharpest instrument available, the Word of God. Applying God's Word, according to the book of Hebrews, can cut to the issue and restore spiritual vitality. The writer of Hebrews says, "For the word of God is [living], and powerful, and sharper than any two-edged sword, piercing even to the dividing asunder of soul and spirit, and of the joints and marrow, and is a discerner of the thoughts and intents of the heart" (Hebrews 4:12).

A skillful and courageous "surgeon," usually in the person of a godly pastor or a biblically astute and wise layperson, must deal with this spiritual disease aggressively. God, of course, allows such intrusions into the church so that the Holy Spirit can confirm scripturally authorized and appointed leadership, by their knowledge of the Scriptures, their burden for the sheep and their boldness in protecting their flock.

Paul the Apostle, addressing the Corinthian church concerning various invasive errors, wrote, "For there must be also heresies among you, that they who are approved may be manifest among you" (1 Corinthians 11:19). This is a day in the Church when those "approved" of God have a serious mandate to be "manifested among us."

Churches who have allowed and encouraged their men to participate in Promise Keepers need to find out if there "is a doctor in the house". Pray that God would raise up men with the courage to "cut" when necessary and with the spiritual perception that can discern the spiritual "snake oil" being peddled by quack doctors who *promise* much but who cannot deliver.

Promise #5
Dopey

"A Promise Keeper is committed to support the mission of his church by honoring and praying for his pastor and by actively giving of his time and resources." [2]

Many pastors sense the condescending nature and subliminal inference of this *"promise"*. This promise, by its intonation, emanates an attitude of spiritual superiority and priority over the local church and pastor. To the thousands of men who have abandoned the biblical demand to prioritize their call and ministries to their local church, this promise is like crumbs from *"Master Promise Keepers'"* (see also Matthew 15:27) table to the subservient and subordinated local church.

Christian men are to maintain a singular priority in their commitment to their local church. This commitment is not optional for an obedient believer. It is a man's divine appointment to pursue an ever-deepening ministry through his local church. God places a mandatory call upon Christian men that must be obeyed to insure spiritual growth, ministry development and blessed stewardship. God calls these men to pour their energies, resources and gifts into their local fellowship. Promise Keepers' other demands on men abort their missions and ministries to and through their local churches. Promise five is a kind but perverse Promise Keepers' acknowledgment of local churches and pastors, and frankly, it is akin to "tossing the dog a bone." The honorable and conciliatory substance of this promise is flatly contradicted by the other tenets of the Promise Keepers' faith.

Men across America have realigned and/or misaligned their focus and commitments onto Promise Keepers. The organization's attitude and condescending tip of the hat manifested in promise five has subjugated the vital importance of the local church in the minds and hearts of thousands of Promise Keepers participants. This promise, with its diminutive effort to acknowledge the church and pastor, brings to mind the lop-eared, goofy looking, "flattery will get you anywhere" dwarf named "Dopey".

"Old Pastor Dopey, bless his heart, he tries but he just cannot get you men excited about being, well, real men" is the feel of *promise five. "But let us Promise Keepers honor and pray for poor old Dopey. He is really doing the best he can for you guys. Let's give him a big hand. Come on down here Brother Dopey and let us pray for ya."*

How very difficult it is for the average pastor to match the multimillion-dollar slick ad campaigns, the theatrics at Promise Keeper Stadium rallies, the dynamic speaking abilities of Promise Keepers' guests and the electricity in the atmosphere that is produced when 50,000 cheering people gather for any *"common experience."* Old Brother Dopey feels a bit out of his league if he even attempts to compete for the energies of his men who have been caught up in this pseudo-spiritual whirlwind of excitement generated at Promise Keepers rallies.

As a pastor and minister for 25 years, I am most appreciative for any and all prayers offered on my behalf. I need them desperately. It is, however, most comforting when I am convinced that those who are praying for me are in tune with the Spirit of God and are praying when being led by a holy motivation that promotes the purposes of God for me and my flock. Promise Keepers' patronization, on the other hand, is not palatable to me, nor is it, I suspect, palatable to most other pastors as well.

Those who have attended Promise Keepers rallies have watched as pastors were asked to stand and or come forward to be "prayed for." As hundreds of pastors respond, it is a moving experience to many of these precious men who, for the most part, are fighting raging battles within their local churches. Among their most time and energy-consuming responsibilities are: keeping members of their church from "scratching each other's eyes out," maintaining the ministry God has given them often among a rebellious people and unceasingly attempting to activate the men in the church to accept their God-given responsibilities within their own church. Most pastors will readily attest, it is a lonely battle. But having 30,000 to 50,000 men stand in ovation while screaming, *"We love you, Pastor,"* can be a touching moment for any lonely, wounded warrior.

How can Pastor Dopey leave such a setting unimpressed and warmed by such adulation, even though it is belated, often fabricated and Promise Keepers-stimulated? Promise Keepers' ministries have, at least subliminally, been elevated to the unbiblical position of spiritual authority that, in the minds of most participants, supersedes that of the pastors and the local church.

To illustrate the deep felt sense of Promise Keepers' infringement by pastors into the local shepherd's arena of Biblical authority, the words of a local pastor best expresses the burden that multitudes have respecting Promise Keepers.

In August 1995 Bill Randles, pastor of Believers in Grace Fellowship Church in the state of Iowa, wrote what is now a well-distributed "Open Letter to Bill McCartney," the founder of Promise Keepers.

Because of the length of Pastor Randles' letter, I quote below the parts relevant to this particular promise. He writes:

Dear Mr. McCartney:

My name is Bill Randles and I am the pastor of Believers in Grace Fellowship Church that I founded in 1982. I am writing to express certain reservations and concerns I have about Promise Keepers. The reason this is an open letter is because there are probably thousands of other pastors who have similar reservations. You know this also because you referred to this at a meeting in Detroit on April 29, 1995. In fact, I have listened to that message carefully, and heard you make some very emphatic statements about the reluctance on the part of pastors to ally themselves with Promise Keepers. You actually went so far as to say that any clergyman who isn't planning to go to your February 1996 Pastors Gathering in Atlanta 'needs to be able to tell us why he doesn't want to go.'

Mr. McCartney, this is my response to your brotherly challenge. I agree that I need to tell you what my reservations and concerns about P.K. actually are. First of all, in the interest of clarity, let me transcribe for you that portion of your speech which promoted the writing of this letter. You said in Detroit:

...'Now, I think many of you are in touch with the fact that we're having a pastor's gathering in Atlanta on February 12th, 13th and 14th. This gathering in Atlanta should exceed 100,000 clergymen. Why? Because we have many more than that, and every single one of them ought to be there. We can't have anybody pass up that meeting. If a guy says that he doesn't want to go, he needs to be able to tell us why he doesn't want to go? 'Why wouldn't you want to be a part of what God wants to do with His hand-picked leaders?' We need to understand that our clergymen, many of them, are reluctant to go. Many of you come from churches and your clergymen have never been to a Promise

Keepers gathering because they're keeping a distance from us. You need to go back and tell them: Promise Keepers wants to come along side you and be everything you need by encouraging [your] men and giving resources.

'Now listen to me men. February 12th, 13th and 14th to me is not a coincidence that comes over Valentine's Day. I think we're going to have another St. Valentine's Day massacre. I think Almighty God is going to rip open the hearts of our leaders. I think He's going to tear them open. And I think He's going to put them back together as one. One leadership. We've got to have one leadership, one leadership only' (Promise Keepers, Detroit Silver Dome, April 29, 1995).

Mr. McCartney, my response to that is a simple question. What do you mean when you call for the clergy to become one leadership? In fact, minutes after, you made another statement about the things that we could do 'if we are in control, if we come together, if our unity of command responds.' You said we can accomplish things like 'pay off the national debt, and feed the poor...we can dissolve gangs,...and be an impact in the inner city.'

These kinds of statements underscore my initial reservations. I am very cautious when the call is made for 'One Leadership' and 'Unity of Command.' On the other hand, I am troubled by this because in actual reality, the church already is under one leadership. Jesus Christ is Himself the Head of the Church! If you and I each submit to His headship through obedience to His Word, we are already in unity and don't need to manufacture it. Evidently what you are calling for is one [human] leadership and one unity of [human] command. Mr. McCartney, there already is an organization claiming that kind of leadership and command: The Roman Catholic Church under the headship of the Pope. Because of this 'One human leadership and command,' almost a billion people are locked in spiritual bondage.

The call for clergy to become one leadership and unity of commands reminds me of the shepherding movement in the 1970's and 80's, which sprang out of the Word of God charismatic community in Ann Arbor, Michigan, and was nurtured by the Fort Lauderdale five: Bob Mumford, Derek Prince, Don Bashum, Charles Simpson and Ernie Baxter. You mention in *Ashes to Glory*, that you enjoyed fellowship with the Word of God Community. Have you perhaps been influenced by that particular vision of church government?

I have a threefold problem with a humanly centralized church leadership, and unity of command: (1) it has to be a man-made unity; and it denies the reality of the Spirit that all Christians currently partake of; (2) another problem I have is that it concentrates a tremendous amount of influence into the hands of well-meaning but sinful men; (3) finally, where there is a centralized, carnally unified command, it makes it easier for deception and manipulation of the Church of Satan. Look at the dark ages under the Papacy! I am glad that the church doesn't have that kind of unity today (yet). Ours is a spiritual unity based on devotion to Jesus, not a political unity based on 'Shepherding' principles. The way things are now, Satan has to deceive the Christians one church at a time, but under a 'unified command,' all he has to do is deceive the leadership.[3]

Pastor Bill Randles is an independent Pentecostal pastor who, while many may hold different doctrinal positions than those represented by his denomination, is a man of keen discernment concerning the heretical and apostate doctrines that now threaten the Body of Christ.

His gracious but forthright letter to Bill McCartney also covered numerous other major conflicts over which a growing number of pastors are deeply concerned respecting Promise Keepers.

Among those issues is one to which I have devoted an entire chapter later in this book. However, since Pastor Randles deals with Promise Keepers ecumenical spirit so articulately in his letter I feel that it is appropriate to include it here, as well. Of this, he wrote:

> Mr. McCartney, a second but closely related concern I have is with the ecumenical unity promoted by P.K. Of course, I believe in the true ecumenism: the communion of the saints everywhere on earth, based on the truth of the Gospel. But I am extremely wary of the 'unity-at-the-expense-of-truth' movement. People are being encouraged to de-emphasize doctrines so they can come together as though doctrine is a meaningless detail. What is doctrine, but the body of the truth entrusted to the saints once and for all?

> Doctrine divides because truth divides. There are many denominational barriers that should be kept in place. The basis for unity of the faith (truth), a faith which has a content and makes specific demands of people. Any other basis for unity, such as maleness, politics, social concerns, etc., will only prove to be a house built on sand.

> Mr. McCartney, do you believe the following statement made by the Pope? 'On this universal level, if victory comes, it will be brought by Mary. Christ will conquer through her, because He wants the church's victories now and in the future, to be linked to her' (from *Crossing the Threshold of Hope* by 'His Holiness' John Paul II). How am I to find common ground with anyone who believes this way? What basis for fellowship is there? Scripture commands us not to fellowship or even wish God speed to those who deny the doctrine of Christ. Another example would be this statement from the 1994 Catechism of the Catholic Church, page 128, section 460:

> 'The Word became flesh to make us partakers of the divine nature...For the Son of God became man so that we might become God. The only begotten Son of God, wanting to make us sharers in His divinity, assumed our nature so that He, made man, might make men Gods.'

Mr. McCartney, we are to refute such heresies! How am I to find spiritual unity with people who worship Mary or believe they will become gods? While I can find all sorts of commonality on the basis of being a human being, or the desire that a man be a better father, husband, have integrity, purity, etc., I would hardly mistake those things for Christian Revival. If P.K. is supposed to be a great move of God, doesn't truth and discernment count for anything? What is to stop the Mormons or Jehovah's Witnesses from starting P.K. chapters in their denomina-tions? Why not? They can make identical promises.[4]

The final lines of Pastor Bill Randles' open letter to Mr. McCartney, read:

I applaud your many charges for men to become 'men of integrity,' family men, 'men of purity' and so forth, but I notice that there isn't much of a call for men to be men of discernment. If you truly want to know where many of us pastors are coming from, I'll tell you. A lot of us don't see the lack of physical unity, nor lack of social action, nor lack of signs and wonders, as the true challenge of the last days church. According to II Thessalonians 2, the ultimate issue facing us is 'will we love the truth, more than the lie, in the face of a false revival of lying signs and wonders?' This is why many of us are seeing truth as the ultimate issue, not tolerance.

Of course, I love all Catholics, Mormons and Jehovah's Witnesses.

All of these 'name the name of Jesus!' But almost all of them worship a different Jesus. I can't claim most of the above as brothers in Christ. If a Mormon keeps all seven of your promises, that could well make him a moral person, but that moral Mormon will go right to Hell. Why? Because in spite of his morality, unity, good father skills and marital fidelity, he is still doomed because he doesn't believe the testimony God gave of His Son.[5]

Millions of pastors owe a great debt of gratitude to Pastor Randles for his courage and true spiritual boldness, demonstrated in his willingness to address these issues to the founder of Promise Keepers. Many thousands of pastors are currently rethinking their position and opinion of Promise Keepers because those among the remnant of God have begun to see His Light concerning Promise Keepers' premises and promises.

It often takes a tremendous amount of integrity and willingness to suffer persecution from one's peers when standing up against popular but errant trends, especially one as popular as Promise Keepers.

A great many pastors now see and sense something else in this focus on "honoring the pastor." They sense the condescension of those who have, through soulish manipulation and "pseudo-honorable mentions," constructed this seemingly sanctified effort at appeasement encapsulated in promise five. As a result, vast numbers of pastors are made to feel like, *"Well, I'm just not being quite as effective as those who are now requesting that the men of my church and others pray for me."* It leaves many pastors flat, empty and with a sense that, after all the years, tears, time, sermons, counseling, visiting and sacrifice that they have invested in "Old Bob" (whom they could not activate in the church with a keg of *TNT*), "Old Bob" is now among those who are applauding his pastor's *"valiant but wasted efforts"* to enliven his church ministries and to get him involved on his home front. "Old Bob" has become an active, ardent attendee, supporter and defender of Promise Keepers, while his energies, resources, and ministry that God intended that he pour into his local church are being siphoned off by his newfound parasitic love. It is an illicit affair.

James, speaking of the believer's need to focus on our biblically established priorities, wrote, "The double-minded man is unstable in all of his ways" (James 1:8).

Many may believe that. *" 'Old Bob' can give a bit to both Promise Keepers and his local church and perhaps even do better than he would by focusing on just his church ministry."* Such an attitude reveals the unscriptural and unfortunate misconception that a great number of men and women have concerning God's demand and the vital and strategic importance of ministry in and through their local church. The church is not an extracurricular or an optional activity for the believer. Scripture clearly demands that each Christian is to know and perform his ministry to and in the local church where he, under the leadership of the Spirit of God, has planted his life. Obedience in this matter is imperative to that believer's spiritual growth, ministerial success and the blessings of God upon his life and family.

Many feel as though they should shop around for any ministry that "turns them on," whether it happens to be a local church or a para-church ministry. But God has already rendered the verdict on that debate, as we shall shortly see. Suffice it to say, the smorgasbord of ministries available which are drawing Christians and resources away from local churches have inflicted greater damage on the cause of Christ than any of the overtly anti-church groups.

Even Christians whose call to home or foreign missions, evangelism or any ministry "outside the church walls" are to maintain a fully submitted heart, mind and ministry to their local church and pastor. This spiritual *"cover"* which God ordained of old is not a matter of choice for those who are called into vocational ministries outside the local church. It is a matter of being in the will of God.

I spent 15 years in evangelism before I began pastoring, which I have now been doing for over a decade. I traveled the world, led and conducted a multifaceted ministry and led evangelistic and revivalistic efforts in local church meetings, city-wide crusades, Bible conferences, a nationwide television ministry, a radio ministry, the publication of a monthly ministry magazine and much, much, more. My family moved three times during those years, and each time we went to a new church.

Among my first priorities upon joining each church was to set an appointment with the pastor, enter his office and, in full humility, submit verbally and actually to him as my pastor and to our new church, our entire ministry, my family and my life. I was fully cognizant that my tithes, offerings and resources were to be invested into the Kingdom of God through my local church. These pastors understood the concept and each graciously and lovingly stood by our work. And because they knew I was fully behind them and my church, they would often ask me to lead crusades, revivals, conferences and other outreaches of our church. Besides providing a spiritual umbrella for my family, our ministry and me, it created a sweet fellowship, as it always does when we maintain God's structure of the biblical chain of command.

On the surface, Promise Keepers Ministries says "honor your pastor." But in reality, every man who chooses to participate in Promise Keepers is simultaneously taking something away from his local church and pastor that *dishonors* that participant and his pastor. In addition, each participant brings back to his local church the contaminated and spiritually polluted philosophies, concepts and doctrines that he absorbs through Promise Keepers' unscriptural ministry and its spiritually corrupt techniques.

The nature of "a little leaven" has never changed and it will eventually "leaven" the whole lump.

One final last thought on this *promise*.

If, indeed, Promise Keepers' ministry was based exclusively on the sound doctrine of the Word of God, and it is not, the scriptural legitimacy of promise five would be contingent upon the kind of church and pastor Promise Keepers is encouraging attendees "to honor and support with their time and resources." Men need to leave churches where the Gospel is not preached, where the Bible is not believed and where there is no Spirit life. To encourage men to honor their pastors and church where the uncompromised Word of God is not taught or preached is but another illegitimate Promise Keepers demand. Rather than fulfilling the biblical demand to reprove false teaching, to warn against false religion, and to stand against the "wiles of the devil" (Ephesians 6:11), Promise Keepers chooses to ignore this responsibility as well.

As a minister, I see nothing Promise Keepers can offer true men of God that is not available in and through a biblically sound and healthy local church. Promise Keepers' vain attempt contained in their fifth "*promise*" to impress is wasted on thousands of pastors like myself.

Although most will not admit it, many pastors, myself included, have much in common with Dopey the dwarf. We are starving for approval and hungry for affirmation and the elusive *"thank you"* for countless sacrificial hours of service that often go unnoticed by most of our flock. How refreshing it is to the unsuspecting pastor to show up to "check out" a Promise Keepers rally, to sense the zeal, to have an opportunity to listen to one of the celebrities preach and to watch thousands of men sing, shout and praise the Lord. Then suddenly, unexpectedly they call, of all things, "little old me, pastor of the First Church of Insignificance" (at least many of us sometimes feel that way) to come forward. They recognize me as important, and then they honor me with a rousing standing ovation.

How do we, at least most of us Pastor Dopeys, handle such adulation and admiration? It does not, at least at that moment, cross our sheepish minds that this perceived approval has been, in all honesty, provoked by those who are often doctrinally polluting the men we pastor or that the manpower and resources of the local church are being drained by the spiritual blood-letting of Promise Keepers. Most pastors simply shrug and respond by saying something like, *"Well, I am just glad to be here with the guys, kind of like, well, kind of like, as Promise Keepers materials puts it... like Jesus, I am enjoying hanging out with all these other "phallic" kind of guys. I am impressed and just watching all the good things that God is doing."*

We pastors, not unlike our little pal Dopey, can often be sucker-punched with a little praise, appreciation and recognition. It, however, would be most wise for us to, in these days of great deceit, be more circumspect and perhaps even more suspect of those who seem a bit overzealous in their commendations to us.

Snow White's Dopey was won with warmth and words but we are warned that "a flattering mouth worketh ruin" (Proverbs 26:28).

I pray for God to increase the number of godly, bold, discerning pastors across America. As a pastor, I know I must *"shake"* myself daily out of that creeping, status-quo mentality and into an awareness of God's call on my life to speak where and what God has spoken.

"For if righteousness comes through the law, Christ died needlessly."

Galatians 2:21b

CHAPTER 14

"For He is our peace, who hath made both one, and hath broken down the middle wall of partition between us."

Ephesians 2:14

Happy and Sneezy

Promise #6
Happy

6. *"A Promise Keeper is committed to reach beyond any racial and denominational barriers to demonstrate the power of biblical unity."*[1]

Happy. It is so good to just be **Happy,** and if everyone would just reach out, love each other and tear down those ugly walls that separate us, then we could all be happy, just like *"Happy, the dwarf"* was always, well, happy.

Promise six is the spiritual anesthetic that numbs the Promise Keepers participant from the stinging conviction he should feel when violating the many biblical principles that his involvement with the organization necessitates.

However, biblical principles notwithstanding, the Promise Keepers' goal of "unity" is paramount and minor obstacles such as Truth and doctrinal purity are expendable. The reality concerning the Promise Keepers' objective which promise six identifies as "biblical unity" remains. There is nothing biblical about the Promise Keepers kind of "unity."

Because this sixth commitment is but another flesh-inspired, emotional appeal, it is most fitting that it be named after our bumbling little buddy, Happy.

I cannot help but remember a few lines of a poem, that as child I was made to memorize. Though I cannot recall its author, I do recall the title and a few of the lines. It was entitled, *"Be Happy"*:

> *"Be happy kid, but not too happy*
> *'Cause it's the happy people that bust*
> *Hard when they do bust*
> *And they do bust*
> *So be happy but not too*
> *Doubled up doggone happy happy."*

The poet's appraisal of happiness is quite correct. Happiness has its limits and can certainly *"bust hard."*

And yet, happiness is very important to our society and fundamentally so in vast segments of the American "church." In fact, we are told that unity among all groups claiming to be Christians, a goal sought by so many in church leadership and promoted by Promise Keepers, would demonstrate to the world the true power of God. This *"unity,"* so we are told, would cause the world to be overwhelmed as it beheld all of those once-quarreling Christian groups joining hands to be one big **happy** family. Why, everyone would be so *"happy and unified and that is what Jesus told us to do, isn't it?"*

Well, is it? We shall see.

Truthfully, God's desire for mankind is neither happiness nor the Promise Keepers' concept of "biblical unity." The goal to get Christian men, through spiritual intimidation, to join together, forgetting their doctrinal differences, may create a union, but it will not create true unity nor will it "demonstrate the power of biblical unity."

Supernatural joy comes to the believer who is One with Christ and thereby in harmony with the Father and the Holy Spirit who resides in all believers. This residual "joy unspeakable and full of glory" (1 Peter 1:8) is not the focus of God's desires for His children but rather the fruit of a believer's consistent fellowship with the Father while walking in obedience to His Word.

Happiness is a human emotion contingent upon happenings and circumstances. It is transient and will come and go to both the regenerate and unregenerate among us. It depends on events that are manipulated by external forces. On the other hand, joy does not depend on externals. *Joy* is *"fruit"* of the Holy Spirit. The events that surround the believer do not dictate whether he has joy or misery. Joy is a residual reality to every believer who is choosing, moment by moment, to abide in fellowship with Christ.

This sixth promise emphasizing once again the need for men to employ the power of their will so that a visible demonstration deemed vital to spiritual success by Promise Keepers can be manifested is nonsensical babble with no basis whatsoever in the Bible. Does it really make any difference at all to Christian laymen, to pastors or ministers that this, along with so many others goals of Promise Keepers, is scripturally illegitimate, and has absolutely nothing to do with "demonstrating the power of biblical unity?" Does it matter at all?

I find it bizarre as well as heart-rending that, in spite of this and the obvious clear assault that the Promise Keepers agenda presents on the Church and the Scriptures, men's hearts, among them the hearts of so many high-profile *"ministers,"* are still set to continue their participation in this dark work. Millions of people in church—laymen and clergy alike—have bought the lie that God wants the Church on earth, all the churches, and all the various religious belief systems that go under the guise of the church, to be unified under one big Christian tent *regardless* of their doctrinal and theological differences. This idea is not, as we shall see, only unscriptural, but was, indeed, prophesied as an idea whose time would come and in fact, will soon be upon us.

This plea for a new unity of all who call themselves Christians often goes as follows: *"Well, Jesus prayed for all of us to be one. We are to join together as one and cease the debates over our differences and strive to be one by dropping these differences and come together on the fact that we all love Jesus and have the same Holy Spirit."*

But is this a biblically sound appeal?

The aforementioned argument does not find support in the Scriptures in any way. Promise Keepers, as well as others who promote neo-unity, most often refer to Jesus' High Priestly prayer in John Chapter 17 as a proof text to support their call for denominational unification regardless of doctrinal differences. The Gospel of John records the words of Jesus, as He prayed, "That they all may be one, as thou, Father, art in me, and I in thee, that they also may be **one in us**; that the world may believe that thou hast sent me. And the glory which thou gavest me I have given them, that *they may be one,* even *as we are one" (John 17:21-22).*

This passage focuses on the relationship between Jesus, the Son, God, the Father, their Word and the followers of Christ. Jesus interceded for those in "the present" as well as those who would receive Him in "the future." Remember, this was Jesus' passionate prayer just prior to Judas' betrayal, His own arrest and ultimate crucifixion. It was before the resurrection as well as the outpouring of the Promised One, the Comforter, the Holy Spirit that gives birth to the Church in Acts, 2.

With prophetic praying at its zenith, Jesus, being fully aware of the events that were about to transpire, poured out His heart to the Father in giving expression to the desires of the Holy Spirit. The Holy Spirit was birthing prayer through the Son. Though God is sovereign, He has chosen to restrain His intervention in the affairs of man and the release of His power to effect change in answer to the prayers of believers who ask in agreement with His will. This is the principle, the Person and the power that Jesus demonstrates in John 17. He prayed the very will of God that man's coming new relationship with God and each other be as fixed, as immutable, as intricately and intimately binding as His own relationship with the Father.

Jesus, especially aware of the coming birth of the Church, prayed in agreement with the mind, heart and will of God that those who choose to receive Him would experience the same kind of deep, full knowledge of and fellowship with God that He, the Son experienced. Jesus prayed for those who came to Him to be "one" as He and the Father are "one" (see also Verse 21-22). What does that mean? How are the Father and Jesus "one?" Certainly not in the sense that either sacrificed any part of their Truth in order to accommodate their oneness. Their sameness facilitated and accommodated their oneness. They had no dissimilarities to forsake in order to be One. Jesus prayed for the believers to partake of this kind of Divine union that was in perfect harmony without need to abandon even the minutest detail of character.

The word "one" in its Greek setting of John 17, means "single, to the exclusion of others of variant root (or source); to be separated from that different in kind."[2] It is critical to the correct interpretation of this passage that we understand that the "oneness" and thus, the *unity* that Jesus prayed for is based upon a consolidation of entities with identical natures and harmonious convictions.

The great scholar Matthew Henry points out in his commentary on this passage that there were three facets in Jesus' request for His people to be *"one."* The first facet, Henry writes, is *"That they all might be incorporated into one body."*[3] This is a prayer for *"all believers, through all time."* Jesus said, "Neither pray I for these alone, but for them also who shall believe on me through their word" (John 17:20). Hence, to imply as does Promise Keepers' application of this passage, that the *"oneness"* Jesus prayed for is the same *"unity"* referred to in the sixth promise and therefore all believers today should *"unify"* regardless of doctrinal beliefs, is sheer exegetical nonsense.

Explaining the second facet of Jesus' prayer, Henry notes that Christ prayed, *"... that they may be made perfect in One (Spirit)"*[4] (John 17:23). The intent, says Henry, is for all believers, through all time, be placed within the same relationship and controlled by that same power and personality that brings a harmony to God the Father and God the Son. Hence, Jesus re-emphasizes this point by praying, "That they may be one, even as We are One." The Apostle Paul knew this prayer of Jesus was realizing progressive fulfillment by the time his own ministry began and, in fact, that it began to be answered on the day of Pentecost and the birth of the New Testament church. He writes in 1 Corinthians 6:17, "He that is joined to the Lord is one Spirit." And later he wrote in Romans 8:9, "Now if any man have not the Spirit of Christ, he is none of His."

Commenting on a third facet of Jesus' prayer, Matthew Henry points out that Jesus prayed, "That they might be knit together in the bond of love and charity"[5] (Verse 26). In the continuing answer to Jesus' prayer all believers are knit together in the "bond of unity" as soon as they are "born of the Spirit." The word "knit" repeatedly appears in the Old Testament and the New Testament when referring to the deep spiritual unity believers have with God through our covenant with the Father. The Old Testament Hebrew word for "knit" is *"berith"* and its Greek counterpart is *"diathëkë"*. Both words, among other things, refer to an immutable, irrevocable reconciliation and joining together.[6] Those who have studied the covenant which every believer enters into with the Father through the Blood of the Son have indeed experienced a foretaste of glory divine. It is an exciting picture of our immutable union with Him and others in the Family of God. This covenant that knits the people of God, whom Jesus was praying for, with the Father and the Son, is an answer to the prayer of Jesus in John 17. And only those who have come to the Father through the covenant blood of Christ are participants in this union but all who have done so need not seek an additional *"unity"* imposed by man through his misinterpretation of this passage.

Many groups such as Promise Keepers constantly misapply and misinterpret John 17 and insist that this prayer of Jesus cannot be answered before He returns unless we drop our doctrinal distinctions and tear down "the walls that have divided the body of Christ for too long."[7] Jesus' prayer for all believers to be *"one"* as He and the Father are One is in no way a divine mandate for those who accept the Bible as the literal, final and inerrant Word of God to "unify" with those who categorically reject it in word, practice or doctrine. This passage in John 17 promotes nothing even remotely related to such a concept.

On the day of Pentecost, as the Holy Spirit baptized those Old Testament disciples of Jesus into the Body of Christ, Jesus' prayer began to be fulfilled. It is not a prayer that *will be* answered when believers are willing to compromise even the smallest *"jot or tittle"* of God's Truth for the purpose of *"helping God"* answer the prayers of Jesus. There, in fact, is no danger whatsoever of any of the prayers of the Lord Jesus Christ going unanswered.

How impudent to even insinuate that answers to the prayers of Jesus, as well as the Second Coming of Jesus, are hindered or postponed by believers who refuse to defile the purity of their commitments, convictions and fellowship by disregarding God's demand for separation from those caught up in false doctrines and heretical and apostate beliefs.

To repeat, the prayer of Jesus is not something that **will be** answered. His prayer began to be answered in the Second Chapter of Acts and will continue to be answered until the last blood-bought saint is snatched from the eternal bondage of sin and Satan and made *"one"*, through new birth, with God the Father, God the Son, God the Holy Spirit, as well as *"one"* with every other true believer since the birth of the Church on that glorious day of Pentecost. In no way was Jesus rebuking future Christians for their disharmony, schisms and divisions. The Apostle Paul dealt with these spiritual conflicts throughout the Epistles. Jesus was dealing with the spiritual union consummated upon the occasion of a believer's new birth where, simultaneously, that believer is made *"one"* with Him, the Father, and all other Christians.

The Father and Son have the same attributes and perfections that the Father, by grace, because of the Son, bestows upon each believer. There is no shadow of spiritual disharmony, no conflict of doctrinal positions and no "wall to break down" that interferes with the unity of true believers, Jesus the Son or God the Father. The *"Spirit of Oneness"* has unified all believers in the Spirit and Truth of God. Any division among believers has nothing to do with the nature and character of *"oneness"* for which Jesus was praying.

Promise Keepers' misapplication of John 17 is a mistake common to dysfunctional, out-of-context, impositional interpretation of the Scriptures. Such twisting of the Word of God in an attempt to fit it into a personal perspective and to use it as a proof text to support an illegitimate doctrinal position is standard operational procedure for whoever writes Promise Keepers' variant, and often conflicting, positional and doctrinal statements.

The unity that Promise Keepers seeks among all Christians who have profound doctrinal disagreements is not going to be achieved until the glorification of all believers becomes a reality. Though, in truth, all true believers are "one in Christ" and have no division at all in that we are "seated together with Christ in the heavenlies" in full harmony, the fact is, while here on earth even Christians have strongholds, heresies, doctrinal confusions, incomplete revelation of the Scriptures and honest differences in understanding and application.

Additionally, every believer is at a different level of spiritual maturity and is progressively experiencing the externalizing of his internalized sanctification.

Hence, until all Christians stand before God with full understanding, there will exist honest and deep rifts on peripheral issues. These differences cannot be overcome by falsely interpreting the Word of God to reach the goal of solidarity at the expense of sacrificing clear and obvious Truths that represent the fundamentals of our Faith. To do so will be to sacrifice *"the Faith"* itself. God's people are commanded to "contend for the Faith." This can be accomplished without sacrificing kindness, Christian courtesies or becoming contentious.

God is still working to exhibit His Life through each believer but He does not do so by demanding that he or she condone obvious doctrinal error and seek compatibility with those who have deviant belief systems.

Jesus also prayed in John 17:17 that the Father would

"Sanctify them through thy truth: thy word is truth." It is clearly not the process of Promise Keepers-style "unity" that will manifest a demonstration of the power of God or biblical unity. It is the believer's unyielding commitment to and love for God's Truth, the Scriptures, that will, in accordance with Jesus' prayer, distinguish the Christian and demonstrate the true power of God.

It is the distinction of every spiritually mature believer that he is adamantly, fanatically and wholly given to God's Word. He will lose it for nothing and sacrifice it for naught. Ask him to forsake God's Truth that has set him apart unto God and you will see the futility of such a request. Ask him to join in a move to unify those who say, *"But we believe in Jesus, too,"* as these *"explain"* that he must not bring his radical love for the Truth of God's Word or his bold declaration thereof and you will see it is a hopeless effort. The rooted and grounded believer has a sacred and correct conviction that all the Truths in the Word of God are to stand together or all of them are compromised. Not one word, jot, or tittle of God's Word is expendable for any reason to those who prize and understand the necessity of scriptural integrity.

This so-called move to "break down denominational walls" for the sake of a union forbidden by the very Word of God is not really an effort to create Christian unity at all. Whether understood by those promoting this unification or not, it is a full-blown, all-out conspiracy against the integrity of the Scriptures and the purity of its doctrine. And sadly, many sincere but undiscerning believers are being deceived.

Students of this century's history are reminded of pre-World War II days when Hitler had loosed his Wehrmacht on various European neighboring countries and had gobbled them up for the Third Reich. Because Britain's Prime Minister, Neville Chamberlain, desired peace more than risking a possible short confrontation with Hitler and his still weak German military machine, he compromised beyond belief. Chamberlain took his now infamous flight to Munich to grovel before Hitler, insuring him that Britain had no desire to go to war as he begged Hitler "to be a good boy and not consume too much more of Europe."

Hitler, whose deception has yet to be matched, sent Chamberlain on his merry way back to London, where, before the masses, the media and the House of Commons he received standing ovations and accolades while he waved his piece of paper signed by Heir Hitler. Chamberlain proclaimed, "I do believe it means peace in our time." "Yes," men like Winston Churchill responded, *"But peace at what price?"* History tells the rest of the story.

Because Chamberlain and most leaders of Britain wanted peace, unity and cessation of their tiring, vigilant, defensive posture, it almost cost the entire free world its freedom. It did ultimately cost the lives of more than 55 million people killed in World War II and an additional 6 million Jews who were turned to ashes in Hitler's ovens and gassed to death in his concentration camps. Some peace that was. Some unity, too.

What price is the *"Church"* paying to follow the spiritual "pied pipers" of today who tell us to "break down those denominational barriers" for peace and unity among the brethren? What price, indeed, to be one, big "happy" family. "Happy", at least until those wearing the woolen cover of the sheep remove their camouflaged clothing and expose the teeth of the wolf.

Promise #7
Sneezy

> 7. *"A Promise Keeper is committed to influence his world, being obedient to the Great Commandment (Mark 12:30-31) and the Great Commission (Matthew 28:19-20)."*[8]

This, the last of our little dwarfed ones who have graciously and aptly aided our analysis of the Promise Keepers' promises, is no less a rascal than the six other midget efforts to reach the standard of God. This is no small matter; rather, it is one of the major failures of Promise Keepers to measure up to the standards that would qualify them as a God-ordained, biblically mandated ministry.

Promise Keepers and its attendees must be challenged to realize that the "Church" has the original plan, design, and call to perform these commands and commissions. Promise Keepers in no way meets the biblical qualifications of a local church and in fact, in doctrinal practice, is totally disqualified to function as either a church or a credible extension of the true Church. The organization simply attempts to persuade men to vow to *do* what God has already told every Christian will *be* the fruit of their relationship with Christ and part of their ministry to and through their local church.

Promise number seven echoes and fraudulently tries to fulfill commissions given to believers and to the Church. Promise Keepers' ministries are open to any who desire to join their activities, regardless of their belief system about salvation. In fact, the ministry does not define its doctrine of salvation at all. The leadership of Promise Keepers then makes the gargantuan mistake of assuming that the men who make a commitment to *do* the promises are true Christians.

So why do I compare promise number seven with "Sneezy", the dwarf who sneezed almost nonstop (allergies, I suppose, poor fella)? Because of a couple of interesting facts about sneezing. First of all, sneezes are caused by a foreign object interfering with and agitating the nasal passages and sinus cavities. And second, it is almost medically impossible for people to keep their eyes open when they sneeze.

This analogy may be a bit of a stretch, but it nonetheless illustrates the fact that the Body, the Church, indeed has experienced a traumatizing, agitating interference of foreign doctrines and alien concepts that have infected its senses and discernment. Preoccupied with our implementation of new pragmatic stimuli for growth, our eyes have been shut to dangerous liaisons between the enemy and our pretended friends. When vast segments of Christians, church leaders and popular ministries close their eyes to the horrendous and savage butchery by Promise Keepers of the most basic tenets of the Christian faith for the sake of a *"bigger tent,"* the floodgates open to every kind of heresy and man-concocted, strange doctrine imaginable.

It is not popular, in fact it is downright *"mean,"* at least according to some, to mention the deception, the fraud, and the counterfeiting of the move of God. Such is the contemporary attitude of the vast majority of America's pulpits. While some privately applaud *"a voice"* that occasionally does call for biblical integrity in popular ministries like Promise Keepers, their silence in the public arena is deafening. Many pastors of America's mega-churches, those controlling most of our nation's major television ministries and Christian print outlets in a concerted, standing ovation, heap praise upon the work of Promise Keepers.

Where are the prophets of God?

As we watch the parade to promote Promise Keepers we are compelled to wonder, not as the biblical saying of old, "Where is the God of Elijah?" but as one, more contemporary observer has noted, "Where are the Elijahs of God?"

The first part of Promise Keepers' seventh promise states the goal for men to love God and their neighbors (Mark 12:30-31). The premise of this promise is flawed because of the faulty concept not only of what it takes to become a Christian, but also because of an erroneous understanding of just how Christian love is to react in an atmosphere where there are so many biblically unsound theologies respecting salvation. If this fundamental doctrine is not stable, then certainly those who build upon it construct in folly. It should be no surprise, then, that since the Promise Keepers' foundation is faulty because of the group's clearly stated premise that *"all roads"* lead to Christ—whether one is Catholic, Methodist, Mormon, homosexual, or whatever—the continuing philosophical structure Promise Keepers builds will also be full of scriptural discrepancies.

Promise Keepers demands that true *"Christian love"* will embrace not only those with doctrines of salvation that are absolutely in conflict with the Word of God, but also that true "Christian love" will embrace all *"brothers"* who are in disobedience. Promise Keepers promotes reconciliation but it is a flawed and scripturally forbidden reconciliation that promotes fellowship between the believer and the infidel and those walking, by their own design, in rebellion to God. That mutual acceptance, regardless of what they believe about what constitutes a Christian, is the true message of love Promise Keepers is promoting. But this is not God-love. It is not *"agape"* but rather a very *"sloppy agape"* that in truth is not related at all to the biblical kind of love that God expresses. It is a pseudo-imitation of the most deceiving sort because of its pretense. It is yet another facet of Promise Keepers' character that causes an inrush of every kind of ill-conceived, man-centered, and demonically religious concept into the "fold of our loving heavenly Father."

I think we used to call that *"universalism."*

While true Christian love longs to see the regeneration of the lost and restitution of an errant believer, God's Word demands the Christian, rather than entering into fellowship, covenant and meetings with such who are walking in rebellion to God and His Word, separate himself from such. The Apostle Paul could not have been more clear than he was to the Thessalonians when he admonished them, "Now we command you in the name of the Lord Jesus Christ, that ye withdraw yourself from every brother that walketh disorderly and not after the tradition (doctrine) which he received of us" (2 Thessalonians 3:6).

We must question the legitimacy of any ministry that refuses to, without waffling, demand that there is no other way to know God and experience eternal life except through faith and by grace in the atoning blood of the Lord Jesus Christ. Yes, some speakers at Promise Keepers do preach the Christ of the Bible. Perhaps some are being born again. But I believe that in no way under heaven does that legitimize, condone or put God's stamp of approval on any ministry that is so tolerant and pursuant of groups, *"churches"* and cults who reject the Cross and the deity of Christ and who believe that their religious system **alone** can guarantee man's salvation. Such fellowship that Promise Keepers fully promotes with heretical and apostate doctrines of devils gives those in false religions and in rebellion to God reinforced confidence in their Christ-less, death-ridden religions. Yet, Promise Keepers insist that their door remain *"open"* to receive those who adamantly and aggressively reject the entire universal plan of God. Not only does Promise Keepers encourage their full involvement; the organization works to insure that its participants do not aggressively confront this spiritual and moral perversion. They insist that all men must come together on the basis of *"Christ."*

Somebody tell me, which Christ?

I appeal to the Scriptures to answer this question. Should Promise Keepers unconditionally accept "men of the cloth and their followers" who preach another Gospel, encouraging them to fully participate with true believers without ever confronting these so-called "Christ-believers" with Truth? And is it really God's will that so many of those participating in Promise Keepers are not *"of the Faith"* at all? This organization encourages, condones and practices the reception of so many groups who would be forced to reject their beliefs if indeed they ever are to know the true Gospel.

I have gone into much greater depth in exposing many of these groups that, though clearly not orthodox in their so-called Christian convictions, are encouraged to fully participate in Promise Keepers as "brothers in Christ". You will find this bizarre "yoking" promoted by Promise Keepers in chapter 21 of this book under its title, "The 'Baskin Robbing' Jesus of Promise Keepers".

The Apostle Paul answered the question when he was forced to deal with a very similar problem in his letter to the Galatians. He said, "I marvel that ye are so soon removed from Him that called you into the grace of Christ unto another gospel: Which is not another; but there are some that trouble you, and would pervert the gospel of Christ. But though we, or an angel from heaven, preach any other gospel unto you than that which we have preached unto you, let him be accursed. As we said before, so say I now again, If any man preach any other gospel unto you than that ye have received, let him be accursed" (Galatians 1:6-9).

Paul was expressing the mind of a Holy God that would not permit any pollution of Truth among the people of God that promoted any other way than the exclusiveness of repentance and faith solely in the finished work of the Lord

Jesus Christ on the cross. He said it twice to make the point clear. Do not reconcile, fellowship, hear, receive, sit with, confess to, participate with or covenant with (as do all Promise Keepers activists) those who preach any other gospel. In a bit we shall see just who these groups are that have found a home in Promise Keepers and thereby been accepted among the *"people of God"* instead of being rebuked and told they are damned except they repent.

Yes, I know. I have already been told, *"That is so unloving."*

No, it is not. What is unloving is to allow people to spread the message of devils without being confronted, to give credibility to false religious systems and to ignore the poisonous doctrines within our midst. And to promote the idea that because men love God they should enter into fellowship and relationship with believers who are out of fellowship with God is also anti-scriptural. In 2 Thessalonians, Paul states, "And if any man obey not our word in this epistle, note that man (i.e. know who he is, name him and his condition) and have no company with him that he may be ashamed" (2 Thessalonians 3:14).

In these days, as compromise becomes the norm, Satan is blinding the hearts of the people of God. They often cannot see that separating from their disobedient brethren is for that brother's spiritual welfare and can result in his repentance and full restoration. Separation is God's demand because that process alone is what *"shames"* the disobedient into full repentance.

The doctrine of separation has another vital purpose, and that is to preserve the purity and integrity of the Church. If a local church loses its sense of spiritual purity and it does not maintain a full expressive commitment to the integrity of the Scriptures, that church's ministry, witness and authority is sacrificed. It may keep going and even numerically growing but it loses the distinctions that make a church the Church.

The second part of Promise Keepers' seventh promise asks for commitment to obey the Great Commission of Matthew 28:19-20. In light of the organization's beliefs and doctrines, this is a charade and a hoax. This commission involves not only preaching the Gospel, but also teaching those who believe... *"To observe all things whatsoever I have commanded you"* (Matthew 28:20). Yet, Promise Keepers' position is that it really does not matter what church or doctrinal creed we attend and believe. It is a "one-size-fits-all" religious organization.

But it does matter where we attend church and what the church teaches people to believe. Paul warned the Ephesian elders in the Book of Acts (Chapter 20:17-32) that he refused to compromise and "he preached the whole counsel of God" to them (Acts 20:21). He warned them day and night with tears for three years (v. 31). His warnings were of grievous wolves and false teachers, who would enter in, "not sparing the flock" (v. 29). He warned of those who would rise from among their own group "speaking perverse things to draw away disciples after them" (v. 30).

The hearts of every discerning man and woman of God in our nation are heavy at this time, as we witness the blindness, apathy, scriptural illiteracy and compromise that is invading the Church.

Oh, that eyes could remain open at all times.

Epilogue

Ever wonder what happened to those seven dwarfs in the Snow White story? Well, they are still out there, haunting the woods, looking for other disenfranchised, unrooted and vulnerable hearts to help. They can protect and please for a while, not unlike the false doctrines that darken man-centered ministries. The seven are there, too, as are the efforts of men who put confidence in the flesh, to help prop up the fallen and caress the wounded soul. Ah, but one soon gets tired of the day-in, day-out routine of depending on self.

Snow White needed far more than seven little dwarfs. She needed Prince Charming to kiss away her death, to sweep her away on his white horse and to deliver her from the vile "wicked one" who sought her life.

But death, yea, desperation ultimately visited Snow White. Even in the fairy tales, it is death, wrought through the failure of the seven to render protection, that finally introduced life. When a man finally gets weary of "one more day of works" and tires of the tune, *"Heigh Ho, Heigh Ho, it's off to WORK we go,"* then he can discover his hope is not in seven or 700,000 promises to please God and man but, rather, in death to efforts, to works and to self.

PART IV

The Terror Within the Trojan Horse

"Brethren, we shall not adjust our Bible to the Age, but the Age to the Bible."
—Charles H. Spurgeon

"It does not matter what your personal deficiency...
God always has one sufficient answer, His Son, Jesus
Christ, and He is the Answer to every human need."
—Watchman Nee

CHAPTER 15

The Evolution of a Revolution

"For no man can lay a foundation other than the one
which is laid which is Jesus Christ."

1 Corinthians 3:11

Early in this century, the theories and presumptions of men began evolving into the latest American-born religion: psychology. No movement has been more responsible for molding the mind of America, at least in this century. In fact, psychology has even invaded Christendom in America with hardly a whimper of protest from major Christian church leaders. This humanistic religion, whose high priest is the psychologist, is a major part of the Promise Keepers doctrinal package.

Paul Vitz, a psychology professor at New York University, wrote, "Psychology as religion exists...in great strength throughout the United States...[it] is deeply anti-Christian... [yet] is extensively supported by schools, universities and social programs...financed by taxes collected from Christians... but for the first time, the destructive logic of this secular religion is beginning to be understood."[1]

Today's variant strains of psychology are increasingly sophisticated-sounding, appealing to the "wounded souls" of millions searching for answers to problems spawned by their increasingly complex lives. In fact, this "science," has recently taken a new "bride." "Miss American Christianity" has wed "Mr. Psychology," and together, they have created an unholy alliance which is producing some "strange children." Jesus, as well as others in Scripture, prophesied of a coming worldwide deception that will blanket this planet before His literal physical return to this Earth. The "deception" will be so convincing that it will mislead "if possible, even the elect." In fact, in describing to His disciples the "last days," Jesus told of this coming, rampant, religious deception: "For there shall arise false Christs, and false prophets, and shall show great signs and wonders, insomuch that, if it were possible, they shall deceive the very elect. Behold, I have told you before" (Matthew 24:24-25).

This prophesied deception is now affecting not only the Church and religious community but every facet of American society as well. No better illustration of this powerful deception can be made than through that of the courts of our land. The new "political correctness," dictated by the "judicial psychologist," requires judge and jury to psychoanalyze the accused before determining guilt or innocence. The new religionist insists it is wrong for society to "re-victimize" the criminal with unjust and cruel punishment simply because he is a mass murderer, thief or rapist. The criminal is "like he is," according to the psychologist, because of circumstances beyond his control; therefore he is not at fault. According to the humanist priest-psychologist, the offender is the product of his environment and represents the sum total of his negative experiences with perhaps his abusive father, cruel mother, or mean siblings. In truth, society often receives the blame for allowing the disenfranchisement of the poor *"victim"*.

This reversal of reason and convulsion of reality has distorted our society, made a mockery of justice and set the majority of the Christian and religious community in America on a new course.

The social acceptance of this unholy religion has been hastened by its deceptive shifting of the blame for humanity's evils from the antiquated Judeo-Christian concept of original sin to the "new bad boy on the block" named *dysfunctionalism*. Dysfunctionalism defines, explains and excuses the human condition by attributing all negative traits, hang-ups, maladjustments and rebellion to the dysfunctional family or perhaps the dysfunctional non-family or even an abstract dysfunctional society.

Ultimately, explains the New Age psycho-priest, no one is really at fault for anything and any guilt one senses is unnecessary self-flagellation rooted in a maladjusted self-image. The solution to all man's problems can be found within himself, and, the psychologist continues, the key to a full and rewarding life is self-actualization.

These are not biblical concepts. The Bible teaches that each of us is responsible for our own conduct and sin. We alone ultimately choose the life we live. Of course, circumstances, environment and the way a person is brought up influence one's character; however, influence is not synonymous with responsibility.

It is easy to recognize the natural evolution of psychology's "the answer lies within one's self" concepts in the man-centered promises that are the premise of Promise Keepers' belief system.

The illegitimacy of Promise Keepers as a credible Christian ministry is established by the enormous influence that well-known psychologists have had and are having upon the materials, books and methods of the Promise Keepers organization. Many pastors and laymen would scratch their heads in bewilderment when hearing anyone speak negatively of Promise Keepers based upon their intimate relationship with psychology. "Why can it be so wrong?" they ask. "So what is wrong with a little psychology," they ask, "especially if it is Christian psychology?"

How strange that men of God, supposedly educated in the Scriptures could pose such a question, and yet the obsession of so many in the "church" with Promise Keepers demands an answer to the question, "What is wrong with psychology?"

Psychology, because it is considered a "science", is based firmly on the theory of evolution, which teaches man evolved from lower life forms. It therefore refuses to consider what I shall call the *"God factor,"* outside of an occasional honorable mention to some abstract "higher power." Some secular psychologists grant, for therapeutic purposes, subscription of their patients to this nameless *"higher power"* but a personal, loving, Holy God that is capable of having a relationship with man is completely out of the equation for any realistic diagnostic purposes.

The efforts made by "Christian psychologists" who do consider the "God factor" often stop short of accepting the whole truth included in the God factor. To acknowledge God's existence or even His involvement in the human stream and to then reject the full and final revelation of Scriptures as the sufficient and exclusive means by which to deal with man's problems is to separate the *"wet"* from the *"water."* While acknowledging the reality that "God is," the Christian psychologist refuses to forsake the fundamental tenets of his ill-founded *"science-faith"* and thereby admit God's Word indeed does contain the answers to all of man's problems. Consequently, the Christian psychologist must come up with "answers" for man's dilemma that are compatible with his subjective Christianity while staying rooted in psychology. He will not believe the Word of God that teaches all of man's need, hurt, pain, failure, guilt and fear stem from the spiritual reality that man is a sinner and that the consequence of that sin is death (Romans 6:23). This death is not one "pending", it is a present reality and resident within each human from the moment of his birth until it is supernaturally dealt with by a Divine intervention. Men, dead in "trespasses and sin" (Ephesians 2:1) cannot, through therapy, discover life and resurrection.

Basic psychology attempts to answer and solve man's **sin** problem and its *"consequences"* through the building up and restoration of man's self-esteem and self-image. Christian psychology is merely a slightly varied and mostly semantical application of the principles in its twin religion, psychology. Both strains, in addition to approximately 250-plus others, must get the man to acknowledge that all of his problems and hurts are not really his fault. He has been *"victimized"* and he is constantly *"at risk"* of becoming more severely victimized until he learns, through the tenets of the humanistic religion of psychology just how valuable he is. The message is *"Hey, you're OK, I'm OK."* **Okay?**

No, according to the Word of God, we are not "okay." We cannot find redemption from our traumas until we are prepared to reach to Someone outside of "self" to complete us. That basic Christian principle is finding less and less acceptance among self-seeking men, in a self-centered society, whose greatest problem is a desire to worship at the altar of *"self."*

Promise Keepers fundamentally accepts and promotes the tenets of the humanist religion of the psychologist. The "slow leak" of viligance in "defending the faith" by millions of once doctrinally sound church members numbed their sense of discernment and has led to the acceptance of the spiritually still-born, scripturally neutered ministry.

The Failure of Early Warning Systems

Have you ever been deceived by someone you really trusted and later, upon discovering the deception, were so ashamed of your naiveté that you could not bring yourself to tell anyone? You were *"conned"* but decided to keep it to yourself, fearful that others would think you were foolish. Often our pride keeps us quiet when we discover we were wrong.

As this book and others being written by some of our nation's true men of God with the courage to speak out become more available, more and more people are going to realize that they have been spiritually raped by Promise Keepers because of this ministry's teachings and beliefs, which violate their basic convictions and entire Christian belief system. Although the premise of Promise Keepers is topically well-camouflaged, I am still amazed at the vast numbers of intelligent and well-read, but obviously philosophically and scripturally shallow Christian leaders who are so blatantly deceived by the ministry. Others who are only casually acquainted with Promise Keepers have not been challenged to look more closely at the organization and its teachings. Public statements by those who realize that they have been misled or remiss in their examination of Promise Keepers would salvage the ministries, energies and resources of massive numbers of men who are currently pouring everything into their involvement in Promise Keepers. But my concern is that far too many in pulpits and in church leadership, like the rape victim who feels ashamed and embarrassed to have been violated, will be reluctant to tell the truth once they learn it. Pride dies hard and few are willing to think.

The fact that this ministry has already made such a tremendous impact throughout the country is evidence of the failure of what should have been the early warning systems of the Church, the tens of thousands of astute, thinking and ordinarily scripturally sound and vocal pulpits across America.

Backup Systems Flash

Can any Christian with an undefiled conscience and the desire to maintain a personal commitment to biblical integrity condone the invasion of darkened, anti-Christian teaching into the very core of our Faith's Holy of Holies, the pure Word of God? Can any scripturally knowledgeable, discerning believer accept the defilement of that which God has elevated above His Name, "His Word?" "...for Thou has magnified Thy word above Thy name" (Psalms 138:2). Do you know anyone who could be so careless with the sacred trust, a trust purchased at no less a price than the blood of the martyrs, as to quietly allow and thereby assist in a completely disfiguring, defacing and defamation of His Word? This is precisely what Promise Keepers ministry and its support base is doing and fully plans to continue, if they follow their stated goals and continue to expand their influence.

The voices of so many pastors ring in my memory as I have heard them endorse and staunchly defend Promise Keepers. They say, "But I went to a Promise Keepers rally...I heard nothing that contradicts the Bible...I do not see anything to worry about...look at all the good they are doing." These testimonies illustrate just how far the church and many of its "shepherds" have strayed from the simplicity, clarity and knowledge of God's Word. Although I am sure these men do not realize it, their comments mark them as either naïve, undiscerning, unread or simply intellectually lazy. It does not matter *"how much good"* any work does if it be born of flesh or devils. Coming to Christ or experiencing a change in life-style does not confirm a minister or ministry as scripturally valid.

The vast majority of pastors across America has not been exposed to the Madison Avenue expertise and slick sales mechanisms that are often attracted to high-profile or successful ministries such as Promise Keepers, which has a highly marketable message. So many may not know that Promise Keepers, with its multi-million-dollar promotional campaign, has some of the world's best sales and marketing professionals at its disposal. These promotional personnel who know how to launch campaigns designed to appeal to the hearts of pastors and laymen are funded by the bottomless pit of cash garnered through the sales of the organization's merchandise and materials. Yet, the wolf under the wool Promise Keepers wears is to be found not in the gigantic, massive rallies, but in its teachings, literature and mentoring techniques.

The Promise Keepers' sales pitch to pastors is, "Look at our numbers, our rapid supernatural growth, our ability to attract men and even our famous speakers and supporters. We must surely be of God or we would not be endorsed by so many well-known men of stature. Nor would we experience such widespread approval and acceptance." I hear this reasoning and recall the words of Jesus, "Woe to you when men speak well of you for so did their fathers to the false prophets" (Luke 6:26).

Promise Keepers knows that the contemporary philosophy which defines the heart of many pastors, captures their attention and fires their vision is "pragmatism." Pragmatism is the belief that truth is discerned and qualified and that the means to an end is justified on the basis of the results that they garnered. The mega-ministry, mega-church mentality is damning commitments to conscience and capturing men of the cloth who are being seduced into compromising for what appears to be successful ministry. The Promise Keepers mentality is leading the charge for those who appear to be far more enamored with results than with theological distinctions or scriptural integrity. If this were not true, then they would have had from their inception an undying, unyielding commitment to fulfill God's objectives for men without the horrendous, spiritual poison and scriptural slaughter necessitated by the employment of methods from Sigmund Freud, Carl Jung and a multitude of other antichrist evangelists in the religion of psychology. Nor would Promise Keepers be calling for the pseudo-unity that attempts to consolidate men with solid doctrinal backgrounds with other men who live by and defend belief systems that are foreign to biblical Christianity. Nor would Promise Keepers have so watered down and redefined the entire Christian faith through their man-made, flesh-reliant, ego-appealing, system of works-based spiritual growth.

The Department of Defense and The Integrationist

Promise Keepers' leadership and the authors of much of the literature written and promoted by Promise Keepers are theological and philosophical *"integrationists."* Like every cult and false religious system since time began, those who have crafted the foundation of Promise Keepers Ministries integrated the Truth of the Word of God with the deceptive doctrine of darkness. The subtlety of this unholy concoction lies in its "Christian" appearance. Promise Keepers' doctrine of salvation is not only non-offending, but non-stated, non-printed, and non-existent. It provides a comfort zone for all in its belief system for the spiritual bedouins wandering around in the nation's religious wilderness. Promise Keepers has far more in common with the Bahai faith than they do with Orthodox Christianity. Bahai's open-door policy encourages all religions to participate in Bahai worship. After all, "do not all of us travel on different roads to the same destination?" Clearly, Promise Keepers would not accept without hesitation, as it surely does, the various false religious systems, perverse sects of neo-evangelical Christianity and other cults if they were unflinchingly and irrevocably committed to the Way and Word of God.

Promise Keepers' doctrine for spiritual development is a maze of contradictory systems of religious babble that caters to everyone from the Charismatic Catholic priests to the cultic Mormon elder to the unrepentant sexual deviate.

This growing phenomenon integrates false *"truth,"* (a misnomer, I know, but one that best defines partial truths and half lies) of psychology with God's Truth and, for most people, so muddles the latter that it is indistinguishable from the former. How can men expect to achieve God-given goals by using God- forbidden techniques? Yet, few large churches in America remain that do not employ a full-time counselor trained in psychotherapy (or psychological counseling) who has not endorsed the ministry of Promise Keepers.

Some may still be asking, "But what is wrong with psychotherapy or psychology if it really helps people?" Obviously, that is exactly what Promise Keepers, its leaders, founder, and, apparently, those who vociferously support it, are asking. Clearly, Promise Keepers would not be doing the things I am about to share with you if they really knew what they were doing, would they?

Well, would they?

Subtle Seditions

Promise Keeper's original seven-page Position Letter written in response to a massive number of inquiries regarding their use of the book, *The Masculine Journey, Understanding the Six Stages of Man* by Robert Hicks, states that Hicks "submitted his work to Navpress and Promise Keepers as a candidate for inclusion in our line of books. We were convinced it would help men pursue Jesus Christ and also the challenge of the twentieth century."[2] However, Promise Keepers' involvement in the Hicks book, which blatantly attacks Christian truths, was not nearly as benign as Promise Keepers' public relations department would have us believe. They originally attempted to imply that Hicks took a personal initiative and basically *"pushed the book"* upon Promise Keepers and their publisher, Navpress. Promise Keepers then infer that they thought, after its publication, that it would be a nice little ministry tool. However, researchers Martin and Diedre Bobgan have since discovered that Hicks' book was a joint effort between Dr. Hicks, Promise Keepers Ministries and Navpress.[3] Promise Keepers refuses at this time to release its original position paper defending *The Masculine Journey*, but it also refuses to renounce its support of the book, which is considered by many to be anti-Christian, sexually deviant and spiritually perverse.

Promise Keepers' office now sends an updated version of its stand on the book, simply stating that they do not currently distribute it. But, of major importance, the ministry still refuses to refute or deny that this anti-biblical publication contains a philosophy central to their theology and that it expresses doctrine that they find redemptive. Once again, to men of the clergy and Bible students who are cognizant of the deep and irreconcilable differences between the message and the methods in the Word of God and those found within the discipline of psychology, it is a most severe philosophical and theological contradiction to suggest that men follow, simultaneously, both the Christian *"faith"* and religion of psychology. Jesus Christ stated it succinctly when He said, "No man can serve two masters; for either he will hate the one, and love the other" (Matthew 6:24).

A Breach in the Lines

The entire ministerial philosophy of Promise Keepers—from the premise of their seven promises to their menagerie of fraudulent doctrinal positions to their unwillingness to disavow the belief that the Word of God and psychology are readily compatible—is riddled with spiritual corruption. Promise Keepers applies anti-Christian, psychological techniques to help "diagnose" participant's problems relating to personal crisis management, relational conflict, and spiritual growth.

This results in a fraudulent diagnosis, which often ends in disaster for the "patient". As men act upon this erroneous diagnosis, their problems are only perpetuated. Promise Keepers' solutions are akin to the age-old practice of *"bleeding."* But instead of bleeding the body, they senselessly and harmfully bleed the *"psyche"*, or, if you prefer, the human soul.

How applicable to these *New Age* priests are the words Jesus spoke to the zealots of His day who were seeking converts to their false religions: "Woe unto you...for ye shut up the kingdom of heaven against men; for ye neither go in yourselves, neither permit them that are entering to go in...you compass sea and land to make one proselyte, and when he is made, ye make him twofold more the child of hell than yourselves...ye blind guides, who strain at a gnat, and swallow a camel" (Matthew 23:13, 15, 24).

Contrary to the message at the core of the systematic psychology and the aberrant doctrine embraced by Promise Keepers, each of us is personally responsible for our sin and the consequences it brings to our lives. Promise Keepers, especially in their materials represented by Dr. Hicks' books, as well as in their guilt-free, conviction-absent mentoring sessions, wants to soften the blow of reality with yet another spiritual placebo.

In their original defense of their aggressive campaign to distribute Dr. Hicks' book, Promise Keepers stated, "What we discovered, *The Masculine Journey* was a biblically-centered, frank and honest account of man's journey with God...we endorsed it because we believed that it would be a tool that challenged men to grow in Christlikeness, to become 'zaken' or 'wise men of God' as Dr. Hicks writes."[4]

As stated earlier, Promise Keepers now refuses to release their letter defending the work and refuses to publicly and openly repent of spending tens of thousands of dollars to help produce, print and distribute it. In the 1993 Promise Keepers Convention in Boulder, Colorado, this book was received by all 50,000 men who attended. Its full title is, *The Masculine Journey, Understanding the Six Stages of Man* and it came complete with the Promise Keepers' logo, information packets and an accompanying study guide. Obviously, Promise Keepers still has no shame in their endorsement of the book.

Christians who understand how important it is to maintain the divine integrity and a commitment to Holy Writ as the inspired, authoritative Word of God are fully aware that they must resist any and every attempt from any quarter to infiltrate biblical truths with alien and foreign philosophy. Dr. Hicks, *"an integrationist,"* combines biblical phraseology and precepts with the fundamentally flawed premises of psychology. Christian theologians with conservative values have long understood that psychologists, such as Dr. Hicks, typically consider their personal character facets, traits, actions, reactions and behavioral tendencies as the common experience of all men and, therefore, universally applicable. But psychological theorists have made a gargantuan mistake in their diagnostic techniques. They impose these generic categories on their patients in order to help them get to the *"root"* of the patient's problem. However, these techniques to therapeutic counseling not only lack scientific data to support their universal application, but, indeed, they have no biblical support qualifying them as a legitimate approach to deal with men's spiritual or emotional needs.

More than 250 psychological counseling techniques or theoretic approaches to counseling exist in the field of psychology. Each includes contradictory theories and teachings and each claims to present "truth". A number of them, as does Dr. Hicks, use the Scriptures as a way to "qualify" their theories. But all of these methods cannot be *"true"*. In fact, of the multitude of ideological interpretations of psychological truth, what chance is there that any of them are correct?

But the integrationist interprets *"truth"* in terms of relativity. Truth, according to psychology, is a variable. It changes. As men psychologically and intellectually progress, *"new truth"* becomes available to replace *"old truth"*, according to the evolutionary philosophical premise of the psychologist. Psychologists and others of *"partially revealed"* fields of *"science"* feel that as our evolutionary process continues, we naturally discover greater truths that nullify *"old"* beliefs about what is true.

Until the beginning of this century, doctors were still *"bleeding"* patients who desperately needed blood transfusions.

Only in recent history did medical science discover what the Word of God had pronounced thousands of years ago: *"the life is in the blood"* (Leviticus 17:14). However, the principle of this *"new truth"* that replaced the *"old truth,"* while applicable in fields where knowledge is still being garnered, does not apply in the field of theology, into which the psychologist has intruded with his sordid, darkened humanistic principles. Truths from the Scriptures speak the age-old Truth of God and are the full revelation of God to man.

The mistake scientists and researchers continue to make because of their deluded and rather arrogant presupposition is that today's discoveries wrought through their investigation of the *"facts"* reveal the whole truth. Rarely do the truths and laws supported by science today support the revelations of truths that follow tomorrow. The law of gravity, set upon by Galileo, was indeed true and yet another law was ultimately discovered that superseded and rendered as incomplete the idea that what goes up, must eventually come down as a result of the law of gravity. The law of aerodynamics, while not abolishing the law of gravity, introduced truths that deeply affected the ancient idea that man, because of gravity's law, was earthbound.

The Apostle Paul referred to the *"law of the Spirit of life in Christ Jesus"* that made the believer free from the *"law of sin and death."* He, as well as Galileo, observed laws that held true only in the absence of higher truth. Both laws were true and yet one was forced to yield to the other.

Man's quest to understand the behavioral sciences has often led to premature conclusions of what is true and what is not. Often these researchers have stopped short when stumbling upon a *partial* truth simply because they considered it to be the *whole* truth. However, no truth is the whole truth unless it incorporates God's Truth.

God's Truth, we know, is complete and absolute. God's Truth is not new truth, except in the sense that it is newly revealed to God's individual people according to His own sovereign timing. There can be no *"new truth"* that contradicts God's ageless Truth that can stand a legitimate test of accuracy. Yet, His absolute and complete Truth is being challenged, not

only by the deniers of God's Word who openly reject the
Truth of Scriptures, but by the subtle integration of *"new
truths"* into *"the counsel of God."* But indeed, these new
revelations are not truths at all. They strive to bring a
compatibility between the wisdom of man, reflected in
psychology, and the wisdom of God, found in the Scriptures.
This is no more clearly demonstrated than in the Dr. Hicks'
book. Even if Promise Keepers would disavow any and all of
their allegiance to this particular book, and they have not,
still the entire foundational basis for the Promise Keepers
ministry is similarly deeply flawed. This flaw is inherent in
their unyielding commitment to extra-biblical beliefs and
practices, much of it inundated with the philosophical baggage
of psychology, mysticism and contemporary impositions upon
the Word of God.

The Insufficiency of God's Word

God's Word has failed, at least in the thinking of many, to
produce spiritually integrated growth, Christian unity and
consequently, a harmonious testimony to the true power of
God. So, at last, to the rescue, psychology rides over the hill
to save us from the insufficiency of Scripture. It is here to
accomplish what Bible-based Christianity has for centuries
failed to do on its own. Although such thinking is a farce, it
sums up Promise Keepers' philosophy; otherwise, they would
not impose extra-biblical demands upon their participants.

We must rededicate ourselves to teaching our families
and fellow believers to distinguish between unchanging,
theocentric, Bible-based Truth and ever-changing, psychological
and experienced-based doctrines that are anthropocentric, or
man-centered. The religion of psychology focuses upon the
"man-self." Self-awareness, self-image, self-actualization and
self-esteem are its fundamental goals. Most of Promise Keepers'
leadership are part of a movement that promotes a subjective
spiritualistic belief system that has no allegiance to the Word
of God as the closed Canon and final revelation of God. The
nature of this belief links them to other religious groups such

as Mormons, the Jehovah's Witnesses, the Moslems, the Catholics, and others. Such is the antithesis to the Truth of God's Word represented in true Orthodox Christianity. It simply facilitates the birthing of yet more false religions.

To mix theoretical psychology with Christianity and simultaneously infer that the Word of God is still being written has birthed a menagerie of strange religions. One such hybrid is the attempted infusion of Marxism into Christian theology. The result of that futile effort was aberrant "de-Christed" Christianity that came to be known as *"liberation theology"*, a misnomer because liberation theology is neither liberating nor is it Bible-based theology.

The same is true of the hybrid religion resulting from the attempt to incorporate therapeutic psychology into a biblical belief system. Such an effort not only contaminates the purity of God's Truth but also results in the idolatry of *"self."* It creates yet another technique for meaningless therapy, and a handsomely profitable practice for the psychologists.

The contradictory nature of these two belief systems make their philosophical co-existence impossible. That does not mean that the particular Truths stolen from God's Truth and integrated into psychology to produce *"Christian psychology"* are no longer true. But this spiritual *"hijacking"* of biblical Truths does not lend credibility to the hijackers. Furthermore, these Truths, when removed from the context of Scripture, often lose their practical viability when integrated into the opposing doctrines of psychology. This philosophical approach to ministry has birthed such things as "Christian" night clubs, "Christian" heavy metal rock music, "Christian" pornography and "Christian" strippers. One woman involved in the latter told an interviewer, "We are stripping under the leadership of the Holy Spirit. We sense His presence when naked on stage." Blasphemous indeed, and yet once we begin to justify the process of rewriting, redefining, recreating or transplanting God's Word into alien belief systems, all truth becomes subjective to one's personal taste, values and preferences. Man, no longer Scripture, arbitrates truth.

This convoluted approach to Scripture allows Promise Keepers to justify such perverse *"tolerance"* as is reflected in its open-door policy to practicing unrepentant homosexuals who claim to be Christians. This lack of commitment to the Word of God as the absolute and conclusive revelation of God allows Promise Keepers leadership to urge heterosexual participants to simply *"receive and love"* homosexual participants without confrontation at Promise Keepers sponsored activities. But it is a "love" foreign to Scripture that *"warns not the sinner"* nor calls him to repent and receive the Savior. The writer of Proverbs states, "Better are the wounds of a friend than the kisses of an enemy" (Proverbs 27:6).

But then, strange theologies make strange bedfellows.

The Sculpting of Manure

The tenor of Promise Keepers' beliefs system insists that the Scripture, while true, does not adequately deal with this age's dilemmas, questions and problems. They tell us that people are no longer struggling with such issues as "forgiveness of sin" and "where will I go when I die?" They tell church leaders that *the church* must *"get relevant"* if they are to reach people. People, they say, are now concerned with discovering their personal identity and the meaning of life as it relates to their present existence. The Promise Keepers' approach to making "real men" through covenants, oaths, group therapy and mentoring—though they would certainly deny it—is rooted in humanistic religious psychology that defies Christian realities.

Many who hold to the traditional message of the church appear to have been out of touch with this generation's needs to a large degree. However, the failure of many in the church to "be relevant" to the perceived needs of contemporary man is not the fault of the Word of God but of those who have yet to discover the powerful, ever-relevant and timeless message that it contains for a *"now"* generation. The writers of the New Testament understood relevancy. The Apostle Paul repeatedly dealt with issues more contemporary than tomorrow's newspaper. He thoroughly dealt with self-esteem, self-image and self-focus. And what he taught flies in the face of books like *The Masculine Journey.*

Paul discarded those seemingly positive attributes that contributed to his pre-Christian personal advancement and high rank in society. He considered that which had been "gain" to him from a worldly, secular perspective and supportive of his "self-realization" and "self-affirmation" to be obstacles to his life in Christ. He considered the advancement and promotion of self as *"dung"* when compared to what he had found in Christ. Not many things are as crass as manure. Nor could Paul have found a better way to illustrate the uselessness of those values and priorities of men without God. He wrote the church at Philippi, "But what things were gain to me those I counted loss for Christ, yea doubtless I count all things but loss for the excellency of the knowledge of Christ my Lord, for whom I have suffered the loss of all things and do count them but dung that I may win Christ, and be found in Him, not having mine own righteousness which is of the law but that which is through the faith of Christ, the righteousness which is of God by faith; that I may know Him and the power of His resurrection and the fellowship of His sufferings, being made comfortable unto His death" (Philippians 3:7-10).

Paul's "self-image" was absorbed in his identity with Christ, being dead to self-effort, feeble fleshly promises and any kind of self-focus. He, through Christ, was able to live as "more than a conqueror." He was not living the "self-life" but the "Christ-life." Christ Jesus is not plagued with traumas, fears, anxieties or a wounded soul. He does not have to deal with the history of a "dysfunctional" father. He is not worried, upset, fearful, angry, bitter, maladjusted, psychotic or neurotic. The exchanged life finds fullness and sufficiency in "dying to self" and "living to Christ."

The solution and answer to every question, every need, every conflict and every fear, is all secured for every believer in the *"allness of life"* that Christ has provided for them and in them. Little wonder Paul proclaimed, *"For me to live is Christ!"* What more could anyone want, than all of God in all of them?

Promise Keepers' unbiblical doctrine and psychology-laced resources, materials and techniques suggest that we have a less-than-adequate Christianity and that it desperately needs additives.

In his excellent book entitled, *Christ-Esteem, Where The Search For Self-Esteem Ends,* Don Matzat expands on these truths when he states the following:

What About Jesus?

It is strange that in the midst of all the criticisms being leveled against the offerings of traditional Christianity, *you never hear anyone criticize Jesus.* I have never read a book promoting the claims of modern psychology as an alternative or addition to biblical Christianity in which the author says, *"Jesus Christ does not have all the answers."* Of course, you hear it said that the "sin and grace theology of the church is not relevant," or even, "the Bible does not have all the answers," but you never hear it said that the person of Jesus Christ is an insufficient solution to the needs of modern man.

Those who promote the integration of psychology with biblical theology have *failed to grasp the basic essence of the Christian faith.* I know that is a very serious accusation, but nonetheless, when you examine the writings of Christian psychologists, it is very evident. They speak of Christianity as a specific, limited body of religious truth addressing the subject of human behavior. For example, a popular book defining the principles involved in the integration of psychology and theology states: "Many individual Christians look to psychology for new insights that will relieve personal discomfort or despair. They hope that psychology will provide answers to *questions not specifically addressed in Christianity"* (Matzat's emphasis).

Dr. Gary Collins writes in his book *Can You Trust Psychology?,*[5] "Some human problems are not mentioned in Scripture. They are not discussed specifically, neither are there examples to show how others dealt with these issues in a way pleasing to God."

According to this way of thinking, the integration of psychology with theology poses no problems. Both disciplines deal with the same subject matter of human behavior and are both dedicated to helping people live more meaningful lives. Since it is philosophically correct to say that all truth ultimately comes from God, it is therefore reasonable to suggest that psychology is able to fill up that which is lacking in the body of Christian truth. This understanding is based upon a wrong definition of the very essence of Christianity.

Contrary to the thinking of Christian psychologists, Christianity is not a religion doling out spiritual wares and adjusting them from time to time to meet user demands! Nor is the Bible a fundamentalist's textbook of psychology offering a potpourri of spiritual and psychological solutions to the needs of hurting people. When confronted with the needs of people, we do not push buttons and pop out appropriate Bible verses. We offer Jesus! Christianity is and always has been a relationship with the person of Jesus Christ who is the same yesterday, today, and forever.[6]

It is not uncommon to hear pastors and Christian counselors say that some psychological propositions in ministry are in harmony with the Scriptures. Such protests indicate a shallow understanding regarding the root and nature of psychology versus that of the Scriptures. It also strongly indicates a lack of understanding about an indwelling and empowering Christ. No human need could ever possibly develop—past, present or future—which the life of Christ working in harmony with the Word of God and an obedient believer fails to meet.

Psychology preaches that man needs to "find himself". On the contrary, man's problems stem from the fact that he has "found himself", and what he has found, he loves—to the point of self-worship. Man is enamored with *"himself."* Psychology, rather than quenching the flame of need and despair in the human heart, further fuels it until it is a raging inferno. Man does not need to *"find himself."* Man needs to discover God's Son and that can only be accomplished when man is willing to *lose* himself. Jesus said, "If a man keeps his life he shall lose it, but if he shall lose his life for my sake, he shall find it" (Matthew 16:25).

A final quote from the book by Don Matzat is noteworthy:

> While our secular society is faced with a meaningless existence, most Christians today are suffering from complacency. There are many miserable, unhappy, hurting, fearful people in the church who simply put up with their condition. They may seek pity, understanding, and compassion from the pastor and their fellow church members, but they are not looking for answers. While they find their identity in their traditional connections and live moral lives by the standards of the Ten Commandments, they lack freedom, contentment, joy, and peace. We cannot say to a secular, humanistic society that Jesus Christ is the answer to their deepest needs until He is the answer to the deepest needs and longing of those who claim to be the followers of Jesus Christ.[7]

Men will become the "real men" that God intends them to become when they discover the fullness of Christ and the richness of God's Word.

The battle to create additives for that which has been completed will continue as long as the nature of man tends to defy the nature of God and refuses to repent of his self-centered, self-seeking, and self-destructive remedies. The *"destroyer"* is at large. His quiet whisper can still be heard in the rustle of leaves in the Garden of Heathens. He still desires to assist us in our quest to *"be as gods."* His enticements are seductive indeed.

"Whom the gods would destroy, they would first confuse their language."

—Author Unknown

CHAPTER 16

The Babble of Babel

"And they said, Come, let us build us a city and a tower, whose top may reach unto heaven... and the Lord scattered them... upon the face of all the earth; and they ceased building... the name of it was called Babel, because the Lord did there confound the language."

Genesis 11:4-9

Men have forever been enamored with building highways to heaven. Often these highways have been paved with the religious works and efforts of man. At other times, such efforts were more tangible, like the building of the Tower of Babel (Genesis 11:1-9). The debris of all such human efforts litters the pages of history as shattered ruins and testify to the futility of man's efforts to play God, much as the scattered remains of the Tower of Babel on the Plains of Shinar. In spite of these failed attempts throughout history, man apparently is still not prepared to surrender his quest to *"be as god"* (Genesis 3:5).

Human attempts to repackage "Christianity" by co-mingling it with extra-biblical demands, principles of psychology, and other additives must be recognized as the saboteur's handiwork. Introducing scripturally illegitimate books, concepts and human reasoning into biblical Christianity's doctrine only derails men who otherwise might go on with God in a deeper capacity. Man, through a relationship with Christ and a walk with God, can experience fullness in his life, home and relationships without the "additives" presented by ministries such as Promise Keepers. But we live in an age when additives to our religion and subjective psychological notions intrigue many people. It is not unlike the casual reading of one's horoscope. A curious flirtation with these flesh-appeasing, pseudo-intellectually teasing additives often becomes a habit, which soon develops into a stronghold of "wrong thinking" concerning God and "self." Throwing in "some truths" from the Word of God to *"sanctify"* the *"whole"* is, again, futile. However, Promise Keepers' material and guiding ministerial techniques do precisely this. By so twisting the Scriptures to make it appear as though the Word of God is the source behind their concepts concerning men becoming *"real men,"* they capture unsuspecting hearts with biblical-sounding phraseology.

As has been noted, Promise Keepers released a statement that, though they no longer give the book away, they have never denied or retracted their doctrinal harmony with Robert Hicks' book, *The Masculine Journey.* In the book, Hicks initially rejects some aspects of psychology but he later weaves the psychological strand back into his developing premise. Whether he does this intentionally or not, those who are rooted and grounded in sound biblical doctrine can easily perceive the deceptive results. Promise Keepers' original, as well as on-going infatuation with such polluted concepts, is systemic to their entire organization's philosophy.

That philosophy is illustrated throughout Promise Keepers' literature and is a most striking theme in Hicks' book. His continued inference that Jesus was a great example and that if we are to be true men, then we must try to be like Jesus is fundamental to the Promise Keepers premise. In fact, Hicks states that Jesus is "the model of manhood for which men should strive."[1] To laymen and churchmen who may not be familiar with the central thesis of the entire Christian faith, which is Christ living His Life through the believer, Hicks' statement sounds solid and logical. But in truth, it is anti-

Christian and unbiblical. God has never called men to *try to be like Jesus*. The call of the Holy Spirit is for men *to allow Jesus to be Jesus in them*. All efforts man might undertake to imitate Jesus result in abysmal failure and frustration. Humanity, especially Christians, must realize that anytime they attempt to *"be like Jesus"*, they are destined for such failure. The results are depression, guilt and further alienation from God's desire. Christianity is *"Christ in you, the hope of glory"* (Colossians 1:27). It is not *me* trying to be more and more *like* Jesus until, through some kind of metamorphic, evolutionary spiritual cycle, I reach the point at which I become God, which is the teaching of many cults. To the contrary, Christianity is the exchanged life; *my* life for *His*.

Hicks' ideas are representative of many of Promise Keepers' theological positions which are riddled with concepts that are alien to the Scriptures. Mr. Hicks boasts of his dependence on truths that he discovered in Daniel Levinson's, *The Seasons of a Man's Life*.[2] Yet this man who so influenced Robert Hicks in his quest to help men discover their *road to recovery* is yet, another psychologist. From 1968 to 1970, Levinson and a group of others studied 40 men between the ages of 35 and 45 years old. The study conducted by this group, which was fundamentally Freudian with one Jungian, was, at best, piecemeal in nature. It involved psychologically testing the subjects according to the interviewer's criteria.

In reporting on Mr. Levinson's techniques for the study, researchers Martin and Deidre Bobgan discovered that one psychological test used during these interviews was the *Thematic Apperception Test,* which uses a projective technique with extremely low validity. "The test was not administered according to strict procedures," the researchers said.[3]

Levinson said, "Our essential method was to illicit the life stories of forty men, to construct biographies and to develop generalizations based upon these biographies."[4] He continued, "We found ourselves full of ideas stemming mainly from psychoanalytic theory about the subject's development in childhood and adolescence. We could make many connections between these early periods and what happened in early periods and what happened at mid-life."[5]

One need not have extensive knowledge of the concepts of Sigmond Freud and Carl Jung in order to understand that Mr. Levinson and his "researchers" were quite simply giving Freudian and Jungian interpretations to their subject's information. This babble, and rightly called *"psycho-babble"* by some discerning people, is, according to Hicks, the pool from which he drew some of his "excellent research" for his book. Perhaps Hicks should have consulted the writings of the Hindu, the Buddhist or even of Confucius. Each of these religions employ variations of the theme that man goes through cyclical stages of life. This "cyclical" concept concludes that all men go through "stages" in their lives and is obviously what attracted Hicks to Levinson, whose book concludes that men evolve through four stages of human development.

Hicks, on the other hand, has opted to identify, more along the lines of Confucius, who believed in a six-stage life cycle. But in order to follow Mr. Hicks' rather bizarre "theology," one must be willing to take quantum leaps of faith from one supposition to another without any contextually supportive scriptural undergirding.

Hicks does explain that the conclusions which form the foundation for his book combined Mr. Levinson's ideas and his personal "recall" of Greek-Hebrew words he learned while in seminary. Hicks obviously conjured up these fascinating concepts on how God wants to develop *"real men"* through a combined, seemingly subjective study of the Word of God and the perjurious philosophy of psychology. The most devastating shock of all is that thousands of spiritual leaders, Christian pastors and educated men fail to recognize or address this severe breach of Christian theology. Many biblically literate individuals are curious as to why this intrusion of darkened philosophies into the belief systems of Hicks and Promise Keepers has drawn such little criticism from Christian leadership.

It is as though the endorsements of such high-profile personalities so impress pastors that they assume Promise Keepers is, as advertised, the greatest move of the Holy Spirit since Pentecost. *"Who are we to question the Holy Spirit"* seems to be the prevailing attitude among those who could and should be sounding the alarms about Promise Keepers' perverse Christianity. But this deadly assumption by thousands of America's church leaders has clearly paralyzed their corporate discernment, captured their instinctive protective passions and contaminated their courage. We cannot know why or how the system promoted in Promise Keepers' various philosophies, and especially Hicks' book, has failed to set spiritual alarms blaring in American pulpits, but the silence of the watchman is appalling. Once again, the wolf, though well-disguised as a sheep, is prowling among the flock and stealthily taking out his prey, man by man, pastor by pastor and church by church.

"Truth Just Needs a Bit of Tweaking"

Those who believe that something fundamental is missing in biblical Christianity see no conflict of interest in combining the variant ideologies of psychology with Biblical Christianity. These individuals welcome the introduction of psychology into the increasingly difficult task of counseling people with major and complex problems. It is much simpler to use the *"pat"* formulas presented by psychology than it is to motivate people to understand and apply the theology of the New Testament. The latter would necessitate a clear understanding of what the Bible teaches concerning men and the root of their problems.

Men with backgrounds in the discipline of theology, if they hold to the essence of orthodox biblical Christianity, will find themselves in an absolute philosophical head-on collision with men whose discipline is psychology. If there be any redemptive qualities to the *"discipline of psychology"*, it is only in the few instances in which it echoes the Scriptures. Like the proverbial broken clock, at least it is right twice a day. However, the marriage of Christianity and psychology always results in an ideological slaughter of one at the expense of the other.

A Viennese psychiatrist and noted specialist in human behavior, Dr. Viktor Frankle, observed the conflict between psychology and religion: "Any fusion of the respective goals of religion and psychotherapy must result in confusion."[6] The opposing sources of orthodox Christianity and of psychology must be completely ignored when attempting to find any compatibility between the two.

Most often, the sacrificial lamb is not psychology, but Christianity. Those who strive to justify this union charge that Christianity is specific and limited in scope and application while psychology more clearly defines and copes with the conflicts of human behavior. This is clearly expressed in a book by Bruce Narramore and John D. Carter, entitled, *The Integration of Psychology and Theology*. They write:

> Many individual Christians look to psychology for new insights that will relieve personal discomfort and despair. They hope that psychology will provide answers to questions *not specifically addressed in Christianity* (Emphasis mine).[7]

Such thinking is the result of one who has no hint of the depth, scope, richness and power in the Word of God or the Christian faith. This reasoning is reiterated by Dr. Gary Collins in his book, *Can You Trust Psychology?* He wrote: "Some human problems are not mentioned in Scripture. They are not discussed specifically, neither are there examples to show how others dealt with these issues in a way pleasing to God."[8]

Thus we see the faulty reasoning that birthed the contemporary effort to fuse Christianity with psychology which is contrary to the Word of God. The Apostle Paul wrote to believers at Colosse to answer such spurious and unfounded charges as those made by Narramore, Carter and Collins. He wrote, "For in Him (Christ Jesus) dwells all the fullness of the Godhead bodily and ye are complete in Him who is the head of all principality and power" (Colossians 2:9-10). Every human need is answered completely and specifically in the Word of God. It stands alone as God's full revelation.

Hicks quotes a host of secular authors who are clearly philosophically aligned with the likes of Carl Jung: inner-healing therapist, Leanne Payne, transpersonal psychiatrist and spiritualist Elizabeth Kubler Ross, and Sam Keen of the

New Age/Eastern Mystical Therapeutic Center south of San Francisco. Keen's books feature vicious attacks on biblical Christianity. The attempt is made to legitimize *"Christian psychology"* and, amazingly, vast numbers of men in leadership in the Christian Church are not at all alarmed about this attempt to neuter God's Truth.

On the other hand, in the field of psychology, it seems only those who would identify themselves as Christian psychologists are open to this union between Christianity and psychology. Secular psychologists vehemently oppose any effort that seeks to find common ground between the two. Christians should be amazed that those in the field of psychology are indignant about attempts by those they consider "ignorant, shallow Christians to impose themselves into the profoundly intellectual and scientific world of the psychologist."

Again, such is very puzzling and it well ought to be. Yet, Hicks, in his effort to fuse psychology into scriptural harmony, plunges forward with his book. But it is an unholy union, an exercise in "spiritual fornication," producing alien offspring.

The Promise Keepers' Jesus and the Phallus

To get a sense of how distant Promise Keepers philosophies of ministry are from the Scriptures, one need only to browse through some of their literature. We can only guess why the organization's leadership refuses to fully renounce, publicly refute and openly repent of their participation in the printing of and distribution of materials that so blatantly contradict and defy God's Word.

One is never shocked with the darkened reasoning and actions of men alienated from God and living without His redeeming Grace. But to observe the rapidity with which those who are among the household of the Christian faith are falling prey to godless philosophies and diabolic reasoning is appalling. It takes no biblical scholar to recognize the psychological thought that permeates Robert Hicks' doctrine of man. Indeed, he feebly attempts to sanctify his diatribe with phrases like, *"created in the image of God"*, but then he launches into a presentation on the importance of such horrendously unbiblical notions as *"self-esteem."*

He writes:

> In my fight for *self-affirmation*, I am revealing the basic fabric of what I am and how I am made. The work of psychologists and self-help writers only affirms this reality…The therapeutic remedies that are designed to recover or develop *self-esteem* and the *self-help* literature, only affirm this *intrinsic deeply rooted but unexplained valve.*[9] (Emphasis mine)

Most slightly informed students of philosophy, theology or simply the Scriptures recognize the *"self-esteem"* origins in Hicks' statements. Yet he unabashedly charges forward to build the case that his six Hebrew words are definitive of every man's evolutionary journey into manhood. His description of the initial stage of manhood calls man a *"noble savage"*, with King Solomon as his biblical illustration. Never mind that the Bible never alludes to or even hints that man is a *"noble savage"*. And never mind that such concepts have their roots in humanism and its belief that all men have some good in them, and that this good is only corrupted by his societal, environmental pressures. After the reader wades through the initial *"noble savage"* philosophical gobbledygook, he discovers Hicks' concept of *"Jesus, the phallic kind of guy."* Hicks uses the Hebrew word *zaker* to identify "man" as the phallic male. Of this he writes:

> We are sexual beings at our most primary (primal) level. The Bible never pretends or expects us to be otherwise. It meets us and describes us where we are, where we live and have our being. To be male is to be a phallic kind of guy, and as men we should never apologize for it…[10]

He then says, "The Bible simply defines man by the phallus."[11] No doubt, like many who rewrite, redefine and reorder Scripture for flexibility's sake, Hicks is attempting to squeeze the Bible into a narrow and bizarre category to accommodate his perverse concept. Three times Holy God is reduced by Hicks to the level of the goddess of sex, Aphrodite, and other ancient deities that focused on the genitalia as objects of worship.

As Hicks leaps further into his sexual preoccupation, he refers to various pagan religious practices and their connection with biblical circumcision. He says, "The phallus has always been the symbol of religious devotion and dedication...we are called to worship God as phallic kinds of guys, not as some sort of androgynous neutered non-male or the feminized males so popular in many feminist enlightened churches."[12]

It is appalling to think that pastors and Christian laymen across America support or remain silent about this miserable, blatant, obnoxious, demeaning and perverse script that Hicks has the audacity to put in print. Obviously, his ignorance of the Truth is equaled only by the blindness of a generation of churchmen who overwhelmingly approve of Promise Keepers' and Hicks' presentation of God's creation and man's development.

He states further that man's sexual hang-ups with pornography and sexual license "reveal how desperate we are to express in some perverse form, the deep compulsion to worship with our phallus."[13]

This book gives a deviant perspective of man and his spiritual development. Hicks' Freudian preference in analysis is overtly obvious. He states that "some men are fixated at the phallic stage of development."[14] Anyone familiar with Freudian teaching is familiar with his fixation on the "psycho-sexual" development of man. He taught that every child between the ages of three and six years of age represses his or her latent desire to have sexual intercourse with the opposite-sex parent and to get rid of the parent of like sex. Though this Oedipus complex, believed by Freud, has long since been proven fraudulent, Hicks manifests a considerable amount of philosophical leakage from it in the book.

He then follows through with the conclusion one would expect from an author who starts down the road of horrendous heresy. He identifies Jesus as being very much phallic as he writes: "I believe Jesus was phallic with all the inherent phallic

passions we experience as men. But it was never recorded
that Jesus had sexual relations with a woman."[15]

For a man to even suggest such as the above is a grief to
the Holy Spirit. Of course it was never recorded that Jesus
Christ, the sinless Son of the Living God, ever had sexual
relations. Why not? Because it never happened. It never
happened because, contrary to Hicks, Jesus never was occupied,
preoccupied with or tempted to engage in sexual impurity.
What a ludicrous and irreverent suggestion. But that is not all
Hicks says about this matter. In the same paragraph, he writes:

> ...He (Jesus) may have thought about it (having sex) as the
> movie the Last Temptation of Christ portrays, but even in
> this movie He did not give in to the temptation and remained
> true to His messianic course.[16]

Hicks' position teaches, as does the Study Guide to *The
Masculine Journey,* which Promise Keepers distributed to
tens of thousands of men, that the Lord Jesus Christ was
sexually tempted as other men.[17] While this is no treatise on
the sinlessness and impeccability of the Lord Jesus Christ,
suffice it to say that Hicks' view, publicly backed by Promise
Keepers, does not represent the Gospel presented in God's
Word. This is another Jesus and crosses the line of blasphemous
rhetoric. The errant and godless description by Hicks of the
nature of man, the purity of Christ, and His *"celebration of
sin"* that is promoted by his book[18] are only a few vivid
illustrations of his warped and ill-conceived, unbiblically profane
views of God's Word prevalent throughout his publication.

I apologize if I have been too graphic in my description
of this travesty of a book written to facilitate the *"spiritual
growth"* of Promise Keepers participants. Be assured I have
considerably abbreviated the many volumes that could be written
to expose *The Masculine Journey* for the sham and shame
that it really is. What spiritual condition would the leadership,
spokesmen, supporters and backers of a ministry have to be
in, in order to condone and recommend such a trashy, disgusting,
obscene perversion of so many holy and precious Truths?

Clearly, just as the Trojan Horse has left its prophetic

footprints in the sands of time, the Tower of Babel is also being reconstructed by those who seek to raise a new monument in this New Age to a very old god. He is not Jehovah God of the Bible, but rather, man's favorite ancient deity, himself. And upon this reconstruction, we once again witness the fingerprints of the satanic saboteour who is seducing humanity to rebuild this highway to heaven via human effort.

It appears more obvious than ever that "there is a way that seemeth right to man but the ends thereof are death" (Proverbs 14:12).

"Sanctify them through thy truth; thy word is truth."

John 17:17

Chapter 17

It Ain't Necessarily So

"All Scripture is given by inspiration of God, and is profitable for doctrine, for reproof, for correction, for instruction in righteousness, that the man of God may be perfect, thoroughly furnished unto all good works."

2 Timothy 3:16-17

A popular song in a Broadway production written some years back best characterized this liberalized Church age at the beginning of the last decade. The cute little ditty with a catchy tune and words said, "The things you read in the Bible...they ain't necessarily so, they ain't necessarily so." Each verse of the song identified a different Bible story that, according to the songwriter, was not necessarily true; among them: the Flood, the story of Noah and the Ark, the record of the fall of Man through satanic deception and that of the parting of the Red Sea.

In days past, most clergymen could be identified by their alignment with the infallibility and inerrancy of the Word of God. It was either *"necessarily so"* or *"not necessarily so."* The issues that pastors and the Church face today have become more complex in that, over time, semantics, phraseology and terminology have become much more subjective and less definitive. Words, especially in theological circles, have lost

their meaning and have often been completely redefined so
that those who enjoy playing intellectual and theological sleight-
of-hand for the purpose of appearing non-suspect among their
more conservative peers can say what they do not mean, while
at the same time, not really mean what they say. Hence, we
have never been through a period of church history during
which, from the pulpit to the pew, people have been so easily
deceived about doctrine and led astray. I call this the *"Babel
Syndrome,"* alluded to in the previous chapter. As a result of
the current confusion created by the use of words that no
longer have a universal definition, multitudes of clergy and
lay persons are finding a new camaraderie with those whom
they would never have fraternized with in days past.

The enemy no longer sings…"It ain't necessarily so." His
new song for our deluded age is…"Sure, it's absolutely
so…without doubt, believe it. But there is more that is absolutely
so as well." In other words, "Close your Bible. We all believe
it, but open your **mind** because God has some fresh new
revelations in **addition** to that Bible."

This tendency to rely upon "special revelation and
experiences" to the exclusion of the Scriptures has created
the diabolical doctrine of the *"open-door policy"* to which
Promise Keepers Ministries is fundamentally and irreversibly
committed.

You Better Take a Closer Look

Promise Keepers founder Bill McCartney has the reputation
of being a kind, driven, and sensitive man. He was a Catholic
whose "conversion" to the Vineyard movement subsequently
led to the birth of Promise Keepers Ministries. Characteristic
of the churches and people involved in the Vineyard movement
is the heavy reliance upon their strong conviction that God is
giving *"new revelation"* today. They hold that we are living
in an age of miracles, as was the New Testament Church
before the canon was closed, and that these miracles should
be very normal for believers today. McCartney has obviously
chosen to accept this Vineyard doctrine, as well as additional

bizarre beliefs in the movement, as his own. While addressing Promise Keepers rallies, he has often shared with those in attendance *"words"* that he claims are direct revelations from God. McCartney claims that these revelations from God are not simply the amplification of Scripture by the Holy Spirit to his heart.

To the contrary, he believes he *receives* these words directly from God and claims that God is speaking to and through him in the same capacity that He spoke to and through those *"men of old"* whom God inspired to pen the Scriptures. That is pretty heady stuff.

The Scriptures, as well as Church history, have established with certainty that God is not continuing to write the Bible. His full revelation to man is complete and final and contained in full in the Holy Bible. He has spoken His *"Thus saith the Lord"* and that Holy Book contains far deeper, richer and more glorious Truths than any single man or group of men could possibly exhaust in a million more millennia. Man does not need a new Word from God or additional revelation. Our problem, as a people, a nation and a society stems from the fact that we have yet to fully obey the old Word of revelation. That old Word, the Scripture, is made new and alive everyday as the believer absorbs and obeys it.

The Scriptures need no additives any more than our salvation needs an additive. The Apostle Paul states, *"And ye are complete in Him"* (Colossians 2:10).

Concerning the powerfully effectual and thoroughly penetrating influence that the Word of God has upon the yielded heart, the writer of Hebrews wrote, "For the word of God is living, and powerful, and sharper than any two-edged sword, piercing even to the dividing asunder of soul and spirit, and of the joints and marrow, and is a discerner of the thoughts and intents of the heart" (Hebrews 4:12).

Those who are under the impression that God's Word needs contemporary updating by neo-Christian revelators are, tragically, increasing in number and influence. Promise Keepers is overflowing with such men, from its founder, to members of its board of directors, to most of its advisors, who are in full harmony with the concept that additional *"words from*

God" are needed because of the insufficiency of Scripture. Such darkened reasoning has opened a floodgate to inconceivable heresies within the organization. Since a major emphasis of the Promise Keepers is to build unity regardless of the doctrinal persuasion subscribed to by participants, there is no accountability system to honor biblical absolutes for what is said or done "in the name of the Lord".

Beatles "Bring Revival"

McCartney's pastor, James Ryle, is on the board of directors of Promise Keepers and a co-founder of the Vineyard Movement with John Wimber, self-proclaimed prophet of God. Ryle is yet another in the Vineyard Movement who is, according to his own claims, a modern-day prophet. As a "prophet of God" he naturally attests to the fact that he, too, regularly receives direct "revelations" and communiqués from God.

Some time ago, he publicly shared one of these "revelations from God" at the Vineyard Harvest Conference in Denver, Colorado. All those in attendance were privy to his "revelations" declaration when he said:

> The Lord has appointed me as lookout and shown me some things that I want to show you...the Lord spoke to me and said, What you saw in the BEATLES, the gifting and the sound that they had, was from ME...It was MY purpose to bring forth through music a worldwide revival that would usher in the move of MY Spirit in bringing men and women to Christ.[1]

Pastor Ryle claimed on yet another occasion that "he had a vision of a Beatles concert where the people were screaming the Name Jesus."[2]

The judicial cliché "ignorance is no excuse" is extremely applicable in the courtroom of the spirit world. Christian men who endorse, praise, support and attend Promise Keepers rallies and who participate in their efforts—especially pastors and Christian leaders—are obligated by the Word of God to fully know who they are endorsing and encouraging the men of their congregations to follow and what those men believe concerning the fundamental tenets of God's Word. We are well past the time when men, regardless of their doctrinal persuasion or denominational background, can simply "praise the Lord for all the good things that Promise Keepers are doing because they do so much more good than bad." Such reasoning is foreign to spiritual discernment and leads one to qualify that which God has disqualified. This kind of rationale, increasingly common among church leaders, indicates the shallow and pathetic condition of American Christianity. Hosea, echoing the heart of God wrote, *"My people die for lack of knowledge"* (Hosea 4:6).

Ryle's statement that "God told him" that the Beatles were anointed to bring forth worldwide revival and to "usher in My (God's) Spirit" is shameful, humiliating and defiant of the Scriptures, the nature of God and of the Holy Spirit. How could anyone, especially one who claims his words come straight from God Almighty, expect others to believe that a true, heaven-sent revival could be provoked by a demonized musical group that promoted anti-christ, drug-ridden, sexually deviant and godless living? Then, unashamedly, this so-called prophet of God proclaimed that the Beatles' music was anointed by the Spirit of God. This is a "prophet of God"? Whatever else Ryle may be, he is the pastor and spiritual leader of Bill McCartney, the founder of Promise Keepers. He is only one of the many *"prophets"* who share his persuasions and sit on the Board of Directors of Promise Keepers.

Promise Keepers Attempts Damage Control

It is clear from the rather consistent flow of new faxes and articles stemming from Promise Keepers' headquarters that knowledge about the lack of Scriptural integrity that permeates the organization is beginning to stimulate more and more people to question a lot of things about Promise Keepers, including the infamous "Beatles Were Anointed of God" message by Pastor Ryle.

Such was the case when Promise Keepers recently released a fax attempting to "explain" Ryle's Beatle comments. It read:

PROMISE KEEPER'S POSITION ON JAMES RYLE'S BEATLES COMMENTS

Thank you for bringing your concerns to our attention in regard to Pastor James Ryle's comments on the musical group the Beatles. We are committed to honoring Jesus Christ in responding to concerns of this nature. We desire to facilitate true biblical unity in the body of Christ, not the division that results from unnecessary and dishonoring debate.

Promise Keepers would like to provide some background in order for you to understand the context in which the comment was made. In 1990, Pastor Ryle spoke at a conference and gave a message entitled, "The Sons of Thunder" containing three main points: 1) God wants the entire world to be evangelized (John 3:16); 2) God wants us to become all things to all men that by all means men might be saved (1 Cor. 9:22); and 3) God provides gifts to all of us through which we can reach out to the lost. Pastor Ryle went on to elaborate on the third point, stating that all gifts are a blessing from God—doctors are gifted with healing, teachers with the ability to communicate information, judges with wisdom, and musicians with music, etc.

Pastor Ryle's message focused on the power of the gift of music. He stated that music is a universal language and it speaks to the heart of men like no other medium. All musicians have received the gift of music from God, whether they are Christians or not. Pastor Ryle used the Beatles as a stellar example of the power of music. These musicians influenced an entire generation and people followed them into drugs, sex and eastern mysticism. Pastor Ryle asked his audience to imagine the tremendous influence that the Beatles could have had if they had been Christians; if they had used their gift to glorify God and to impact His kingdom.

In fact, this message has led numerous musicians (including some prominent secular names) to write to Pastor Ryle saying things like, '...at last I know why I was born with the gift of music.'

In his reference to the Beatles' gift of music, Ryle referred to that gift as an 'anointing'; indicating only that the gift was from God. Pastor Ryle regrets that his comment was misunderstood by believers who thought that he was endorsing the message and lifestyle of the Beatles. He only intended to convey his understanding of the power of music and that it is a gift from God. Pastor Ryle did not mean to imply that he believed that the Beatles were used by God, only that their gift was from God and it could have been used for the glory of God.[3]

The theology in this fax is so incredibly out of sync with scriptural Truth that addressing all its discrepancies would require another book. Just the fax's defense that focuses on Ryle's assertion that the Beatles' music is a "gift that was from God" disqualifies the pastor's entire "vision," his message, and the Promise Keepers' position paper from being scripturally valid. God does not give spiritual gifts to unregenerate, lost men. These gifts accompany the Holy Spirit in the life of truly born again people.

However, the veracity of the Promise Keepers' fax and position paper on Ryle's comments is what is immediately brought into question. Is Promise Keepers telling the truth or simply attempting to employ more damage control?

In September of 1996, *The Christian Conscience* magazine published a revealing article entitled, *"The Promise Keepers Fax Scandal "*, by Carl Widrig, Jr. Widrig tells of his firsthand experience with Pastor Ryle and the *Kansas City Prophets*, his cohorts in the early 1990s who were all circulating around Vineyard churches at the time.[4] He writes as an eyewitness and ear-witness of the matter.

The article begins with a quote Pastor Ryle made during his message at the Harvest Conference in November 1990 in Denver, Colorado.

Ryle, sharing various apparitions that appeared to him in his "visions," said:

> It looked like a Sergeant Peppers Hearts Club jacket...it 'looked like a military jacket, and it started floating back and I knew that that represented the anointing, the mantle, the covering that was coming to the 'Sons of Thunder.' And not long ago, the Lord said, 'I'm giving you the permission to pass the jacket out.'[5]

The Widrig article, entitled, "The Promise Keepers Fax Scandal," continues as excerpted below. The article in its entirety has been reprinted in the Appendix "A" page of this book.

The Promise Keepers Fax Scandal
by Carl Widrig, Jr.

...Suns of Thunder

During the latter half of 1989, at the height of the "Kansas City Prophets" nationwide tour of Vineyard Christian Fellowship, Vineyard pastor James Ryle had three dreams involving the Beatles which God allegedly interpreted for Ryle after he woke up from each dream. By February 1990, Ryle was sharing the contents of his Beatles "anointing" dreams, and the alleged God-given interpretation thereof, with other Christians—a "revelation" concerning a musical "anointing" that God gave exclusively to the Beatles to usher in a worldwide revival, and then took away from them in 1970 to be reserved for Christian musicians ("The Sons of Thunder") in the 1990's, for the purpose of ushering in a worldwide revival.[1]

---

[1] The part of Ryle's "revelation" about God giving Christian musicians in the 1990's revival-ushering musical "anointing" was nothing new at the time—such was commonly "prophesied" by the "K.C. Prophets" who were circulating around the Vineyard at the time. I was an eyewitness to these events, and the object of one such "prophecy" on March 7, 1990, by the assistant prophet to Larry Randolph, a man named Howard Jones, who "prophesied" that God would place an "anointing" on me and I would play "a new song" with my guitar at beaches and in parks and people would gather around and God would "manifest" his presence and the people would get saved.

On July 1, 1990, at the local Vineyard he pastors, and also in November 1990, at the "Harvest Conference" held in Denver, Colorado with "K.C. Prophet" Rick Joyner, Ryle, in a message entitled, "Sons of Thunder," shared the details of his Beatles' "anointing" dreams and their interpretation. The latter message (especially) has since been accessed via audio tape by multitudes and become   the subject of much controversy.

By 1994, Promise Keepers was becoming very popular in the evangelical church in America. In February 1994, James Ryle, who by this time was a rising star Director of Promise Keepers, wrote a piece for *Charisma* magazine (published by the same publisher as the PK organ, *New Man*) titled "The New Sound of Music," wherein he toned down quite a bit what he had emphasized on earlier occasions about the Beatles' exclusive "anointing." Instead he attributed their success to the "social climate" of the time, not unlike contemporary 1990's culture. Thus in the name of "history repeats itself" he claimed that

> we will see musicians who are anointed by God and gifted with even greater ability than The Beatles...these musicians will not fail to glorify God and therein will be the secret of their success. (Charisma, 2/94, p.14).

This was a much more reasonable-sounding-to-evangelicals rendition of his original "Beatles were anointed by God" "revelations" circa 1989-90.

Later, in 1995, Bill Randles, a Pentecostal pastor in Cedar Rapids, Iowa, wrote what has become one of the most well-known critical pieces on Promise Keepers, "An Open Letter to Bill McCartney," wherein Randles voiced numerous concerns (many of which PK has responded to via fax), including one about Ryle and his Beatles dream interpretation (specifically Ryle's aforementioned "Sons of Thunder" message at the Nov. 1990 Harvest Conference).

Then on January 11, 1996, Steve Chavis, National Spokesman for Promise Keepers and co-host of the "Promise Keepers This Week" radio program, appeared on a local Denver/Boulder radio program called, "The Grant Connection", claiming that, "It's not true" that "James Ryle said, 'The Beatles were anointed by God.'"

In more recent months, Promise Keepers released a fax titled, "JAMES RYLE'S COMMENTS ON THE BEATLES," that specifically refers to Ryle's 1990 "Sons of Thunder" conference message as the sole subject of their fax. This fax they have been distributing to their Ambassadors, this time admitting to the word "anointing" in Ryle's Beatles' revelation, but spinning what Ryle said into this:

> Ryle referred to that gift [the Beatles had] as an "anointing" indicating only that the gift was from God.

As the reader who considers the historical record to be further elaborated on might notice, James Ryle and Promise Keepers seem to be making a unified and concerted effort to tone down and "spin-doctor" what Ryle actually said God showed him earlier in the decade about an alleged musical anointing that God gave exclusively to the Beatles and then took away from them in 1970 to be reserved for Christian Musicians ("The Suns of Thunder") in the 1990's. Coincidentally (?), the toning down and spin-doctoring has taken place alongside the growing popularity of Promise Keepers which Ryle is a Director of, and of which Bill McCartney and Randy Phillips (who both call James Ryle their "pastor") are the Founder and President respectively.

Lack of Integrity

My own examination of the evidence has yielded several items of interest. I compared what Ryle was actually saying circa 1990 with what PK has been saying of late via

Steve Chavis and this PK fax. I have come to the conclusion that this PK fax is a blatantly skewed portrayal of the historical facts. It's as if they didn't think those who read the fax would ever become privy to the facts via listening to the audio tape recording of Ryle's "Sons of Thunder" message—the most interesting part of which (having to do with Ryle's three dreams) was also virtually transcribed verbatim in Rick Joyner's *Morning Star Prophetic Newsletter*. The whole thing has to leave one wondering why PK has suffered such a lapse in the integrity department.

1. Important Contextual Information

The background provided in the PK fax, regarding the context in which Pastor James Ryle's comments about the Beatles were made, is unbelievably misstated, so much so that they must have thought that the reader would never actually hear the "context" with their own ears.

...What the PK fax doesn't tell the reader is that moments before Ryle gave his "Sons of Thunder" talk, Rick Joyner spent many, many minutes setting up the crowd to be open to "weird revelations" (having to do with "new music") they were about to hear about from James Ryle. Joyner even went to the point of emphasizing that Ryle's prophetic message was particularly for Colorado at that particular time. Ryle's own message contained the same effort to set up the crowd to find what he was about to share to be reasonable, based on the theme of "evangelism" (as if "evangelism" would make whatever he was about to share legitimate). The set-up concluded with these words:

> Now, all that so I can tell you these three things [his three dreams]. I just had to set that as a framework as to the burden of the Lord and the passion of the Lord towards evangelism.

"Framework" is a long way from the PK fax's "three main points." There is no way even a casual listener of Ryle's message could think that Ryle was merely "elaborating" when he finally brought up the Beatles "gift." Nor did Ryle even mention *a single word* about "doctors," "teacher," "judges" or "musicians" as historical examples of those who have "gifts" like the Beatles had—that suggestion by the author of PK fax is a blatant attempt to completely revamp the message Ryle actually spoke in history.

2. The Result of Dreams

Ryle's "Beatles" thing came about from dreams Ryle, after much careful deliberation, claimed God personally explained to him and appointed him to "report":

> Isaiah 21:6 is a verse that the Lord quickened to me at the outset of this year, and this is what it says: "This is what the Lord says to me: 'Go post a lookout and have him report what he sees.'" And what I'm going to tell you right now is three separate dreams that the Lord gave me over a period of several months. And I say that up front because I want you to realize that what you're about to hear is not the fruit of zealous immaturity. This is something that has been thought out, it's been prayed over, it's been examined, it's been investigated, scrutinized, and laid before the Lord and shared with others who are certainly more esteemed than I am in these types of seeings and it has, to this point, stood the test. And so I am confident in saying this much, that the Lord, to a degree, has appointed me as a lookout and has shown me some things and I want to show you and tell you what he showed me. (James Ryle, Harvest Conference, Nov. 1990)

One would hardly know about this context upon reading PK's recent fax on the issue which makes it seem as if James Ryle simply picked the Beatles on a whim, as a mere "example" to make the unobjectionable-to-any-evangelical-ear point that the Beatles had a God-given plain-Jane musical "gifting" that could have been used for honorable evangelistic purposes, which "gifting" God later took away. The problem with this spin is that the gifts of God are irrevocable (Rom. 11:29), and we all know that John, Paul, and George didn't suddenly lose their musical gifting in 1970 (assuming Ringo never had it in the first place).

3. Ushering In A Worldwide Revival

The Beatles "anointing" that Christians were hearing Ryle talk about in 1990 was supposedly so special and powerful that it could have ushered in a worldwide revival—an anointing that God allegedly held back for over 20 years and soon planned to "release" to the Church. That anointing is quite a different animal than Ryle's 1994, "greatly gifted by God", and PK's recent fax, "gift as an 'anointing' indicating only that the gift was from God." Following this line of thought, if Ryle's 1990 "anointing" was really just a plain-Jane musical "gifting" that has been held back for over 20 years now, that would also logically imply that no one has had this plain-Jane musical gift since 1970!

4. Gifting the Rebellious?

Ryle misquotes Psalm 68:18 which actually reads (NKJV, NASB, NIV),

> When you ascended on high, you led captivity captive, *you RECEIVED gifts FROM men, even AMONG the REBELLIOUS, that God may dwell in our midst.*

Ryle, in both his Nov. 1990 Harvest Conference presentation, and in the *Morning Star Prophetic Newsletter*, misquotes Psalm 68:18 as saying,

> *When you ascended on high, you led captivity captive, and you GAVE gifts TO men, even TO the REBELLIOUS, that God may dwell in our midst.*

Ryle needs Psalm 68:18 to say 'gave' to justify his teaching that God really could have given the Beatles this special "gift"/"anointing". Ephesians 4:8 (which Ryle never acknowledges) quotes a portion of Psalm 68:18 and then reads, "and gave gifts to men", but in context this is clearly referring to grace given to each one in the Body of Christ (cf. Eph. 4:7), and the passage omits any mention of "the rebellious."

This leads to an important point: It is not in accord with God's Word that God would clumsily and unknowingly give a special, worldwide, revival-ushering anointing to unbelievers like the Beatles, who would then pull a fast one on God and use it for the devil's purposes (preaching a false message accompanying the anointing) while God just sits there and lets it go on until 1970 (!) before taking it away from them. Using this logic, Ryle's "God" could just as well give this type of anointing to end-times false prophets and the antichrist to work lying signs and wonders to deceive, if possible, even the elect (Matt. 24:24)!

5. Strange Gospel for Evangelism

The fact that the PK fax gives the impression that PK finds no trouble with the content of Ryle's "Sons of Thunder" message is itself a witness against the discernment of PK. For example, the PK fax highlights that Ryle's message was all about "evangelism." But the evangelism Ryle speaks of is not your typical "preach the gospel that Jesus died for your sins and rose again and is coming back unto salvation, and then those whom God has appointed to salvation are regenerated and believe and are saved."

As Rick Joyner was prepping the audience to receive Ryle's "intense" prophetic message at the 1990 Harvest Conference, he stated, "We've had a lot of our concepts about evangelism, and I think the Lord is going to change some of them." Minutes later, Ryle was saying the following

which makes evangelism seem more like a Vineyard healing service than the evangelism we know of per the Bible:

> ...a light shines from above and there's a woman
> standing in the midst of the church, and she stands
> up and she begins singing this song under the anointing
> of the Holy Spirit. And the song had one sentence
> that she kept singing over and over. And the song
> was this: "In the name of Jesus Christ the Lord we
> say unto you: Be saved!" And she would just start
> singing that, she would sing it up to that part of the
> balcony, and I started watching, and it was like wind
> blowing on a wheat field. The people in that whole
> section just began to swoon under the presence of
> the Holy Spirit, and many of them would collapse into
> their seats, sobbing, proclaiming, "Jesus is Lord."

> And then she would sing it over here, "In the name of
> Jesus Christ the Lord we say unto you: Be saved!",
> and salvation was spontaneously and sovereignly
> happening all over that place. And that was the end of
> the dream.

> [After waking up] the Lord showed me some things,
> and I submit these to you for your prayer and con-
> sideration and discussion. But this is the thing that he
> showed me.

Ryle's "gospel" as per his "Sons of Thunder" article in the
Morning Star Prophetic Newsletter is likewise troubling:

> The Lord said, "Say this to the church: 'Stand in the
> light. Lift up your voice and sing in the streets. Sing
> the simple message of the gospel—In the Name of
> Jesus Christ the Lord, be saved. Lift up your voice as
> a witness to Christ and the Spirit of God will cause
> people to be converted.'" (Ryle, "Sons of Thunder",
> *The Morning Star Prophetic Newsletter*, Vol. 1, No. 4.
> (Winter 1991), pp. 23-29.)

This cross/resurrection/hope-absent "evangelism" and "gospel" of James Ryle doesn't seem to trouble PK according to their fax. Instead, one would think based on the PK fax that Ryle had spoken a wonderful Scriptural message on evangelism that no genuine Christian could have any trouble with, and therefore must have "misunderstood."

6. A Straw Man

The PK fax presents a "straw man" of the objections that have been raised by Christians who judged Ryle's Beatles prophetic dreams as false:

> Pastor Ryle regrets that his comment was misunderstood by believers who thought he was endorsing the message and lifestyle of the Beatles. He only intended to convey his understanding of the power of music and that it is a gift from God. Pastor Ryle did not mean to imply that he believed the Beatles were used by God, only that their gift was from God and it could have been used for the glory of God.

Again, here the PK fax is bypassing the fact that the things that Ryle actually said—rather than being Ryle's mere "comments" and "his understanding"—were emphasized by Ryle himself in 1990 (the time period under consideration in PK's fax) to be prophetic dreams interpreted by God Himself, thus implicating GOD (!) in "endorsing the message and lifestyle of the Beatles" via His unique "gift" to the Beatles of a worldwide-revival-ushering "anointing."

Any student of the Bible knows that God doesn't give decade-long worldwide-revival-ushering anointings to unbelievers or false teachers, since such an anointing would obviously tend to give credibility and/or added impact to the message accompanying the anointing. Would God endorse the Beatles' message?! Read the sidebars! One would think from Ryle's "revelations", however, that God's priority is an "at-least-something-is-happening" anointing, while meanwhile God can be quite tolerant (for a decade, at least) with a false message accompanying His worldwide-revival-ushering musical anointing.

The PK fax also conveniently avoids specifying exactly who had thought that Ryle was "endorsing the message and lifestyle of the Beatles" and "believed the Beatles were used by God," so that the reader can't confirm the claim. It gives the reader the impression that these are the *only* two possible "misunderstandings" known to Promise Keepers, and thus Ryle is easily cleared of all charges laid against him. Such is not the case, however.

For example, perhaps the most well-known voice objecting to Ryle and his Beatles dreams is Pentecostal pastor Bill Randles, who wrote, "An Open Letter to Bill McCartney," which focused particularly on this "anointing" issue that Chavis and the PK fax seems so focused on themselves to deny or spin-doctor. Sometime in 1995, Randles wrote,

> Frankly, Mr. McCartney, another huge reservation that I am having with P.K. is the fact that James Ryle, a man who claims that God told him the Beatles were anointed to bring forth a worldwide revival and "usher in my (God's) Spirit," is your pastor and mentor. According to Ryle, it wasn't until 1970 that God removed His anointing from the Beatles (*Sgt. Pepper's Lonely Hearts Club Band* was anointed by God? 1970 was the year the Beatles broke up!). I am leery of a "prophet" who discerns the demonic as anointed.

The details of Randles' objections here are based on what Ryle actually said—Randles had listened to the audio tape and is judging Ryles' Beatles dream interpretation as Ryle himself instructs his readers to do in his two books on dreams (cf. May '96 CC). But PK doesn't appear to be the least bit interested in even acknowledging the existence of what Ryle actually said, since it is so obviously unbiblical and indefensible—thus they have propped up a straw man of the criticisms to give the appearance of having dealt with the situation when in fact they have not.

No Repentance

Ryle's circa 1990 "revelations" about the Beatles' potential worldwide-revival-ushering musical "anointing", that God then waited until 1970 to take away from them to be reserved for and "imminently" distributed to Christians in the 1990's doesn't at all sound like something the God who inspired the Scriptures would do and say. Ryle's "revelations" rather cast some dark shadows on God's holy character. Does PK know this? It appears they are going out of their way to equip their Ambassadors with misrepre-sentations, both regarding what Ryle actually said and wrote in 1990 and what the critics have been saying since.

Ryle himself hasn't repented of his 1989-1990 Beatles "revelations" either (why would he need to repent if he was simply "misunderstood" as the PK fax would like us to think?)—such a repentance would entail him publicly admitting that he lied or was otherwise massively deceived when he, Director of Promise Keepers, "Pastor" of the founder and President of PK and the rest of those who attend the Boulder Valley Vineyard, and author of two books on the subject of "revelatory" dreams (cf. May '96 CC), in true "humility" (defined according to Ryle at the 1990 Harvest Conference as, "agreeing with what God says about you"), went around claiming to multitudes of people, many of whom "went up to the front" and embraced this "word" to their own spiritual deception, that God has appointed James Ryle as a lookout to both "report" about and "pass out" this worldwide-revival-ushering Beatles "anointing" to 1990's Christian musicians.

Ryle does seems to have toned down in the last few years his extravagant claims and reporting of "what God showed" him, as evidenced by what he had to say in his one-page Feb. 1994 Charisma piece. But such doesn't change the historical facts, that PK has seen fit to "spin-doctor" in a public relations fax what Ryle was openly emphasizing earlier in this decade.

We are obviously asking James Ryle and Promise Keepers to face up to, and respond with an exemplary display of integrity, whatever the cost, to what James Ryle was actually saying and writing in 1990 on this Beatles "anointing" issue. No more lies, no more spin-doctoring, no more straw men—we want the truth; the Ambassadors of PK, and those the Ambassadors are currently funneling misinformation to, deserve the truth and nothing but the truth.

In the meantime, and even if Promise Keepers was to actually repent and begin to behave with integrity on this matter, the take-home message of this whole incident has got to be something like this: PK is more than willing to play fast and loose with the truth, even to the point of equipping their own Ambassadors with false information, in order to cover the errors of their leadership who are guilty of misleading Christians with their false doctrines and false prophecies."[6]

The related supportive material, endnotes and documentation to this article is, as previously mentioned, reproduced with the Appendix.

If there were a more widespread knowledge of all the false prophecies and the clearly fraudulent *"moves of the Spirit"* attributed to God by Promise Keepers' leadership and their associates in the Vineyard Movement, then surely the many pastors from varied, conservative, evangelical, Bible-based churches who support and defend Promise Keepers would be horrified and repulsed over how they have been scripturally deceived and spiritually raped. Discernment is not on the list of manly attributes Promise Keepers calls for. On the contrary, the organization's insidious, contaminated menagerie of doctrine prohibits men of discernment from participating.

Bill McCartney and Pastor Ryle are only two of several pillars upon which the entire Promise Keepers system rests. Their extreme, bizarre and far-fetched doctrinal positions represent the very core of Promise Keepers origin, existence and agenda.

An objective, biblical examination of the doctrinal positions and theological perceptions of McCartney, Pastor Ryle, John Wimber, Promise Keepers' President, Randy Philips, and other influential men in Promise Keepers, reveals an obvious and undeniable, disturbing common denominator. These men do not subscribe exclusively to the traditional, historic, orthodox Christian Church's position that tenaciously adheres to the fact that all men are clearly forbidden *"to add to or take away from"* the closed and final revelation of God that we have in the Word of God.

The core of Promise Keepers leadership not only, as we have clearly established from the Scriptures, directs the focus of men on extra-biblical standards, works, experiences and fraudulent guidelines for godliness, but they are also widely known among spiritually discerning and biblically know-ledgeable men for their inconceivable perversions of and license with the sacred Holy Scriptures. I have no reason to doubt or demean the character, motive or moral integrity of these particular men. I commend and applaud their desire to call men to what they perceive to be a process that will make them men of God. However, we must never forget that sincerity, pure motives and nice thoughts are not the standard by which God, or His Church, is to measure the credibility or legitimacy of those who would lead the Christian Church or ministries. The standard and final measuring rod that determines a legitimate Christian leader must remain that one's full acceptance of, and confidence in the Word of God.

Tragically, Promise Keepers and other like ministries will ultimately leave in their wakes massive amounts of wasted energies, resources and lives. These ministries are promoting a satanically inspired, counterfeit plan for godliness. The imposing volume of additional heretical and apostate values, doctrines and beliefs that are riding *"piggyback"* on this *"Trojan Horse"* called Promise Keepers is shocking. As an organization camouflaged under the cloak of Christian ministry, Promise Keepers ranks among the most fraudulent, spurious and dangerously pretentious deceptions in more than 2,000 years of Church history.

The Wizards of Ahs, Oohs and Praise the Lords

To understand any ministry, especially one like Promise Keepers, it is necessary to look back to its origin and beyond. In this case, we have seen that founder Bill McCartney and his pastor, James Ryle, are participants in the Vineyard Movement, which was started by John Wimber. Learning more about who Wimber is and what he believes will give inquisitive hearts another insight on the nature, doctrine and vision of Promise Keepers.

Millions of undiscerning, hungry-for-supernatural-expression church members have listened in awe as John Wimber told of miracles he has seen and been a part of. A chorus of *"Oohs, Ahs"* and *"Praise the Lords"* echoes through the audience as he speaks.

I am a staunch believer in the miracles of God and the God of miracles. I know that God operates in a powerful and miraculous capacity in our day. Miracles are not, however, God's arena for the communication of His Truth, nor do they validate His presence. *"God is a Spirit and they that worship Him must worship Him in spirit and in truth"* (John 4:24).

God used miracles during specific Old Testament times, in the life of Christ and in the beginnings of the early Church for explicit reasons. His primary means of communication before the Scriptures, which are the total revelation of God, were completed, was through unusual and miraculous acts. So, while indeed God has used miracles to announce His presence and confirm His Word, today we have "a more sure word" in God's written Word. The Bible is full of warnings to the people of God to stay alert and not be fooled by those who would impose their personal agendas upon it, even if they can manufacture the miraculous.

The Apostle Paul repeatedly cautioned the recipients of his epistles who were bombarded with those claiming to be "operatives of the Holy Spirit" in their performance of the supernatural. He warned the church at Galatia against the rush of believers to receive additional revelation from other sources, even from one appearing to be an "angel from heaven" if that person expressed any variation from the gospel that they had received. He wrote, "But though we, or an angel from heaven, preach any other gospel unto you than that which we have preached unto you, let him be accursed. As we said before, so say I now again, If any man preach any other gospel unto you than that ye have received, let him be accursed" (see also Galatians 1:8-9). At Philippi, a woman who followed Paul as he preached the gospel was clearly demon-possessed. Even though she was "confirming" that Paul was sent from God to show them "the way of salvation," she was, according to Scripture, possessed of a spirit of divination. After days of tolerating this wicked spirit, Paul spoke to the demon to leave the woman and it did. (see also Acts 16:16.) Even though this woman was confirming the Truth, still she did so under the influence of demon spirits in an effort to establish, like many today, her own credibility.

Another individual who had "believed and was baptized" followed Philip as he preached in Samaria. This man, named Simon, was a sorcerer who went through the motions of becoming a Christian and joined the ministry of Philip so he could behold the *"signs and wonders"* over which he marveled. Finally, his spirit of witchcraft was manifested in his request to Peter and John that they sell him this power to perform signs and wonders. (see also Acts 8.) Of course they, with great indignation, told him he was still in satanic bondage and needed deliverance. He was just another in a long line of many who, from external words and walk, seemed to belong to God's people, but had experienced a false conversion to Christ.

Charlatans, frauds, false prophets and the demon-possessed who performed the supernatural, claiming it to be of God, have been with us throughout the Scriptures, as well as Church history. The Bible clearly points out that the hallmark of the last days will be false miracles with an incredible power to deceive. Jesus forewarned us in Matthew 24:24: "For there shall arise false Christs, and false prophets, and they shall show great signs and wonders, insomuch that, if it were possible, they shall deceive the very elect."

Our world has seen periods of great spiritual darkness, but none so dark as that period which we are now entering. Prophesying of this, the last generation, Jesus clearly meant to alert believers to the massive and unprecedented assault by the religious spirits of darkness who would aggressively focus their deceptive efforts upon the *"elect"* of God. Jesus, Peter, Paul, James and every other person of notoriety in the New Testament stressed that this latter days deception would not come from the obvious enemies of the Church, rather, the "great assault" would be initiated from within.

Luke, who was used of the Spirit of God to pen more of the New Testament Scripture than any other individual, repeats the urgent warning of the Apostle Paul to the Ephesian elders.

"Wherefore, I testify unto you this day, that I am pure from the blood of all men; For I have not shunned to declare unto you all the counsel of God. Take heed, therefore, unto yourselves, and to all the flock, over which the Holy Spirit hath made you overseers, to feed the church of God, which he hath purchased with his own blood. For I know this, that after my departing shall grievous wolves enter in among you, not sparing the flock. Also of your own selves shall men arise, speaking perverse things, to draw away disciples after them. Therefore, watch, and remember, that for the space of three years I ceased not to warn everyone night and day with tears. And now, brethren, I commend you to God, and to the word of His grace, which is able to build you up, and to give you an inheritance among all them who are sanctified" (Acts 20:26-32).

Paul warned of those wolves among the sheep and of their deception. Then as a protection against deceivers and their snares, he commended the Ephesians to "God and to the word of His grace" which would sustain, build and sanctify them.

How clever is the enemy to disguise his deceit in the warmth of pretended camaraderie. And, once again, we watch with amazement our previously established illustration of the *"Trojan Horse"* as it becomes reality. The treachery of the enemy has worked yet again.

Jesus spoke of the same in Matthew 7:15, when He warned, *"Beware of false prophets, who come to you in sheep's clothing, but inwardly they are ravening wolves."* Apparently this deception will be so powerful that many will stand before God at the Great White Throne Judgment and insist that they belong to Christ as they say, "Lord, Lord, have we not prophesied in Thy name? And in Thy name have cast out demons? And in Thy name done many wonderful works?" (Matthew 7:22). To their amazement, He will respond, *"I never knew you; depart from me, ye that work iniquity"* (Matthew 7:23).

Millions of people across America who claim to know Christ are chasing the supernatural expression of what they are being told is the miraculous move of the Holy Spirit. Jesus said to the religious crowd of His day who perceived themselves to be among the elite of God, "If, therefore, the light that is in thee be darkness, how great is that darkness!" (Matthew 6:23).

In spite of God's efforts through Holy Writ to sober the heart of believers, still we are witnessing massive, unprecedented spiritual treachery among many of those claiming to be Christians.

Paul also warned the church at Corinth of the aggressive, invasive nature of those who desire to "draw away disciples after themselves" and simultaneously reject the Truth of God. He wrote them in his second letter, "For such are false prophets, deceitful workers, transforming themselves into the apostles of Christ. And no marvel; for Satan himself is transformed into an angel of light. Therefore, it is no great thing if his ministers also be transformed as the ministers of righteousness, whose end shall be according to their works" (2 Corinthians 11:13-15). It should not surprise us in days ahead when we discover that some of the most prominent, sought-after preachers and popular Christian media personalities in the world are among these false apostles and deceitful workers who are busily transforming themselves into apostles of Christ. The scope of this deception will devastate millions of people, blinded for a time, by the dazzling brilliance of a nation overflowing with false angels of light.

Ironic, it is, that the birth of the true Messiah was announced by the sign of a Bright Star in the East and yet today, it is the West from whence comes the *"signs and wonders"* that point to a messiah. Indeed, a new kind of messiah, though he pretends to be the other, and in some ways resembles the other. But then, maybe he does not.

Many say, "Oh, but what difference does it really make, as long as a Jesus of some kind is being preached...right?"

"Wrong!"

Promise Keepers' heresies which have been rapidly deteriorating into apostasies pushing "another Jesus," continue to be nursed by several popular ministries in Western civilization. However, the most obvious father figure is John Wimber, a man I met several years before Promise Keepers was born. The organization is the theologically and doctrinally illegitimate offspring of Wimber and his Third Wave wonders.

"To the law and to the testimony! If they speak not according to this word, it is because there is no light in them."

Isaiah 8:20

CHAPTER 18

The Big Daddy of Promise Keepers and the Third Wave Wonder

"My people are destroyed for lack of knowledge; because thou hast rejected knowledge…"

Hosea 4:6

The tendency of Promise Keepers' founding fathers to affix eccentric extra-biblical accessories to the Christian faith in the form of demands upon participants is a trait inherited from their *"mother church"* in the Vineyard movement.

This spiritual gene is passed down from John Wimber, the man whose beliefs and doctrines fathered a national revival of that *"signs and wonders"* movement. The *"denomination"* of churches born out of this movement, now more than 600 local congregations across America, all bear the birthmarks of Wimber. Without this pioneer of doctrinal terrorism, the groundwork for Promise Keepers' foundation would not have been so easily laid.

A few months before my experience at TBN (see also

Chapter 8), Wimber and I appeared as guests on a *Praise The Lord* program. After spending two to three hours with Wimber before and during the program, I found him to be gracious and charming. He was humble, gentle and easy to be around. His disarming manner and amiable demeanor lent him credence as a natural leader.

During the program that evening, we appeared at the same time in a dialogue format with the host. Though, at the time, I had become aware of the profound scriptural discrepancies in John Wimber's theology, nothing he said that night was particularly out of character with the Word of God. In fact, in light of his rather scripturally out-of-sync beliefs, that evening's program was rather benign.

Some weeks later, I saw a video and received a number of other Wimber tapes and written materials that stunned me. Soon after that, I read a statement, documented in the endnotes, by Chuck Smith, pastor of Calvary Chapel in Costa Mesa, California. John Wimber had at one time been associated with Pastor Smith, who, in discussing the Wimber Wave with a researcher, said, "John Wimber has absorbed every aberrant teaching developed by Pentecostals into his teaching."[1]

In spite of their obvious supra-Charismatic, scripturally-extrabiblical beliefs and practices, the leaders of this movement have convinced vast numbers of non-charismatic, conservative evangelicals as well as many classic Pentecostals, that the movement is not really part or parcel of the supra-extreme factions of the Charismatic persuasion, though it most assuredly is. The founder and leadership of Promise Keepers, the Vineyard offshoot, are deeply and fanatically committed to the extra-biblical excesses of Vineyard theology. They have gone to great lengths to deceive non-charismatics into believing that their doctrine is innocuous and non-charismatic.

Incidentally, a professor of church growth at Fuller Seminary and a major supporter and leader in the Vineyard movement, C. Peter Wagner, came up with the term, "Third Wave". According to Wagner, "The first wave was the Pentecostal Movement, the second, the Charismatics, and now the Third Wave is joining them. The Third Wave being, of course, those mainstream evangelicals, now aware of the possibility of the power of God, but not wanting to identify with Pentecostalism."[2]

The less-than-casual attempts of Wagner and others in the Third Wave movement (including Promise Keepers), to camouflage their identity which is firmly rooted in the paranormal, psychosomatic and bizarre beliefs of Wimber and his Vineyard churches is puzzling. Their unwillingness to forthrightly and aggressively publish and proclaim the true nature of their extremist theology is no mere oversight. Promise Keepers' theology, as well as that of the Vineyard Third Wave, is simply Charismatic theology run amok and gone awry, with no link to a biblical anchor. In fact, Wimber stated, "I believe Dr. Wagner's Third Wave is not so much another wave as the next stage of development in the Charismatic renewal."[3]

While its proponents claim old-fashioned Pentecostalism as its heritage, the doctrine of the Vineyard movement's Third Wave theology, as well as that of their up-and-coming stepchild, Promise Keepers, represents far more. It is a doctrine of extra-biblical extremism that focuses on seeking sensually-oriented experiences and utterances directly from Almighty God. Most often, the "prophet" names the individual these utterances are directed to and he sees visions in which personal appearances by Jesus and other well-known Bible characters are not uncommon. Outlandish and unbelievable extremes, practices and conduct, all in the name of the moving of the Holy Spirit, have sprung from the aforementioned, humble, early practices of Promise Keepers' mother church.

These inherent extremes and the incredible, obvious abuses of the Scriptures which have attached themselves to this "movement" as it evolved from the Charismatic into the Third Wave, shock even most old-line Pentecostals. Many of these precious people have desperately tried to distance themselves from this *"Wimberology"*; yet, to many pastors, the number of people attracted to their churches as they "open up" to this sensual search for spiritual highs is extremely tempting. Again, pragmatism is winning the day.

Third Wave Vineyard tacticians, as well as Promise Keepers' public relations departments have perfected invasive techniques in order to reach into otherwise biblically balanced denominations and infiltrate them with this doctrinal *"leaven"* by refocusing their spiritually naïve victims on the propaganda calling for unity, harmony and the church's need for "real men." This is a well-planned, strategically designed conspiracy to doctrinally invade those of extremely dissimilar theological positions. Their hope is that these target groups will swallow the hook of "Doctrine is no big deal. Let's just love Jesus and unite for Christ." Their plan is to bring to bear on all groups— Pentecostal and non-Pentecostal, Protestant and non-Protestant—the teaching and extra-biblical philosophy that enslaves, excites and drives them with an evangelistic fervor. Thus an influx of Vineyard-type speakers and Third Wave-influenced ministers and materials has been invading otherwise conservative Bible-based churches on the false and deceptive premise of Promise Keepers.

To insure that non-Third Wave men, pastors and churches "bite" the Promise Keepers' bait, they have exposed a serpentine wisdom by including well-known speakers, preachers and authors who, though tolerant and broad-minded, are not of any Charismatic persuasions.

As a pastor and host of a nationwide television ministry, I have on many occasions been approached by those involved in Wimberism who were seeking a place to speak and minister. On each occasion, as I investigated the person, I discovered their root beliefs and, of course, refused to allow them my pulpit or air time. Others among my Bible-believing colleagues, without understanding the perverse nature of this movement, have allowed these people to "minister" in their churches. Usually, just one experience convinces the pastor of the overt and aggressive excesses of these people. The deception such people exercise by maintaining membership and fellowship in denominational or nondenominational churches renowned for their anti-Third Wave positions proves their desire to spiritually ambush unsuspecting believers and churches.

This is a disturbing but obvious characteristic of Promise Keepers. Thousands of laymen from biblically sound churches have been swept up into, via their participation in Promise Keepers, heretical Third Wave Vineyard theology. Rarely is this a result of the larger Promise Keepers rallies where Promise Keepers' true doctrine keeps a low profile. The doctrinal trap is sprung in many of the smaller meetings and the one-on-one relationships promoted by Promise Keepers *"mentoring"* efforts.

The Promise Keepers Tie to the Wimber Wonder Wave

According to Wimber and Third Wave activists, this "new movement" of the Holy Spirit is birthing through them a great revival predominately marked by "signs and wonders." They insist the Christian Church is without God's power unless its evangelistic efforts are supplemented with miracles of biblical proportions, visions of another world, prophetic utterances and, of course, speaking in tongues. According to this group, evangelism that will ultimately lead the world to Christ is that evangelism which must be accompanied with far-fetched, supernatural, miraculous events. It is the Third Waver's conviction that if people come to Christ in any lesser "spiritually charged atmosphere" then they are not "thoroughly" Christian and, at best, they are spiritually retarded.

Wimber and cohorts in churches, conventions and on television relate unbelievable stories of *"miracles"* they have participated in while traveling the world, and mostly, Third World countries. Interestingly, in the settings where the Third Wave healers have chosen to do their healing, there are few, if any, doctors to validate the physical miracles, the supernatural manifestations or the boasted of *"moves of God's Spirit."*

Wimberites in Vineyard churches, of which Promise Keepers' leadership is made of, are expecting a worldwide response to *"evangelization"* as a result of what Wimber calls *"power evangelism,"* the manifestation of signs and wonders. An article by Andrew Shead in *The Briefing* summarizes what was shared at the Sydney Spiritual Warfare Conference by John Wimber. Wimber said, "We are at a crisis point in history. In the next decade the world will turn to Jesus as never before in any era. Neutrality toward the gospel will be a thing of the past. How will this happen?

Through a revitalized church which by its unity, faith and godliness will recover the lost apostolic powers and with them will cure AIDS, emancipate the underprivileged and impress the gospel upon hundreds of millions of people."[4]

This is why we hear various Vineyard, Third Wave speakers and many of Promise Keepers leaders and featured guests report on the miracles that they regularly participate in. These reports have included such phenomena as eyes appearing in a man born without eyes; decayed, rotted, or absent teeth growing back perfectly whole in an instant; and a nice gold filling suddenly replacing a cavity. Why not another new tooth? Oh well. And then there are testimonies of amputated arms having grown back and, lest I forget, some of these men also claim to have literally raised the dead. Of course, these incredible so-called "signs and wonders" have never been scientifically or medically documented.

More amazing than the fact that these and others like them are on television 24 hours a day boasting of these "miracles" is the fact that millions of Americans obviously believe the reports. The most biblically abusive and scripturally unsound teaching in the Church today is this one-and-the-same doctrine which is subscribed to by Promise Keepers' top leadership.

Dr. John MacArthur, in his book, *The Charismatics,* addresses the Wimber and Third Wave phenomena and their fascinating claim to miracles. He writes,

> The most dramatic miracles come with sketchy details and are always nearly anonymous. Rarely do they even involve people who are known personally to those who report the miracles. Collaborating eyewitness accounts are sometimes cited but never documented. Most UFO sightings come with more convincing evidence.

> A group of five Christian medical doctors attended a recent conference led by John Wimber in Sydney, Australia. These men were hoping to establish the truth of Wimber's claims that miraculous healings were taking place in his meetings. One of them, Dr. Philip Seldan, reported,

"The fact that John Wimber knew we were present and observing may have served to "tone down" the claims which we understand were made at previous conferences... Mr. Wimber himself referred to bad backs and indicated that people could expect pain relief, but no change which could be documented by a doctor. He (Wimber) admitted that he had never seen a degenerated vertebra restored to normal shape...

As I suspected, most of the conditions which were prayed over were in the psychosomatic, trivial, or medically difficult-to-document categories:

> problem with great left toe
> nervous disorders
> breathing problems
> barrenness
> unequal leg length (my favorite - I can't measure legs
>   accurately)
> bad back and neck, etc."[5]

The doctor concluded, *"At this stage, we are unaware of any organic healings which could be proven."*[6]

Perhaps Wimber has not yet thought through his own theology of healing. Evidently, he rejects the biblical principle that physical ailments may be part of God's sovereign plan for believers but he struggles to explain why so many are not healed. The reality is that the Third Wave, with all its emphasis on signs and wonders, has produced nothing verifiable that qualifies in the New Testament sense as an authentic sign or wonder.[7]

One of the most amazing things Wimber has said in terms of "power evangelism" is that he insists "signs and wonders" must accompany true conversion to the Gospel. More puzzling is why so few theologically educated people say anything to correct him. The Bible says "the gospel is the power of God for salvation", not signs and wonders (Romans 1:16). Enforcing

God's Truth, Paul writes, *"Faith cometh by hearing and hearing by the Word of God"* (Romans 10:17).

In recent months, perhaps Wimber has modified his theology, as he has been fighting a battle against cancer. All of us, regardless of our doctrinal positions, should be praying with him.

Promise Keepers, a ministerial and spiritual prodigy of Wimber's Vineyard movement, is clearly compatible and harmonious with this Wimberology, which is doing more to grieve, quench and defame the true work of the Holy Spirit than any other hindrance to revival in our land.

Spiritual Arsonist and Strange Fire

It would not be proper to conclude this discussion of the Vineyard Movement, the Promise Keepers progenitor, without mentioning another "wild and crazy" so-called move of God that is sweeping the world. A brief glance at this, yet another Vineyard-spawned, biblically unrooted and ungrounded, so-called spiritual revival will help us understand the spiritualistic mutation that can be expected of Promise Keepers, a first cousin of the infamous *"Toronto Blessing."* The Wimber-founded Vineyard Churches, numbering over 600 worldwide, have the new paradigm in American Christianity.

The Church of the Living God used to determine true and correct doctrine by testing it against the Word of God. Today, however, it is the Word of God that is held suspect in the heart of America's neo-Christians. The Bible is now the focus and the subject of the *"test."* The validity of the Scriptures is being tried against "experiences" that are rampant among those of this persuasion. The trend is to choose personal experience over the Scripture. The truth is, however, biblical doctrine will never contradict any legitimate experience that is born of God.

The *"anything goes"* attitude dominating the perverse theology of millions of laymen and tens of thousands of pastors has allowed Promise Keepers and its proponents to walk through the Church door undetected as the biblically-abusive, scripturally-errant seducers of God's people that they are. The baggage accompanying them, though by design not obvious at most of their major rallies, is weighted with spiritual contraband from enemy territory. Men who become involved in Promise Keepers' philosophy and doctrines become *"carriers"* of the germ of deception. They continue to take this germ back to their home churches, spreading the epidemic of spiritual AIDS, and rendering those churches impotent to resist the spiritual infection of polluted, poisoned concepts of God and doctrines of devils. Beneath the attractive facade, Promise Keepers is laden with everything from Christian humanism and damnable heretical and apostate beliefs to a total disregard for the integrity of God-established scriptural doctrine.

The recent ABC prime-time special, *In The Name of God*, dealt with the bizarre belief systems and practices of John Wimber and the *"laughing"* revivalist, Rodney H. Brown, and others. The program featured the silly and puzzling antics going on in churches across our land as a result of the doctrinal insanity of such men. The end of the piece showed footage taken in various church services where "signs and wonders" were supposed to be happening and featured various interviews with the movement's leaders, among them John Wimber. ABC anchorman Peter Jennings astutely observed:

"Our goal was to find out if these new methods were making Christianity more relevant...or were they just an attempt to dilute the message to get more people in the door. As these churches strive to bring in a sell-out crowd, are they in danger of selling out the gospel?"[8]

If Peter Jennings was perceptive enough, as an unregenerate man, to observe that the church's current national trends are compromising its message and "in danger of selling out the gospel," it must be obvious. In fact, if he had the advantage both of the Spirit of God and a discerning heart, he would notice that such a "sellout" of God's Truths has already occurred. And the sell-out crowd attracted to ministries like Promise Keepers is what facilitated the sale.

In spite of the spiritual storm alerts sounded by a shrinking number of voices, few are heeding the warning signals.

The following reveals the extremes to which accommodation of Third Wave theology can lead. *"Grab your board"* because the Third Wave surf is up!

Spiritual Barking, Soaking and Laughing: It's All in the Family

Mysticism has subtly crept into American Christendom and has been adopted by Third Wave and Promise Keepers' theology. Over the last few years it has produced a generation of spiritually shallow churches, pastors with misplaced priorities and Christians who are convinced that they must experience God on a sensual level if they are to know Him at all. This, of course, absolutely contradicts the Word of God and for those who believe such a deception, it topples great doctrinal mountains of truth in preference for experiential *"mole hills."*

Such a convoluted understanding of the nature of God stems from statements like that of John Wimber in his book, *Power Evangelism*: "God is greater than His Word."[9] That sounds like profound spiritual knowledge until we turn to Psalm 138:2, in which God tells us, "I have elevated my Word above my Name." But *"Wimberology"* has won the fascination of millions of people who are, as those infatuated with Promise Keepers, too apathetic, unlearned or unskilled in handling the Word of God to test men's utterances or experiences. So, since God, according to both *"Wimberology"* and Promise Keepers' theology, is not restricted to His Word, then anything and everything can be "of God." Few keen observers of the Christian "scene" in America are strangers to the proponents of this widely-accepted, scripturally-deviant doctrine.

The millions of seduced followers who support the growing number of popular "Christian" healers on television and in healing revivals across America speak of the massive deception sweeping our nation. And why not believe what we see and feel? There is no reason to question the validity of any *"experience"* simply because it is not validated by Scripture, so we are told.

John Wimber addressed the subject of healing at a Bible conference. "In the Catholic Church for over a twelve hundred year period, people were healed as a result of touching the relics of the saints," he said. "We Protestants have difficulty with that...but we healers shouldn't, because there is nothing theologically out of line with that."[10]

You bet I have some "difficulty with that", Mr. Wimber! This heresy of the most diabolic origin is 100 percent theologically out of line, not with *"Wimberology"* but with biblical theology.

Little wonder a *"Wimberite"* Vineyard Church in Toronto, Canada, has been the source of some heartbreaking and unfathomable false manifestations of the Holy Spirit. Even Wimber thought it was a bit excessive and finally, because the Church's leadership would not submit to his correction, he dismissed them from his fellowship, but not before the following manifestation of what has been identified as a great and powerful revival started sweeping America and the world from the Toronto church. These "evidences of God's Spirit moving" are only a sampling of the many, as the church leadership has called them, "visitations of God." We must test the legitimacy of such visitations of God against the Scriptures. We can, of course, come to our own subjective opinions. However, below is a summarized list.

The Laughing Revival - originated, supposedly, in South Africa with Charismatic evangelist, Rodney Howard-Brown. This *"holy laughter"* movement is one of the most outrageous so-called manifestations of the Holy Spirit in Church history. Riotous and uncontrolled laughter from those in attendance who claim to be *"drunk on God"* shakes the masses into hysteria. Speakers often attempt to continue in spite of the distraction of the crowds who are bowled over with screaming, hysterical laughter.

Soaking - Multitudes of people travel thousands of miles to sit and do what is called "soak in the Spirit." This requires, they tell us, "major carpet time" where one is "out of this world and caught up in the Spirit world." Even my eleven-year-old daughter, when hearing of this, said, "That sounds so New Age-ish." Yes, the perceptive child is quite right.

Barking - "Barking in the Spirit" just like a dog is one of the latest Holy Spirit manifestations. Getting down on all fours and barking at others who are rolling on the floor in uncontrollable "holy laughter" is a sure sign, we are told, that God is present.

Roaring - This new phenomenon is participated in only by those who have very "tender hearts" and are extremely open to God. It is supposedly a lion's roar. After all, Jesus did have something to do with, as one woman pointed out, "a Lion of the Tribe of Judah." And those who are full of the Spirit are surely as bold as a lion. The roaring is supposed to be a clear manifestation of God's Spirit.

Also included in this pseudo-revival are several other now-popular activities such as making all kinds of **animal noises** "in the Spirit." Senior Pastor Arnott of the Toronto Church said, "We see it as a prophetic message...the people tell us how they felt the strength of the Lord while doing it."

And then, of course, there is the experience with the **Holy Ghost Glue**. This encounter with God's power or, "the Spirit", causes the believer to literally "stick" to various objects such as the floor, chairs and altar areas. They cannot break free of the object to which they are adhered by this Holy Ghost Glue until God is ready to "release them."

These excessive and scripturally abusive activities alert even a nominally biblically literate individual to the horrendous, heretical nature of these "new manifestations."

It requires no exaggeration to connect the outlandish *"Wimberology"* and Vineyard Church doctrine with those in leadership at Promise Keepers who are equally and deeply involved with the entire Vineyard, Third Wave movement. Though Wimber says he has distanced his "Vineyard" churches from the *"Toronto Movement,"* there is no lack of similar doctrinal "distortion" pervading his beliefs system, his movement, and all the churches and organizations, such as Promise Keepers that nurse at his *"doctrinal bosom."* The facts illustrate that Promise Keepers' doctrinal foundation is built upon rapidly shifting sands. But until men across America realize this, even those with profound, scriptural, personal convictions that are doctrinally sound will continue to applaud, participate and promote Promise Keepers.

The pressure upon true believers in America's increasingly hostile anti-Christian social environment contributes to the willingness of many who have been true to the Scriptures in the past to follow the new trend of a denominational and varied religious confederacy. However, nothing is worth the Church forsaking and abandoning God's Truth or being silent when His Word is being "rewritten" and maligned. Leaven cannot help but leaven and there is a very high price to pay when the way, will and Word of God are compromised.

The result of this compromise will always be similar to that of the frog who was preparing to cross a swelling river. By chance, the frog came upon a very sad Mr. Scorpion. "Mr. Scorpion, why are you so sad?" asked Mr. Frog.

Mr. Scorpion replied, "I have no way of crossing the river. Would you mind carrying me across on your back?"

"Oh no, I could never do that" said Mr. Frog. "Why, you are a scorpion and you would sting me."

"I certainly would not," answered Mr. Scorpion indignantly. "In fact, I would be most grateful, indeed."

So Mr. Frog, convinced of Mr. Scorpion's honesty, said, "Okay Mr. Scorpion, hop on my back and let's get going."

The froggy-backed scorpion and Mr. Frog had almost reached the opposite side of the river when Mr. Scorpion raised his stinger high and plunged it into the back of Mr. Frog.

"IEEEYI" cried Mr. Frog. "Why, why, oh why Mr. Scorpion did you sting me?"

"Because" said Mr. Scorpion, "I am a scorpion."

Spiritual scorpions among us are raising their stingers full of doctrinal venom, ready to bury them in the back of those in the Church who, like the frog, are becoming more tolerant than prudence would dictate.

Many well-meaning but naíve Christians allow that natural-born enemy of Truth to ride piggyback upon them. Yet those who are deceived by doctrines of devils cannot resist any opportunity to *"enlighten"* such immature and unsuspecting believers.

The aggressive nature of error mandates an evangelistic fervor. Hence, God has defined the ground rules, instructing Christians to have no fellowship with those who choose to reject the absolute and obvious foundational tenets of the faith so clearly defined in the Word of God. Biblical admonitions concerning piggy backing scorpions reads, *"And have no fellowship with the unfruitful works of darkness, but rather reprove them"* (Ephesians 5:11).

Indeed, instead of entertaining the idea of carrying scorpions on our backs as Christians, we should rather be treading upon them under our feet.

"I'm eradicating the word "Protestant" even out of my vocabulary...I'm not protesting anything. It's time for Catholics and non-Catholics to come together as One in the Spirit and One in the Lord."

—Paul Crouch on TBN[1]

CHAPTER 19

Is It the Beauty or the Beast?

"It's time for Protestants to go to the shepherd (The Pope) and say, 'What do we have to do to come home?'"

—Robert Schuller[2]

The quotes above parrot Promise Keepers' ecumenical call to unify the world's divided religious systems.

The organization has become a major player in this contemporary endeavor to unite laymen and clergymen from some of the most extreme and polarized denominations. Of course, they would consider such a statement a compliment of the highest order. Promise Keepers boasts of the diverse denominational makeup of their participants. Many of the men active in Promise Keepers come from fundamentally sound, Bible-believing churches, while others come from cults, liberal denominations and even *"churches"* which claim that their belief system is the exclusive way to eternal life. Every man who regularly attends Promise Keepers crosses the welcome mat of acceptance laid out at the organization's threshold. No group, regardless of their theological or doctrinal persuasion or their lifestyle need fear any challenge to personal beliefs. By design of Promise Keepers' leadership, those who attend are insured a spiritual comfort zone. They will never, if regulations and ground rules are followed, be personally confronted by Promise Keepers' trained mentors respecting their denomination's preferred plan of salvation. Promise Keepers rallies and local sessions are a theological smorgasbord of dissimilar, deviant and deformed expressions of *"Christianity,"* fellowshipping with those who are truly born of the Spirit. Promise Keepers' uncontested acceptance gives credibility to every attendee's church and belief system, whether apostate, cultic or biblical.

Throughout the New Testament epistles, identical attempts were made to "unite" various beliefs and practices with the pure message of the young church. As the churches of Galatia were being inundated with teachers attempting to weave their message into the Gospel, Paul passionately responded in a letter stating his shock at their *"tolerance"* of those who were attempting to *"improve"* the Gospel with man-made additives and their own warped religious preferences. He wrote: "I am surprised and astonished that you are so quickly turning renegade and deserting Him Who invited and called you by the grace (unmerited favor) of Christ (the Messiah) [and that you are transferring your allegiance] to a different [even an opposition] gospel. Not that there is [or could be] any other [genuine gospel], but there are [obviously] some who are troubling and disturbing and bewildering you [with a different kind of teaching which they offer as a gospel] and want to pervert and distort the gospel of Christ (the Messiah) [into something which it absolutely is not]. But even if we or an angel from heaven should preach to you a gospel contrary to and different from that which we preached to you, let him be accursed [anathema, devoted to destruction, doomed to eternal punishment]! As we said before, so I now say again: If anyone is preaching to you a gospel different from or contrary to that which you received [from us], let him be accursed (anathema, devoted to destruction, doomed to eternal punishment)!" (Galatians 1:6-9, Amplified). Paul was adamant about this matter and demanded that there be absolutely no tolerance of anyone who attempted to pull down the God-ordained, **biblically mandated walls that separated** the true Gospel from the fraudulent message and messengers with their cunning heresies and tired, tried-and-failed religious laws.

In the Statement of Faith, Promise Keepers articulates their *"God-given"* mission. They claim that their "call" facilitates a new confederation which consolidates those who hold diverse, and it might be added, deviant doctrine, with those who hold to sound doctrine. Scripture clearly forbids such a unity as unholy and despotic.

Born in the Belly of Deception

The Promise Keepers' Statement of Faith says, "We believe that we have a God-given mission to unite Christian men... the biblical directive... compels us to break down the walls that have divided and polarized the body of Christ for too long."[3] To justify this scripturally-forbidden effort which ultimately results in an attempt to consolidate Christian, pseudo-Christian and non-Christian men, Promise Keepers has placed two Scripture references below the statement hoping to qualify their insidious goal as a sacred call. The passages are John 17:20-23 and 2 Corinthians 5:18-19. I have already dealt with the false and erroneous interpretation Promise Keepers has attempted to extort from the passage in John 17:20-23. To see why Promise Keepers' doctrinally felonious attempts to use this passage are so obviously illegitimate, refer to chapter 14 entitled, *Happy and Sneezy.*

The second reference Promise Keepers uses to sanctify their efforts to bring men with opposing belief systems into a spiritually harmonious oneness is found in 2 Corinthians 5:18-19. This verse reads:

"And all things are of God, who hath reconciled us to himself by Jesus Christ, and hath given to us the ministry of reconciliation; To wit, that God was in Christ reconciling the world unto himself, not imputing their trespasses unto them, and hath committed unto us the word of reconciliation."

Promise Keepers' use of this passage to support their stated goal is most puzzling. One wonders if Promise Keepers' printers made a "typo" here or perhaps the writer did not consider the possibility that someone might look up some of the references. Whatever the reason for Promise Keepers to take such license with the Word of God in their attempt to prove *"right"* their perceived call to *"unify"* all men of varied doctrinal convictions, they should be extremely embarrassed at this particular imposition upon the Scriptures. These verses to the church at Corinth focus on men being reconciled to God through new birth and their subsequent evangelistic lifestyle that will point others to that reconciliation. The attempt to so twist the intent of this passage into a proof-text to support their *"call from God"* to bring all professing Christian men together even though many of them are caught up in such deviant doctrines as the denial of the deity of Christ and the rejection of the blood atonement is a bold, defacing mis-application of this Scripture. In fact, this passage teaches quite the opposite of what Promise Keepers attempts to impose upon it. Here and in the corresponding passages of Ephesians 2:14-18, Colossians 1:20 and Romans 5:10, the Apostle Paul is dealing with man's reconciliation to God (the Greek word is *katallagg,* which most literally translates to the English word "atonement"). This atonement, or reconciliation, is a God-initiated work that, once completed, leaves that man with a desire to be an ambassador or representative "for Christ" (2 Corinthians 5:19) bearing the "word of reconciliation" or atonement to others that they, too, may "be reconciled to God" (2 Corinthians 5:20).

The ministry of reconciliation is not the result of, as Promise Keepers would have us believe, Christian men forsaking doctrinal distinctions and entering fellowship with men who hold deviant unbiblical doctrine. Paul does not intend to say in this passage what Promise Keepers pretends it says. Clearly, Paul is not, in any way, encouraging Christian men to come together with other men who reject the fundamental tenets of the Christian faith for the sake of unity. God has never called believers to set aside even a single Christian doctrine for the purpose of *"reconciling"* with those who believe incorrectly.

The Promise Keepers' misrepresentation of Paul's words in this passage perverts their original purpose. Again, God's Word here does not even remotely suggest that God's people reconcile with, unify with or tolerate those who believe or teach a counterfeit gospel or who have beliefs that add to, take away or contradict the Word of God. To the contrary, God's Word commands us to vociferously and aggressively confront such false prophets and doctrines of devils as anathema, cursed and damned (see also Galatians 1:6-9).

The touchy-feely sensitivity toward men and systems which defy the Scriptures is a damnable, blasphemous, anti-Christian tolerance. Such strong contending for Truth in light of today's appeal from organizations like Promise Keepers is downright unloving, intolerant and perhaps even unchristian, or so we are told. Yet again, the bastardly nature of Promise Keepers philosophy shows its true character by its contempt for correct exegetic biblical interpretation. Their ill-conceived desire to bring unity and harmony to what they call the Body of Christ causes them and their participants to "turn a blind eye" to the horrendous heretical and apostate groups and denominations who flood into their ranks.

President Randy Phillips, when pressed to explain why Promise Keepers encourages Christian men to interact, fellowship and even *"covenant"* with men who are laymen and leaders in cults and false religious systems, has simply said "We are not...mandating theological issues beyond the clear biblical foundations we stand on."[4] The primary concern among an increasing number of pastors and lay leaders across America, contrary to Promise Keepers oft-repeated *"defense"* of their lack of doctrinal clarity, is that they have no *clear* or *biblical* foundation on which to stand.

Promise Keepers' leadership believes denominational and doctrinal distinctions have always hindered "true revival." They fail to understand that *"doctrinal distinctions"* sought by the Reformers, and others, have for centuries protected God's true remnant from being absorbed and assimilated into deviant Christianity such as apostate Romanism. The doctrinal markings that Promise Keepers so desires to eradicate are peculiarities necessitated by and born of the inspired Word of

God. In fact, one of the main charges that God places upon His Church is to guard, protect, secure and defend the purity, integrity and completeness of God's Word as His full and final revelation to man. The Church has little to offer a lost and dying world if our Gospel becomes polluted with the vulgarities of men's religion through the efforts of groups such as Promise Keepers. If Promise Keepers' philosophy runs its course, the Gospel of Jesus Christ will no longer be preached as a narrow Way that is the only Way. It will become simply another way.

Promise Keepers' subjective interpretation of the term "Body of Christ" is no doubt the most fundamentally flawed and deceptively dangerous of the phrases in their Statement of Faith. It is a sordid, ungodly concept of Promise Keepers, that all who assume the name of Christ as part of their religion, are, regardless of what they believe to be the way of salvation, a part of the Body of Christ. Bringing all of these so-called Christian groups and denominations together with some who truly are born again for interaction, interpersonal ministry, mentoring and covenant-making is a dangerous liaison. Promise Keepers' most obvious failure is their unwillingness to define a full theology or body of truth with which to identify them. Theirs is a doctrine without distinction born in the belly of deception.

The Seed That Bore This Fruit

John writes in the New Testament of the great need for believers to "test the spirits" (1 John 4:1). In testing these spirits, it is necessary to investigate origins. Jesus assured us that "by their fruits" we will be able to determine the validity of any message or messenger. As it is in the world of biology, so it is in the spiritual realm. Interestingly, the fruit carries the seed for each successive generation. Fruit drops its seed and the process of kind producing its own kind is perpetuated.

Perhaps you have heard people, who, attempting to excuse their blind acceptance of ministries and ministers without a biblical analysis boast, *"Well I am no fruit inspector."*

My response is, *"Why not?"* If indeed we are commanded to examine "fruit" in order to determine legitimacy, then it behooves us all to become fruit inspectors.

Jesus also taught repeatedly that externals are deceptive. In Matthew 23, He addresses the Pharisees, the most externally, moral, ethical men on earth at the time, as "hypocrites, fools and blind guides who appear beautiful on the outside but are full of dead men's bones on the inside, as whited sepulchers" (Matthew 23:27).

Externals are, by design, meant to impress. To discover the truth we must look beyond the surface.

So it is with the organization, Promise Keepers. Promise Keepers' initial presentation of their goals and positions easily convinces the casual observer that this organization is committed to the fundamentals of Christian faith and the orthodox theology of the conservative evangelistic church. The truth is, there exists an incredible deception concerning Promise Keepers' basic doctrinal beliefs. The cover-up of their true beliefs and the reason for their "low profile" is by the design of Promise Keepers public relations. This tendency to *"lay low"* with their ultra-extremist, extra-biblical doctrine, as previously pointed out, is a characteristic innate within the parent church of Promise Keepers' leadership.

It must be remembered, Promise Keepers' founder, Bill McCartney, and president, Randy Philips, and many who share in the leadership of the organization are deeply rooted in the Third Wave Vineyard churches of John Wimber. A Christian Research Institute paper entitled, *"The Vineyard,"* describes the theology of the Third Wave-Vineyard ministries.

It states:

> Another disturbing aspect of the Vineyard's ministry is their lack of any written Statement of Faith. Because Vineyard members come from a variety of denominational back-grounds, the leadership has avoided setting strong doctrinal standards. This de-emphasis of doctrine is also consistent with the leadership of John Wimber...whose background theologically includes association with the Quakers, who typically stress the inner experience of God and minimize

the need for doctrinal expression of one's understanding of God.[5]

The leaders that spring from Third Wave-Vineyard seed who have theological training and/or a wide exposure to the academic Christian community are keenly aware of the conservative scholastic attitude toward the Third Wave-Vineyard theology. Conservative theologians look upon this theology as extra-biblical, academically dishonest and intellectually unengaged.

No doubt thousands of pastors and laymen would immediately withdraw from participation in Promise Keepers if they were aware of the organization's deviant doctrines. The subtlety of the doctrinal land mines hides the danger from most of those attending the rallies. Until one begins to participate in local Promise Keepers meetings, delves into their materials and becomes acquainted with their subjective use of biblical terms and phrases, the truth remains hidden.

My personal experience with those who have become involved in Third Wave ministries has been that they vehemently deny that its doctrine is either hyper-Charismatic, extra-biblical or outside the traditional doctrine of mainline denominations. It is fascinating to see how seductive semantic juggling can be when used to smuggle heretical contraband into the heart by persuasive, convincing and widely applauded men of the cloth.

Dr. John MacArthur, in observing the apparent contradiction between what is said versus what is **practiced** by those in the Third Wave movement, wrote:

The Third Wave movement is broadly ecumenical, even syncretic. The truth is, the evangelical veneer of the Third Wave is a carefully crafted image, another crucial element of the skillful marketing campaign that is attempting to sell the movement to non-charismatic evangelicals. In Power Points, Wimber acknowledges the extreme caution that was exercised to keep the book's doctrinal content within the parameters of historic evangelicalism: "This project took a year longer than we anticipated. In part this was because of our concern to root our comments about spiritual growth in historical, orthodox theology."

But is "historical, orthodox theology" really at the heart of Third Wave teaching? No.

Wimber is as comfortable with Roman Catholic dogma as he is with evangelicalism. As we have noted, Wimber defends the Catholic claims of healing through relics. He advocates the reunification of Protestants and Catholics. A former associate says, "During a Vineyard pastors' conference, [he] went so far as to "apologize" to the Catholic church on behalf of all Protestants." In his seminar on church planting, Wimber stated, "The pope...by the way is very responsive to the charismatic movement, and is himself a born-again evangelical. If you've read any of his texts concerning salvation, you'd know he is preaching the gospel as clear as anybody is preaching it in the world today".[6]

Most biblically astute believers will vehemently disagree with that statement by Wimber, and rightly so. If the Pope believed, preached, practiced or adhered to the Gospel of Jesus Christ, he would not only be excommunicated by the Roman Catholic Church, but he would also be marked as a heretic and condemned to hell by the Catholics. Such was the fate of hundreds of thousands of Catholics during the Reformation when they rejected the Catholic religion and received the true Gospel of the Lord Jesus Christ. The New Testament Gospel is not the message of the Catholic Church or its Pope. Such statements by Wimber reflect Vineyard's bizarre, outlandish and darkened reasoning.

Promise Keepers walks doctrinally hand-in-hand with Wimber and his Vineyard movement. Yet, if there is a single characteristic that hallmarks Promise Keepers, it is their tendency, inherited from its mentoring "mother church," Vineyard and its fondness of their "father figure," John Wimber, to look upon defined, sound, biblical theology as restrictive, binding and grievous to experiencing God. Such a theology concludes that nobody is wrong; everyone is right if he has shaken off the shackles of that "dead old doctrine stuff." Promise Keepers offers an open-door, "outcome based" doctrinal policy that "liberates" the varied theologies represented by participants to function in a non-confrontational atmosphere. The trend points, as does Promise Keepers' clearly stated objectives, toward one big spiritual family in which everyone is "hassle free" to relax among his "brothers" who are uncontentious, receptive and warm. However, when he rejects the absolute, expressive and defined theology of the Scriptures, he will embrace, as there is no other alternative, the undefined ideologies and philosophies of men and doctrines of devils.

It seems like there is something about *one big happy worldwide family church under one central authority*, somewhere, isn't there?

Many believers, especially the ardent defenders of Promise Keepers, seem to be so busy sitting around and "enjoying the fellowship of the brothers" and "lapping up those Holy Ghost experiences" that many of them have misplaced their Bibles. They seem to be thinking, "Oh well, who needs a Bible when we have unity and when we can hear from God from such a multitude of other 'sources'?"

But toward what kind of *"Christianity"* is Promise Keepers moving us? It is a *"Christianity"* that Promise Keepers has envisioned from its very inception: *"To break down the walls that have divided and polarized the Body of Christ for too long."* This brand of *"Christianity"* ignores the mandates of God's Word. It is a mutant *"Christianity"* which is no *"Christianity"* at all.

Covenantalism and Kool-Aid

As men are drawn into the Promise Keepers' web, they begin to discover what *"men of integrity"* who keep their promises are expected to do. One of the most important Promise Keepers expectations, they learn, is that "vital relationships among men are critical to helping each other become Promise Keepers."[7] Relationships between men are developed by the Promise

Keepers' concept of covenant partnerships. A Promise Keepers man learns that an essential ingredient needed for his spiritual development is that he be held accountable to another man. This requires each man to be open and forthright in exposing all facets of his life, including, spiritual, domestic, financial and sexual matters. Each man's *"covenant partner"* has complete liberty to inquire about any subject in his life, any time he so chooses. The man holding the other accountable is responsible, under the Promise Keepers plan, to rebuke, correct and instruct his partner.

The Promise Keepers workbook, *"Seize the Moment"*, from the 1994 Portland, Oregon Men's Conference, instructs Promise Keepers attendants on covenantalism with these words:

"In the context of covenant relationships, a man willingly grants other men the right to inquire about his relationship to God, his commitment to his family, his sexuality and his financial dealings. Together they form a team that is committed to advance God's Kingdom."[8]

The application of this concept as a technique to "further one's spiritual development" is foreign to the Word of God. In fact, Christians are explicitly forbidden to make oaths or enter into covenants with one another. The Word of God admonishes us against such oaths and vows because they presume upon the future. God does not want us to make presumptuous commitments that we may not be able to honor. Commitments to God by believers who are simply entering into agreement with the indwelling Holy Spirit through prayer is a different matter, as are our marriage vows.

The few covenants in the Old Testament which were entered into between men such as that between David and Jonathan were divinely designed to illustrate the depth of God's covenant with His people. These typified the blood covenant that God was making through the life and work of Jesus Christ that was finalized on the cross. Unlike the oaths, covenants and promises which Promise Keepers encourages men to make, these Old Testament types demonstrate the faithfulness of God's promises to man rather than man's promises to God or to one another. No covenant of the Old or New Testaments incorporate the use of New Age, psychology-based techniques of mentoring which are employed by Promise Keepers.

In an earlier chapter, we looked at why it is spiritually fraudulent as well as dangerous for men to make flesh-born, prefabricated and religiously orchestrated promises to God. But to teach, as does Promise Keepers, that, in addition to those other ill-conceived promises to God, man must *also* "covenant with other men" to achieve spiritual growth is patently wrong. Such teaching contradicts the Bible and every principle given for spiritual maturity therein.

Repeated admonitions in the Scriptures concern covenants consisting of verbal commitments between two people in which the covenant maker is sworn to a particular action. The New Testament allowance in man-to-man commitments is addressed in James, where he writes:

"...you who say, today or tomorrow we will go into such and such a city and spend a year there and carry on our business and make money. Yet you do not know [the last thing] about what may happen tomorrow...You ought instead to say, if the Lord is willing we shall live and we shall do this or that [thing]. But as it is, you boast [falsely] in your presumption and your self-conceit. All such boasting is wrong" (James 4:13-16, Amplified).

No Christian should make oaths, vows or *"covenants"* with another human, except, of course, during the covenant of marriage. The Scripture reiterates throughout both Testaments the absurdity of doing so, as the boasting of a fool. Proverbs states, "Even a fool, when he holdeth his peace, is counted wise; and he that shutteth his lips is esteemed a man of understanding" (Proverbs 17:28).

This Promise Keeper demand upon participants also interferes with the biblically-ordained structure of authority which God has set as a protective cover over each believer. Christians are to be accountable in their lifestyles to those who are in their own local churches. Under no circumstances is a believer to feel that Scripture demands that he is to share personal matters with anyone—believer or non-believer—or to allow any one to feel free to inquire about such things as financial dealings, spiritual struggles, or sexual activities. Each Christian is free to, without priest, mentor or counselors, enter into the presence of God and find resolution for any and every need or question. Within each believer's local church, any need for another Christian's input or godly counsel can be met without the legalistic yoke that Promise Keepers' mentoring places upon one.

Additionally, Promise Keepers' principle of mentoring clearly defies the concept of the "priesthood of the believer." These matters are not to be placed at the ready disposal of anyone except those inside a Christian's immediate family or those he willingly chooses to confide in who are a part of the spiritual chain of counsel at his local church. Such "clear and present danger" exists within the Promise Keepers' covenant system because the man involved in the process has no way of determining if the one to whom he is "accountable" is even truly born again or if that one has the spiritual depth and maturity to qualify as a competent, confident counselor. Additionally, the Promise Keeper demand that such "share time" be conducted with men of different doctrinal backgrounds creates the very real probability that many of these Christians are being forced to violate the biblical admonition of Psalm 1: "Walk not in the counsel of the ungodly, nor standeth in the way of sinners, nor sitteth in the seat of the scornful..." (Psalm 1:1).

God fully expects our "counsel" to come from biblically qualified, doctrinally sound and spiritually mature persons. Such qualifications are not nearly as subjective as some would have us believe. Christian men must rediscover the biblical principles of spiritual authority and exercise extreme caution when seeking counsel.

A decreasing number of pastors and church leaders are even aware of the biblical truths concerning spiritual authority ("cover" is here synonymous with the word, "authority") and the great benefit and protection it secures for all true believers in the local church. Because the principle of spiritual authority is so rarely preached or practiced, for numerous reasons, millions of otherwise doctrinally stable believers in doctrinally sound churches are being doctrinally polluted and spiritually consumed by the ravening wolves who are running amuck in theologically undisciplined organizations like Promise Keepers.

These *"innocents"* who are spiritually immature and often scripturally malnourished often gravitate to such groups and become infatuated with new spiritual "father" figures who appear to have "all the answers." They often fall for charming, smooth-talking, pious-sounding "leaders" and are willing to defend them "to the death," regardless of the facts.

Many of us remember some years ago the catastrophic results in the jungle compounds of Guyana. Followers of the false prophet, Jim Jones, had "covenanted with each other" to grow up spiritually and to "stick" together through the *oaths* that they made to one another, to have all things in common and to share their private lives, their hearts and their all. The tragic result was that more than *900* of these "covenant brothers and sisters" gulped down their cyanide-laced drinks on the command of another self-proclaimed prophet, Jim Jones, and then dropped dead where they stood.

Though more so now in the spiritual sense, if one's spiritual ears are tuned they can faintly hear, reverberating through America's tangled doctrinal jungle, the continuing echo as the false prophets pipe to their followers, *"Drink your Kool-Aid children. Drink it all. We are all in this together, so drink your Kool-Aid."* Poison, regardless of the attractive package it may come in, is still deadly. Kool-Aid is fine in and of itself, but the sweet waters of Guyana turned bitter. Such will always be the results when attempting to mix light with darkness.

"The soundest reasoning leads to the wrongest conclusions when the premises are false."

—Vilhjahmur Stevansson

CHAPTER 20

Dances with Wolves

"For I know this, that after my departing shall grievous wolves enter in among you, not sparing the flock."

Acts 20:29

It is not yet the Age in which the lamb may lie down with the lion or when the nature of man is in harmony with nature's predators, such as the wolf. Danger exists when humanity attempts to fellowship with nature's predatory beasts. Hence, the uniqueness of a recent movie in which a man alone in the wilderness befriends a wild wolf. Upon seeing this friendship in action, the American Indian inhabiting the territory named the White man *"Dances with Wolves."* Reality removed from the celluloid tale, however, plays out quite differently. Civilized men and savage wolves do not usually develop close friendships.

Today, many in the church of the living God are *"dancing"* and fellowshipping with wolves. *Wolf* is repeatedly used in God's Word to identify false prophets and the danger they present to *sheep*, the people of God who often accept these predatory beasts into their flock.

No less applicable is the story of *Little Red Riding Hood*, whose wolf cunningly concealed his identity in a grandmotherly disguise. This illustration holds fast in Christendom today as many pastors and Christians observe the wolves among us. And, like Little Red Riding Hood, though we observe *"Oh, what big teeth you have!"* many still do not realize the profound, spiritual danger presented by our tolerance of this strange *"bedfellow"*.

"Yeah, But Everybody Is Doing It"

Many churches, denominations and religious groups are discovering an ever-increasing number of reasons to drop their contention over the issues which have distinguished them from others. Many groups who, in the past, were very opposed to anything that hinted at ecumenicalism have now become more flexible and "tolerant". Social, political and moral crusades against such horrors as the homosexuals' rights movement and abortion rights have brought together Catholics, Baptists and others with extremely diverse theological positions for the purpose of consolidating their resources so they can make a more powerful social and political impact. These kinds of common causes weaken the resolve of those who were once far more vigilant in defending the distinctions that separated them from those with a more liberal theology.

As was pointed out at the beginning of this book, a major factor contributing to the rapid numerical growth and the popular appeal of Promise Keepers is that it was born at the most opportune moment in America's social and domestic evolution. It also happened at the best possible moment in America's spiritual evolution. (I use the word "evolution" in a strictly sociological context.) The socio-political and spiritual life of a society is constantly changing, most often for the worst. Each successive cycle brings a weakening of social sensitivities to moral purity. But the forerunner of moral decline has always been the ever-growing weakness of the Church's resolve to maintain its commitment to moral and spiritual absolutes. Thus, the character of each successive age, unless an intervention of a spiritual revival temporarily suspends the decline, is a more dramatic spiritual and moral compromise.

The pulpit's lessening resilience for the bold declaration of biblical truth and virtue results in the gradual moral decay of the pew, which ultimately lowers the standard for the entire society. Those in the church who were once the champions of doctrinal purity and godly living have been more and more willing to cease contending for the faith. Promise Keepers, as well as other ministries we have looked at, was simply there at the right place and the right time to "seize the moment" when this doctrinal, philosophical and moral drift was at its sociological zenith.

How desperate is the need for a new reformation in this hour of Satan's most intensely deceptive assault! Those men and women among us who are willing to *"cry out and spare not"* and who love God's Truth unto death are the true contemporary reformers. However, the threats we see, unlike those in the days of Rome's Inquisition, are hardly restricted to the blasphemous Catholic traditions. The current assault is deeply rooted and quickly fixed in evangelical Protestantism and is so widely popular that opponents are seen, as were those early Reformers, as rabble-rousing, mean-spirited ignoramuses.

Today, those who raise the standard of biblical integrity and call for a continued vigilance in the spirit of the original Reformation are in a small minority. Intimidation is heaped upon them by the majority who have pragmatically chosen to go with the crowd. Many of those *"holding out"* are tiring quickly and have either chosen to be silent or to quietly slip over to the side of those whom they once valiantly opposed. However, while it may be easier at any given moment to choose compromise over standing alone, those who do cross that line must pay an extremely high price.

John Calvin spoke eloquently of the nature of compromising the Scriptures when he called it the appeal to *"Custom against Truth"* in his prefatory address to King Francis. As he authored his *"Institutes"*, he wrote:

Even though the whole world may conspire in the same wickedness, He has taught us by experience what is the end of those who sin with the multitudes. This He did when He destroyed all mankind by the flood, but kept Noah with his little family; and Noah by his faith, the faith of one man, condemned the world (Genesis 7:1, Hebrews 11:7). To sum up, evil custom is nothing but a kind of public pestilence in which men do not perish less though they fall with the multitudes.[1]

Tolerance, the Betrayer of Truth

Promise Keepers' Statement of Faith speaks for itself: "We believe we have a God-given mission to *unite* men who are separated by race, *sectarianism*, age, culture and economics."[2] This statement is not compatible with the principles of the Christian faith and provokes conscientious believers to ask some probing questions: Does God give men missions that contradict His Word and the nature of His character? Is it the will of God that all men be spiritually, regardless of their doctrinal beliefs, "united," as Promise Keepers tells us? And on what *premise* does Promise Keepers' leadership have the right to assume the mantle of a *"divine revelation"* that so absolutely and arbitrarily contradicts the "Thus saith the Lord" of Holy Writ?

Pastors and Christian men with an iota of spiritual depth should be standing up all across this nation demanding that Promise Keepers' leadership repent of their flagrant violations of the Christian faith and the Canon of God. The one sentence in Promise Keepers' Statement of Faith stated above is sufficient to disqualify them, their mission and their self-fabricated call to minister to men. The quantum leap that Promise Keepers takes from their stated desire to "unite men "separated by *race* to those separated in a *sectarian* sense cannot be justified by any stretch of the Scriptures.

For the record, we should note that there exists no separation of true Christian men in spite of or regardless of their race, age, culture or economics. Promise Keepers pompously imposes themselves into an area of ministry that can only be accomplished by the Holy Spirit as men of varied race, age, culture and economics enter their relationship with Christ. Paul explained this spiritual reality when he clarified the unity with which Christ has enjoined men of different races: "For He is our peace, who hath made both one and hath broken down the middle wall of partition between us..." (Ephesians 2:14). Promise Keepers' desire, however, to equate denominational and sectarian differences with distinctions such as race, age, culture and economics that are placed upon men by the sovereignty of God is intellectual and theological grand larceny.

Like the vast majority of Promise Keepers doctrine, such reasoning could only come from one of two sources. The first possible source for such nonsensical statements is out of the hearts and minds of those who are scripturally and semantically illiterate. The second possible source that could bring one to write such absurdities for public consumption is the latent hope that people would not read it and that if they did, they would not **think** when doing so.

Promise Keepers' desire to *"unify"* men of all denominations also ignores the facts of church history. Throughout that history, men of God have been, on occasion, moved by legitimate conviction to establish fellowships committed to the maintenance of doctrinal purity. The reasons for God's clear call for *"separation"* of the church from polluted anti-scriptural practices that would hinder His purposes far outweigh any advantage the advocates of Promise Keepers-style *"unity"* could ever invent. The original protesters against the corrupted church system came to be called *"Protestants."* Their protestations stemmed from their relentless love for the Truths of God and they could not, in clear conscience, remain unified with a system so diametrically opposed to the expressly defined Truth of God. These courageous men and women who often faced torture and martyrdom are those patriarchs of the *denominationalism* that Promise Keepers so disdains and blames for the "lack of biblical unity". This, says Promise Keepers, is the roadblock to a "demonstration of the power of God". How tragic that thousands of pastors and laymen can be so easily persuaded to cast off the heritage of the forerunners of our faith and trade in Spirit-born distinctions for a *"stillborn"* pseudo-move of God.

If Promise Keepers' leadership is as enamored with spiritual unity as they say, then they should seek out and join a local church in which the pastor and people are wholly committed to the will and Word of God. There these men could witness a precious unity. This, in short, is called "the church" and its unity is a result of the *"knitting together"* of the whole without compromising the individual or his pure commitment to the maintenance of the integrity of the Scriptures.

Promise Keepers is under an age-old delusion concerning the diversity that the Holy Spirit birthed into the Body of Christ, a diversity that accommodates the *"oneness"* and *"completeness"* of that whole. Scripture is clear that each autonomous New Testament church is complete and that its body life is self-contained to supply for every need that local body develops. Each local church is fully functional as it aligns its doctrine and conduct with the scriptural prescription.

Paul, in writing to the Corinthian church, went to great lengths to emphasize the uniqueness of the divine unity that already existed with which they were and we are to cooperate. He wrote, "For as the body is one, and hath many members, and all the members of that one body being many are one body, so also is Christ; for by one Spirit [were] we baptized into one body whether we be Jews or Gentiles, whether we be bond or free and have been all made to drink into one Spirit" (1 Corinthians 12:12-13).

Again, the *"unity"* Promise Keepers advocates is an innate characteristic of the local church where the people are led by their burden to fellowship with other believers who hold in common sound biblical doctrinal convictions. Thus, many denominations develop and perpetuate the beliefs held by that particular group. One would think that so many different churches represent a disharmony, but this is not true. Each Biblically rooted church is unique in its call and ministry and different is not always wrong. Local churches have different visions, various focuses of ministries and burdens for different mission emphasis. Yet their spiritual unity is a Divine expression that can only be born of God. If it is true that what God has put together man should not separate, it is equally true that what God has *not* joined no man should attempt to put together. Promise Keepers' drive to build their ministry is much like that ancient Tower of Babel: unnecessary, as well as redundant to an already accomplished work of God.

The Lady or the Tramp

"Come out of her my people, that ye be not partakers of her sin *and that ye receive not of her plagues.*" Revelation 18:4

It has been said that "he who stands for nothing will fall for anything." Few men of the clergy today are willing to stand alone in the face of the popular and appealing temptation from their compromised peers to join them and become a "team player." Everyone wants to be liked; no one enjoys being branded a "narrow-minded, stubborn fundamentalist". But those men who resist such peer pressure and courageously stand in vigilant defense of God's Word act as the adhesive which keeps the church's fundamental integrity and spiritual effectiveness intact.

Another *church* is being built today. It is, according to those in it, an assemblage of the broad-minded, tolerant ones who have separated themselves from the nay-saying, negating, narrow-minded and divisive defenders of the Scriptures. John the Revelator, while on the Isle of Patmos looking through the portals of time, saw this false church. He wrote: "So he carried me away in the Spirit into the wilderness and I saw a woman sit upon a scarlet-colored beast, full of names of blasphemy, having seven heads and ten horns" (Revelation 17:3).

The Promise Keepers' philosophy, reflected in their oft-repeated desire for a conciliatory unification of men of all denominational and sectarian groups, is a darkened "touchy-feel-good" philosophy that "opens the mind" but closes the Scriptures. This "unity" represents the new and growing confederation upon which will be built the "woman" who sits astride that scarlet-colored beast. This false religious system of the last days is pictured in John's vision as cooperating with the antichrist political system and will be built upon the universal brotherhood of man. This *"last days"* religious system whose foundation is already laid has spawned contemporary efforts such as Promise Keepers. The organization and other ecumenical efforts of the past 25 years have acted as a spiritual *"softening"* agent so that the transition into a consolidated one-world "church" will be more palatable to that fading *"intolerant fundamentalist"* resistance.

From the moment of its birth, the New Testament Church has suffered persecution because of the unique distinctions conveyed in the message of its leaders. That message has been simultaneously inclusive and exclusive. It has been *inclusive* because it welcomes all who will believe and receive the salvation it proclaims without respect to color, creed, race, economics or social status. *"Whosoever will"* can come, choosing to die to themselves, that they might live unto Christ. Their message has been *exclusive* because it is absolute and its demands are non-negotiable. Those who desire to partake are *excluded* if they refuse to enter on God's terms. Ultimately, most of humanity will be excluded. Jesus said of those who enter into the narrow gate of eternal life: *"Few there be who enter in..."* (Matthew 7:14).

God's promises regarding salvation and the living out of its abundance are conditional upon men obediently fulfilling the *premises* accompanying these promises. The faith, power, motivation and knowledge needed to perpetuate this divine fellowship is discovered in the wisdom attained from the Word of God, passed down and compiled under the direction of the Holy Spirit by godly Church Fathers.

The Apostle Paul wrote to young Timothy, "All Scripture is given by inspiration of God, and is profitable for doctrine, for reproof, for correction, for instruction in righteousness, that the man of God may be perfect, thoroughly furnished unto all good works" (2 Timothy 3:16-17).

These pages allow neither space nor time to adequately relate the vital, absolute and eternal need for the Church and the individual believer to be wholly given to the instruction, teaching, absorption and focus upon the Word of God. While we do not worship the Bible, without it we cannot worship God aright. It enlivens the life of God in our hearts and minds as the indwelling Holy Spirit brings its great Truths to revelation and application in our living. It is impossible to live a spiritually maturing, Spirit-controlled, abundant Christian life apart from a commitment to study, know and to obey the Scriptures. The psalmist wrote, "Thy word have I hid in my heart that I might not sin against thee" (Psalm 119:11). God's Word insulates believers against a "crooked and perverse generation." The advantage that an irrevocable commitment to the Bible as the authoritative and final Word of God brings to a believer is incalculable.

God promises that our commitment to study, hear and be led by His Word guarantees:

Life - Psalm 119:50b	*Comfort* - Psalm 119:50a
Cleansing - Psalm 119:9	*Revival* - Psalm 119:25
Understanding - Psalm 119:28	*Mercy* - Psalm 119:41
Liberty - Psalm 119:45	*Good Judgment*-Psalm 119:60
Knowledge - Psalm 119:60	*Wisdom* - Psalm 119:98
Protection from evil - Psalm 119:101	*Light* - Psalm 119:105
Deliverance - Psalm 119:134	*Peace* - Psalm 1:1
Stability - Psalm 1:3	*Prosperity* - Psalm 1:3

The pages of this Book of God boasts that "faith cometh by hearing, and hearing by the word of God" (Romans 10:17) and that "without faith it is impossible to please God" (Hebrews 11:6). These are but a few of the characteristics of a life that is consumed by God's precious Holy Word. The true Church is a church that understands the vital necessity of speaking only what is written in the God-breathed record, the Holy Bible.

The contrast between the individuals who know God's Word and those who are ignorant of It is stark. The Word of God, Its message, Its all-encompassing Truths, with Its full supply of instruction that meets every need and answers every question, is the non-negotiable, irrevocable and thoroughly complete revelation from God to man. Without It, no church and no Christian are equipped to prevail in the unceasing spiritual warfare that is their call and destiny.

The system of the Antichrist world, the old nature of the believer and the demonic host of hell are unrelenting enemies that will destroy the witness and ministry of any Christian who fails to recognize the crowning importance of God's infallible Word to their life and their need to use its inerrant principles as a source of power and strength. The prophet Hosea spoke the mind of God when he penned, *"My people are destroyed for lack of knowledge"* (Hosea 4:6). The knowledge that God's people have historically ignored, compromised and rejected is that which is burned onto the pages of the Bible by the very Spirit of the living God through "holy men of God who spoke as they were moved by the Holy Spirit" (2 Peter 1.21).

The satanic effort in these last days as his time draws to an end and he faces eternal damnation is not to cause men to overtly deny God's Word; rather, Satan desires to influence them to subtly redefine its meaning, modify its contents and add to its message. His strategy questions the finality and exclusivity of this single, authoritative Book. However, God repeatedly warns the church to be on guard against this insidious, infectious deception. That Edenic appeal of Satan to Eve in which he asks, "hath God said?" (Genesis 3:1), has echoed through the pages of human history and it now crescendos in this final stanza of these closing days.

Satan will have a *"last days"* church that is bedecked with religious decor and led by pious-sounding false prophets. He and his false priests, appearing as ministers of righteousness, will use the Word of God as a bait to ensnare the unsuspecting, scripturally illiterate masses. The Word of God, much like our nation's flag and our national anthem, has an emotional appeal that tugs at the heartstrings of Mr. & Mrs. America. Few people, however, who claim to believe in the Ten Commandments can name even more than two or three. We are a nation full of unbelieving believers who are functionally illiterate when it comes to applying the Holy Scriptures to our lives. Men who are capable of using the right catch phrases, who appear to be spiritual and who are cunningly adept at throwing out Scriptures that "sanctify" their fraudulent ministry will lead more and more people into error.

The Bride of Christ will retain her distinction as the "Bride without spot and blemish," but this satanic impostor, the harlot of Revelation 17 will be received and lauded by the world. The massive worldwide deception that sets the stage for this *"Tramp"* pretending to be the *"Bride"* will be a direct result of the current widespread cry for *"unity"* that resounds from ministries like Promise Keepers.

Accentuating the Positive and Eliminating...the Truth

The church's effort to enhance its *"numerical drawing power"* has resulted in a neutering of the message that it is called to deliver. Attempts to make the Gospel increasingly marketable and more widely palatable has birthed a new growth strategy. Men can preach this neo-gospel without hurting feelings or upsetting man's self-image. The focus, so we are told by the neo-gospel gurus of contemporary ministry and the church growth strategists, should be one that highlights the positive aspects of Christianity while eliminating the negative aspects. Promise Keepers is a leading proponent of this philosophy and their efforts to unify men, regardless of their concept of new birth or their attitude about the Word of God, should not alarm students of the Scriptures who perceive the prophetic character of our Age.

The shock to the true believers, however, that so many of those in high-profile positions of leadership within the church have joined the supporting cast of Promise Keepers and its accompanying theological travesty should be devastating. But for decades many leading pastors and church leaders have flirted and fraternized with compromise. It should come as no surprise that they would entertain a proposal for marriage from such seductive attractions.

The new evangelicalism touted by Promise Keepers as the wherewithal needed to "demonstrate biblical unity" is a subtle, conspiratorial assault upon the Word of God. Promise Keepers and like-thinkers obviously feel that *unity* is more vital to the life of the Church than is the *Truth* of Her message. Every Christian man and woman who condones the ministry of Promise Keepers and their goals must understand that he or she is, inadvertently, condoning the false doctrines, lying spirits, and anti-biblical methods that inundate this organization.

Promise Keepers calls for all men to come together beneath an umbrella which, on the surface, appears to be Christian. And yet Promise Keepers refuses to deny those bizarre belief systems that are powerfully represented in their organization. The ministry makes no distinction between Mormon followers who deny the deity of Christ (and who happen to be one of the world's fastest growing cults) and the true believers who are deceived into participating. Nor does Promise Keepers confront the Catholic Church's false doctrines of salvation that are deceiving millions of people this very moment.

The practicing homosexuals who attend Promise Keepers professing to be "Christians" are not intentionally confronted by Promise Keepers or informed that the Scripture, without question, clearly condemns this lifestyle. Promise Keepers' doctrine is as spiritually blasphemous and perverse as homosexuality is sexually blasphemous and perverse. (see also page 303 for a more in-depth discussion of this matter).

The popularity of this new evangelicalism, of which Promise Keepers is so intricately a part, is one of its appealing characteristics. When the leading men in evangelical circles of the day repeatedly condone and endorse the ministries of organizations like Promise Keepers, they also condone everything Promise Keepers believes, practices and condones. Such men give credibility to the apostasy and the heresies that are pouring into America's church life. As Promise Keepers' participants return to their churches and families with their hearts full of poisoned, illicit impositions into the Scriptures, this leaven is acting to *"leaven the whole lump"* (1 Corinthians 5:6).

The real damage is done by so many of the men who appear at conferences and rallies as Promise Keepers speakers who privately do not even share the supra-beyond-charismatic doctrine of Promise Keepers. It is their deafening silence on critical issues that the church and Christians across America are wrestling with that inflicts so much spiritual harm. The controversial issues that they have been encouraged and convinced by Promise Keepers' unitarian approach to ignore are issues that are critical to maintaining the integrity and purity of God's Word. Yet, for unity's and harmony's sake, the errant, doctrinal and theological issues remain unchallenged by popular ministers which participate in Promise Keepers and seem to be *"the truth"* to at least the vast majority of attendees.

The growing trend of unwillingness to stand up and speak out against Promise Keepers' doctrinal terrorism is aggressively being promoted in each of their conferences, rallies and local assemblies. This popular new philosophy of tolerance prompts participants and speakers to ignore the negative aspects of Christianity. The *negative* aspects of Christianity are the *"Thou shalt not's"* of Scripture. While Promise Keepers and their supporters seek to be tolerant of error, aberrant theology and perverse beliefs, God, indeed, is not so tolerant.

Men are "sanctifying" their fear of speaking out and their compromise by the neo-evangelical motto "let's not be judgmental." That seems to be the Promise Keepers' battle cry for men to rally to a battlefield where the participants have surrendered the essentials and hence, there is no battle. This "pseudo-peace and unity" among the brothers has alas been realized through Promise Keepers' elimination of discussion on any issue that could cause conflict. Obviously, the crucifixion of Truth did not cease on an old rugged cross 2,000 years ago.

The Truth of God's Word must be trashed if the satanic seeds of deception, sown in the hearts of rebellious men, are to take root and blossom in the fertile fields of this popular new kind of unity. This illicit fruit is needed to nourish the coming New Age church. This last days *"church"* seen in John's vision will have the right words, the right terminology and speak the familiar sounding language of Zion, but it, indeed, is the devil in disguise.

Never has a moment existed in the life of the true church when men's allegiance to *"be separate"* from this creeping, deceptive, doctrinal darkness has been more important. Men of courage and conviction must rise up and support each other against this spiritual tyranny. The Church must experience a rekindling of its tenacious and bold commitment to, at all costs, defend the faith once delivered to the saints (Jude 3).

We, as the people of God, have our orders and should once again apply the motto of the French Foreign Legion: *"If I falter, push me on. If I stumble, pick me up. If I retreat, shoot me."*

The people of God *"have come into the Kingdom for such an hour as this"* (Esther 4:14). Such a moment demands that we be driven not by the popular, trendy claims of a compromised religious system but, that we, in spite of our fears, speak out. The cost of standing alone, of being willing to speak out and stand firm can create isolation caused by the ostracism of our peers.

Napoleon often referred to Marshall Ney as the bravest man he had even known. Yet Ney's knees were trembling so badly on the morning just before a major battle that his men saw him having great difficulty mounting his horse. Finally, after he had struggled into the saddle, he contemptuously shouted, *"Shake away; knees, you would shake worse than that if you knew where I am going to take you."*

If reprisal, isolation or retaliation from our compromised peers is the price we must pay for standing up for the Truth, then so be it. If, indeed, we are forced to carry the standard alone into the arena of battle and we find that we go stricken with terror, still, we must not falter. Too many saints have paid too much in blood for the preservation of Truth for the people of God to refuse to resist this current assault upon the Word of God.

".... truth is perished, and is cut off from their mouth."
Jeremiah 7:28

CHAPTER 21

The Baskin "Robbing" Jesus of Promise Keepers

"Upon her forehead was a name written, MYSTERY, BABYLON THE GREAT, THE MOTHER OF HARLOTS...
Revelation 17:5

Promise Keepers' dream of a *"more perfect union"* among men regardless of their denominational, sectarian, and apparently, even different religions, is not an original idea. It has been around since before the flood. This "open-door" policy to any group who uses the word "church" or "Christian" to identify themselves, is a telling characteristic of Promise Keepers. Such a policy, without doubt, not only violates numerous biblical principles and demands concerning Christians' participation in ministry and fellowship, but it also puts Promise Keepers in league with every diabolic ecumenical group from the left-wing, liberal National Council of Churches to the thoroughly despotic and demon-ridden membership in the World Council of Churches.

The goal of the ecumenical movement is to accomplish a one-world religious community by consolidating religious groups that are separated, as Promise Keepers' Statement of Faith points out, by *"race, **sectarianism**, age, culture and economics."* Unlearned students of the Scriptures and naíve Christian leaders and laymen may find that statement to be quite biblical-sounding. We have already dealt with the fraudulent "unification" efforts of Promise Keepers and their efforts to sanctify it with their illegitimate use of the Scriptures. Ultimately, such a movement will succeed in bringing almost all "religions" of the world together. Promise Keepers' open-door policy has already "tested their metal," so to speak. They have demonstrated their willingness to tolerate a wide variety of religious preferences and conflicting doctrines. And the Promise Keepers' standard for what is to be "tolerated" under their banner and brand of Christianity stretches the comfort zone of even many on the extreme theological left.

The Promise Keeping Mormons

Promise Keepers rallies feature not only numerous speakers from varied, doctrinal backgrounds but numerous "Jesuses" as well. The organization's tolerance of various strains of theology allows men to choose their own flavor of Christianity or, in fact, in some cases, non-Christianity. Promise Keepers' doctrine-free gospel is so appealing that even leaders in the Church of Jesus Christ of Latter-Day Saints, the Mormons, are comfortable with participating in Promise Keepers. The ecumenical, interdenominational, non-descript, undemanding message and atmosphere orchestrated by Promise Keepers has made Mormon leaders comfortable enough to encourage Mormon church members to fully participate in Promise Keepers.

The *Los Angeles Times* printed Mormon stake President Chip Rawlings' endorsement of Promise Keepers. This attorney said, "The movement's Seven Promises are like something straight out of the men's priesthood manual for the [Mormon] Church". In the same article, Rawlings indicated that several Mormon leaders would be attending the Los Angeles Promise Keepers Conference.[1]

I know of no Bible-believing, Bible-preaching church in

which Mormon leadership, with their perverse Christology and their blasphemous cultic beliefs, would feel so compatible with that church or ministry's teachings that they would leave with an excitement that would provoke them to encourage other Mormons to participate. Yet that is the effect that Promise Keepers has had upon Mormons who preach *"another gospel"*, which is not the Gospel of Jesus Christ.

The *"Mormon Jesus"* was, according to Mormon doctrine, the brother of Satan. This Mormonized Jesus was also the offspring of sexual intercourse between Mary and the Mormon God. No further commentary on this anti-biblical, antichrist cult and its sordid theology is necessary here. However, they, with their cultic, extra-biblical revelations, many of which are in the Book of Mormon, the Mormon Bible, have much in common with the Promise Keepers founder, his pastor, the organization's president and much of the Promise Keepers leadership who are members of Vineyard churches (see also Chapter 16).

Both of these groups believe in and regularly receive "fresh-new" and, might I add, biblically contradictive, "revelations from God." Though certainly one or both may on the surface deny it, both groups also consider the Canon, the Word of God, to be incomplete and in need of additional truths. But the Mormons represent only the "hem of the garment" when it comes to Promise Keepers' choices of religious flavor.

Promise Keepers Try Face Lift

If one is to accept an October 1996 article in Promise Keepers' magazine, *New Man,* entitled *The Culting of Christianity*[2] by Craig Branch as Promise Keepers' position paper on cults, then the Promise Keepers organization is vulnerable to charges of hypocrisy. Perhaps the intense amount of criticism Promise Keepers leadership has been forced to endure from Bible-believing Christians (is there any other kind?) concerned about Promise Keepers open-door policy to scripturally deviant groups stimulated their response in *New Man.*

The article, a well-written treatise, attempts to define a

cult. The contradictive nature of the article lies not in its content, but in its publication in the Promise Keepers magazine, whose own doctrine, as well as their reception of others with equally distorted views, is so compatible with the very characteristics identified in the article.

The characteristics which identify what author Craig Branch calls *Christian* cults point to three primary cultic beliefs or practices.

The first among them is *"elitism—*the belief that our group alone has authority or salvation."[3]

One would think that the use of this first "plumb line" would be seen as the double-edged sword that it is. Could not this be said, and truthfully, of the real Church of the Lord Jesus Christ? Most Christians are convinced that where Scripture speaks of commitment to the Divine birth, Life and the subsequent atoning death, burial and resurrection of Jesus Christ as God's exclusive way to eternal life, that such represents the only way to salvation. Is the Church, therefore, a cult because of the exclusivity in the Bible's absolute claim concerning salvation?

Of course not. They echo the Truth that God's redemption is to be found in none other than the Lord Jesus Christ.

Branch, in writing this article, assumed that those reading it would hold certain "presuppositions" respecting the article. I am certain he was right about the majority who read it. However, when articulating Truth, as Branch is clearly attempting, precision in terms is an absolute necessity.

If, however, one follows the spirit of the Promise Keepers article as opposed to the letter of the article, its intent becomes more clear.

That causes one to ask which popular religious groups fall into the category of *elitism* to which the article refers.

The largest and most popular group in the world, which claims to hold exclusive and absolute authority over the "keys" to heaven and hell, is the Roman Catholic Church. No doubt the cults dealt with by name in the Promise Keepers article also claim to represent the only way to true salvation, and yet, the marks of a cult pointed out by Craig Branch are hardly restricted to those he named, among them, Mormons and Jehovah's Witnesses. Nor, as of this writing, has Promise Keepers publicly demanded the withdrawal of Mormon-affiliated men, or in fact, any man who belongs to one of the groups identified by the article as a cultist, to no longer participate in its rallies, meetings, mentoring sessions or other *fellow-shipping* which the organization promotes for Christian men.

Branch defines the second characteristic of a cult as a group that believes in and practices "extra-biblical revelation—the adding to Scripture, elevating personal revelation to the level of Scripture, or treating a leader's interpretations as infallible."[4]

How can such hypocrisy between what Promise Keepers publishes in *New Man* and their open arms-policy toward Roman Catholics and/or Mormons possibly co-exist? Why does not this blaring inconsistency draw a deafening cry of protest from Biblically astute believers?

Yes, the Roman Catholic Church as well as the Church of Jesus Christ of Latter Day Saints (*LDS*) believes and practices extra-biblical revelations and elevates their authority's pronouncements to be inspired and as infallible as Scripture.

The extent to which Catholics are irrevocably chained to their *confessions of faith* is irrefutable. The following is an example of extra-biblical Catholic demands which they extract from their members. It binds them to accept all that is added to the Word of God by the Catholic church authorities. It reads:

> I admit and embrace most firmly the apostolic and ecclesiastical traditions and all the other constitutions and prescriptions of the Church...Besides I accept without hesitation, and profess all that has been handed down, defined and declared by the Sacred Canons and by the general Councils, especially by the Sacred Council of Trent and by the Vatican General Council, and in a special manner concerning the primacy and infallibility of the Roman Pontiff...This same Catholic Faith, outside of which nobody can be saved, which I now freely profess and to which I truly adhere, the same I promise and swear to maintain and profess...until the last breath of life.[5]

The Catholic Church claims the divine inspiration and infallibility of the Pope's statements. The Catechisms required of Catholics add much to the Word of God and, in themselves, breach God's specific commands. "Ye shall not add unto the word which I command you, neither shall ye diminish [anything] from it, that ye may keep the commandments of the Lord your God which I command you" (Deuteronomy 4:2). "But above all things, my brethren, swear not, neither by heaven, neither by the earth, neither by any other oath; but let your yea be yea, and your nay, nay, lest ye fall into condemnation" (James 5:12).

The well distributed Book of Mormon, and other man-authored works considered by Mormons to be infallible, classify the *LDS* as the cult it truly is, if one applies the article's litmus test for cults.

The third belief or practice that the Promise Keepers magazine identifies as cultic is *"authoritarianism*—the manipulative use of fear, guilt, isolation, or control of information which often results in psychological or spiritual abuse."[6] Since I have dealt with the contemporary church's application and illegitimate use of the word "psychological," I will not repeat the fraudulent concept it represents when Christians attempt to wed such concepts to biblical Truth.

But once again, as we shall later more fully see, this third belief clearly identifies not only a number of other cults that Promise Keepers allows to participate as though they were in Christian fellowship, but also describes the Roman Catholic Church which Promise Keepers boasts is among their most ardent and faithful participants.

There is not time or space to expose the further inconsistency of Promise Keepers *New Man* article as compared to their actions. It should however, be noted that many among Promise Keepers leadership, as well as a vast number of their public supporters and speakers, are deeply involved in practicing and believing one, two or even three of the things which Craig Branch identifies in his article as cultic beliefs and practices. Those persons, beliefs and practices are noted with quotes, documentation and illustrations throughout this book. These are not subjective opinions, but are submitted as the absolute facts so the honest investigator may weigh them and, based upon a biblical analysis, come to Scriptural and God-honoring conclusions concerning the source of Promise Keepers' true root and fruits.

In attempting to unravel the Promise Keepers' theological spaghetti bowl, one can only be reminded of 1 Corinthians 14:33, in which Paul wrote, "For God is not the author of confusion".

While Craig Branch's article, *The Culting of Christianity*, rings true, it should set off alarms when considering its truths against the beliefs and practices of the Promise Keepers organization.

Once again, Promise Keepers have clearly shot themselves in the foot, having damaged their credibility with yet another clandestine attempt to cover their true nature.

"Kissing Papa's Ring"

Promise Keepers founder Bill McCartney left the Roman Catholic Church. However, upon considering the relationship Promise Keepers has with Romanism, we must ask, did Roman Catholicism leave Bill McCartney?

Priests, bishops and even cardinals of the Catholic Church find Promise Keepers an attractive arena for perpetuating Catholic doctrine and fellowship among men. Promise Keepers encourages, welcomes and invites Catholic participation in its ministries. However, Promise Keepers does not encourage Catholics to participate so that they can explain to them how deviant Catholic doctrine is. Rather, Promise Keepers considers the Catholics to be brothers in the faith.

In a letter responding to a Catholic layman promoting Promise Keepers rallies, Cardinal Mahony of California went on record with his admiration and support of Promise Keepers Ministry. He said, "I would be very interested to know how the Archbishop of Los Angeles and I could be of assistance in the fuller promotion of Promise Keepers, and how we might be able to work closely together to encourage the deeper level of discipleship for our Catholic men throughout the

Archdiocese...This seems to be a wonderful way to prepare for the Third Millennial of Christianity which begins in the year 2000."[7]

In April, 1995, the Charismatic Catholic magazine, *New Covenant*, did a cover story on Promise Keepers entitled "Bands of Brothers." Throughout the article the writer expressed hope that men, through the ministry of Promise Keepers, might be brought back into the Catholic system.

Some, especially the more liberal in various denominations, applaud this new and unique confederacy developing between so many *"Christian"* churches and groups. They tell us, as does Promise Keepers' Statement of Faith, that it is time to "break down the walls that have divided the Body of Christ for too long."[8] The surprising endorsements of this highly ecumenical effort are those coming from the more traditionally conservative evangelical leaders, which we will discuss shortly. However, what these people fail to admit and to recognize is that Christianity cannot be lived or propagated without *"the walls"* that result in *"dividing."* The Christian faith is built solely upon the doctrines espoused in the Word of God. That doctrine divides because Truth divides. It is misguided, unscriptural and a diabolically conceived effort that seeks to tear down all denominational barriers. A multitude of denominational walls should and must be kept in place.

The only legitimate appeal to unity is on the basis of the whole counsel of God, not for the sake of unity, mankind, societal issues or political expediency. Otherwise, the resulting hybrid religious system will be as scripturally tainted and theologically poisoned as that of the Catholic Church, from which millions of discerning people, since the Reformation began, have withdrawn. Many of these people of the faith were butchered, tortured, slaughtered, disemboweled and burned at the hands of the Roman Catholic Church as martyrs for the Truth of God.

Promise Keepers and the Catholic Church, as well as those aforementioned Mormons, walk in harmony in their extra-biblical beliefs and *new revelations*. It is difficult to conceive that Promise Keepers can in good conscience live with the apostate pronouncements of the Catholic Church in general and the current Pope in particular. Pope John Paul II recently said, "On this universal level if victory comes, it will be brought by Mary. Christ will conquer through her because He wants the Church's victories now and in the future to be linked to her."[9]

So, Promise Keepers and its advocates now yield to the hellish doctrine of *"Maryology"*, which establishes her as co-redeemer and part of the Godhead. The Doctrine of Immaculate Conception teaches us, at least according to the Catholics, that Mary was also virgin-born and sinless. These are religiously spawned doctrines of devils. Is fellowship with people whose leader in the Vatican declares such demonic theology fulfilling the Biblical admonition to "Be ye not unequally yoked together with unbelievers; for what fellowship hath righteousness with unrighteousness? And what communion hath light with darkness? And what concord hath Christ with Belial? Or what part hath he that believeth with an infidel?" (2 Corinthians 6:14-15).

Additionally, on October 24, 1996, Pope John Paul II sent a statement to the Pontifical Academy of Sciences, which was convened in Rome, Italy at that time. His statement stamped the authority of the Roman Catholic Church on the insidious antichrist teaching of Charles Darwin's "Origin of the Species".

Released on the Catholic World Wide Web page of the Internet on that date, the following article, entitled "Pope Yields on Evolution," written by Bruce Johnson in Rome appeared:

> The Pope said yesterday that Christian faith and theories about evolution were compatible, providing these were spiritual as well as material in nature. The acknowledgment, made for the first time, was contained in a message sent by the Pope to a convention on evolution in Rome. Scientists welcomed it as a major step forward in the Church's project to close the centuries-old gap with the study of science. The Pope's message to the convention at the Pontifical Academy of Science read: 'Today new discoveries lead one to acknowledge that the theory of evolution is more than a hypothesis.' But the Pope said that of the two

interpretations of evolution, only the spiritual one was reconcilable with Christianity. 'If the human body has its origins in pre-existing living matter, the soul was created directly by God'.[10]

It is confusing, to say the least, that this Pope did not address the apparent conflict between evolution and the biblical story of creation. Pope John Paul went on to say that "...fresh knowledge leads to recognition of the theory of evolution as more than just a hypothesis".[11]

Neither the Vatican nor the Pope elaborated on just what this so-called "fresh knowledge" might be.

The truth is, evolution not only contradicts the Bible, but it contradicts every related scientific discovery in the last three decades. Overwhelming scientific evidence proves that evolution is a fraudulent hoax. Research in the fields of genetic engineering, the DNA molecule, and the digital code has now established, without doubt, that evolution is a scientific impossibility. As a result, thousands of non-Christians and multitudes of atheistic scientists are renouncing the theory of evolution.

In fact, Dr. Michael Denton, a scientist and one-time supporter of evolution, recently wrote the book, *Evolution—a Theory in Crisis.*[12] In this book he explains how he was forced to abandon his once-ardent belief in the theory of evolution.

But this Pope is now believed by millions—including even many conservative, Bible-believing Christians and much of the leadership of Promise Keepers—to be a great man of God. It is significant, indeed, that Bible prophecy teaches us that the last world-deceiving religion will not be satanism or witchcraft, but false Christianity.

Promise Keepers' solicitation, reception of, and adulation of Catholicism's many aberrant beliefs proves that they have accepted yet another kind of Christianity that is not *true Christianity* at all.

I recently tuned in to a Christian radio station and heard well-known speaker and author Chuck Colson of Prison Fellowship Ministries, speaking at a Promise Keepers rally in

Charlotte, Nortrh Carolina.[13] I suppose the first shock I received as I listened to Colson's message was when he said, "This is no time to be divided up. When we are marching in front of abortion clinics we are marching as brothers and sisters, whether we are Catholic or Protestant".[14]

I first thought I had misheard. Surely thousands of Christian men would not applaud anyone who suggests that the common denominator of Christian brotherhood is a shared grievance against abortion.

Upon closer examination, one discovers that Colson, who is a major proponent of Promise Keepers, has a religious background that is quite compatible with Promise Keepers' agenda and goals.

It was Chuck Colson and a Catholic priest, Father Richard Neuhaus who came up with the manifesto called, *Evangelicals and Catholics Together: The Christian Mission of the Third Millennium*.[15] These two men worked, according to their report, in secret for two years on this project.

Their plan was to get the world's top evangelical and Catholic leaders to sign up and endorse the manifesto before the momentum of opposition to the manifesto could fully develop.

To date, over 50 well-known evangelical leaders have signed this ungodly document, including Pat Robertson of the 700 Club, Bill Sieple of World Vision, Bill Bright of Campus Crusade for Christ, J.I. Packer of *Christianity Today* and a large number of Roman Catholics including cardinals, archbishops, bishops and priests have also signed on.

Reports in various media outlets have also revealed that well-known Southern Baptists, the chief executive officers of Southern Baptist agencies, the Home Mission Board and the Christian Life Commission, had signed the *Evangelicals and Catholics Together Manifesto (ECTM)*.

These two men, Richard D. Land of the Christian Life Commission and Larry L. Lewis of the Home Mission Board, later asked that their names be removed from the document. It was reported that both had undergone extreme criticism, as well as intense pressure from other Southern Baptists to have their names removed as signees of the *ECTM*.

Both men gave into the pressure to do so only to follow that move with a statement reaffirming their deep heartfelt convictions that the *ECTM* still had their full support. Their statement reads in part:

Statement Regarding
Evangelicals and Catholics Together
by
Richard D. Land, Executive Director, Christian Life Commission
Larry L. Lewis, President, Home Mission Board
April 6, 1995

We continue to believe in efforts which consolidate the influence of Evangelicals and Catholics in addressing critical moral issues. We believe the document *Evangelicals and Catholics Together (ECT)* signifies a new era of cooperation...

...However, we have concluded that a significant number of Southern Baptists have been offended by the misperception that our respective agencies have endorsed the document. No matter how many times we explain that we signed *ECT* as individuals, not on behalf of our agencies or Southern Baptists, many do not understand...

...we have decided that as chief executive officers of Southern Baptist agencies, we should remove our signatures from *Evangelicals and Catholics Together*...

...In so doing, we are not personally rejecting the intent of the document, nor are we agreeing with unjust criticism of it.[16]

The penetrating truth that men who so miscomprehend the mission and call of the Church and are so ready to support clear violations of biblical demands are at the helm of one of history's greatest denominational defenders of the Faith, the Southern Baptist Convention (SBC), speaks clearly concerning the rapid deterioration of institutional pursuit to maintain the Scriptural integrity within their jurisdiction.

In years past the SBC, its pastors, its local churches and its governing entities would have never tolerated that kind of compromising, double-speak and spiritually contaminated insolence at the helm of their denomination's major agencies.

The deceptive approach of this clever instrument calling for unity avoids the use of the word "protestant," substituting for it the word "evangelical".

In his writings, Colson is known for his criticism of terms such as "born again", saying that it is offensive to Catholics such as his wife.

The puzzling thing concerning the manifesto by Colson and Neuhaus is its insistence that "evangelicals" should never seek to convert Catholics. It is a fervent call for those who in the past have witnessed to Catholics to now repent of this "sin". The manifesto reads, "We confess our sins against the unity that Christ intends". The manifesto insists that "There are different ways of being a Christian". Of course, true Christians see that for the falsehood it is.

However, as one understands Colson's positioning on such critical issues, it is easy to see how he is so very compatible with Promise Keepers. His participation in and vigorous support of Promise Keepers underscores once again the organization's deep commitment to the unification of the world's Christian religions regardless of their doctrines. Colson freely admitted to the Promise Keepers' rally in Charlotte, NC, that he was the recipient of the renowned Templeton Award for the "Prize for Progress in Religion".

The ties of financial guru John Templeton to New Age efforts and ideology are no secret. His appearance at the Charlotte Promise Keepers rally gave Colson the opportunity to again promote the shotgun wedding between Protestant Christianity and Catholics by the use of their shared moral concerns, particularly that of abortion.

As horrid as abortion is, and as incensed as many Americans are, correct convictions on vital issues do not Christians make. Nor do such shared convictions provide sufficient reason to consolidate religious systems at variance with biblical Truth.

The efforts, lectures and books of Chuck Colson, however, clearly and repeatedly call for this new unity and tolerance among all groups who claim to stand under the banner of Christendom.

As I was grieving over Colson's indiscreet and careless application of the term Christian, I then heard him further clarify his liberal definition of what it takes to become a real Christian. As he praised the credibility of Catholicism's claim to Christianity, he mentioned the famous Mother Teresa. My thoughts flashed back to Dr. John MacArthur's story of how he had met Mother Teresa while he toured India. He asked her if she was born again. She replied, "I have no idea what you are talking about. I do not know what you mean".[17]

My attention was then brought back to the Promise Keepers radio broadcast as Colson said, "Some have said Mother Teresa is not [a Christian]. But I was at the National Prayer Breakfast two years ago when that 90-pound Albanian nun walked up to the platform and turned, didn't look to either side, in a crowd of 3,000 people, with the President of the United States on one side and the Vice President on the other and she said, 'Abortion is the greatest destroyer of peace in the World' and I watched the President squirm and I want to tell you, that woman was my sister when she did that".[18]

Then thousands of men at the rally gave a standing ovation to Colson's assertion, that because Mother Teresa is against abortion and bold enough to say it to the President of the United States, she is, therefore, a "sister in Christ".

This stunned me and it should shock true Christians who understand that one becomes a "brother or sister in Christ" through the atoning grace of God, by faith in the shed blood of the Lord Jesus Christ and a full surrender to Him as the resurrected Son of the Living God. What is going on in the hearts and minds of Promise Keepers' leadership and those who endorse this organization?

A quiet reminder of other *whorish* beliefs of the Catholic system may serve to remind all of us of the damnable apostasies promoted by the Vatican and its Papacy.

Does Promise Keepers' leadership have no knowledge of such matters? Are they simply uninformed respecting the deep and severe anti-Bible, anti-Christian dogma and doctrine of their Catholic partners in **promise 3** or is it that they are simply in compliance or in agreement with the Vatican's theology?

Perhaps Promise Keepers' leaders just consider Catholicism's belief system irrelevant to their true and stated goal of "breaking down the walls" and forming their pseudo-Christian alliances. Whatever the reasons for Promise Keepers' casual acquiescence to such "doctrines of devils" those will not support the ignoring of such blatant refutations of the clear Gospel of the Lord Jesus Christ and of the Word of God.

Transubstantiation

No belief in all Catholicism's multitude of heresies more clearly distinguishes the Roman Catholic Church from evangelical Christendom than that which the Catholics refer to as the sacrifice of the Mass. Most are aware of the flamboyant boast that the Catholic priest and he alone is able to cause the elements of the Lord's Table, the bread and the wine, to transubstantiate into the literal Body and Blood of Jesus Christ so that when received as spiritual food it results in the entering of Jesus into the Catholic. Vatican II put it this way, "...in the Eucharist we become partakers of the Body and Blood of God's only Son...[and] the partaking of the Body and Blood of Christ has no less an effect than to change us into what we have received."[19]

Of course, this is a fraudulent and deceptive teaching. The partaking of the Lord's Table was never intended to play a part in the redemptive process. It is yet another "work" of the flesh invented by Catholic leaders to intimidate Catholics into resisting the temptation, during the Reformation, to leave the Catholic Church. It is an intricate part of Catholic teaching that any and all who are not members of the Catholic Church, non-Catholic Promise Keepers included, are damned to hell.

The Apostle Paul told the Corinthians when instructing

them of the Lord's Supper that Jesus had commanded "Do this in remembrance of me...for as often as ye eat this bread and drink this cup ye do show [proclaim] the Lord's death till He comes" (1 Corinthians 1:24-25). Christians cannot and should not attempt to duplicate the finished work of Christ on the cross as do the Catholics each time they perform the Eucharist. We are told to *"remember"* at what price our salvation was purchased as we partake of this precious and intimate memorial meal that we call the Lord's Supper.

The Catholic heretical teaching of transubstantiation was fabricated in 1215 AD by the Pope in Rome and ever since, Catholics, under the tyranny of such deviate Popes, were forced to believe this fantasy and others just as bizarre or face excommunication from the Catholic Church. Again, being shut out of the Catholic Church, according to the Vatican's doctrine, guarantees eternal damnation.

Promise Keepers has no desire to take any stand whatsoever against the occultic practices and beliefs of the Roman Catholic Church and, in fact, calls those in Catholicism *"brothers."* For many involved in Promise Keepers or any others condoning Catholic doctrine which is not the Gospel of Jesus Christ, it may well be that they are "brothers" but certainly not "brothers" in the Christian faith. No one can deny the exclusive, biblical doctrine of salvation as God's only way to eternal life and still lay legitimate claim to being part of the household of faith. Neither Catholic priests nor the Catholic Church teach that men are exclusively born again by grace through faith. Not one of the Reformers, Luther, Calvin or Wycliffe supported the Catholic plan of salvation. In fact, throughout history, millions were literally butchered and/or burned by the Popes of Rome for rejecting transubstantiation's power to save.

Brave Reformers such as John Wycliffe aggressively defended the Truths of God against the unrelenting and foolish papal edicts and revelations. In 1381, Wycliffe published "his twelve propositions" that specifically attacked transubstantiation as "unscriptural and offensive to the senses." He was tried for heresy before his peers at Oxford and boldly proclaimed the biblical argument against the doctrine of transubstantiation. His eloquent defense silenced his prosecutors and laid the groundwork for other great men to take up the cause and defend the faith against the Catholic perversion of the Gospel. When threatened by his prosecutors with death by immolation, Wycliffe stood up in the courtroom and proclaimed, "Should I live to be silent? No, let the blow fall, I am ready."

Wycliffe lived long enough to translate the Word of God into the English language and for the first time, the Scriptures were put to the hands of common people. The Catholic leadership vehemently resisted putting the Word of God into the hands of their pliant church members. Those members had become used to believing that the church and the Pope represented the voice of God. They accepted the papacy's dogma and rule that the common people do not need the Bible because "they have us." And, indeed, the Catholic Church still has millions of people in bondage to a religious system that wholly guarantees *eternal paradise* for the "faithful" and that turning away from the Catholic system will result only in their *eternal damnation*. Wycliffe was only one among millions to defy Catholic heresies, and most of those who dared to do so paid with their very lives.

In considering the cost Wycliffe and others paid to defy the godless, antichrist Catholic Church, one wonders how Promise Keepers could possibly condone and commend such a system. But they do.

As a result of Dave Hunt's scholarly work, *A Woman Rides the Beast*, thousands of Catholics have reportedly received Christ and Protestants now have a clearer understanding of the horrible, occultic beliefs of the Roman Catholic Church. In his book, Hunt exposes the atrocities of transubstantiation and its blasphemous teaching. He writes:

> Let us consider only one further reason why transubstantiation is a hoax. The psalmist declared (and Peter quoted this prophecy in his Pentecost sermon, as did Paul later): 'Thou wilt not...suffer thine Holy One to see corruption' (Psalm 16:10; cf. Acts 2:27; 13:35). Christ's body did not decay in the grave. Yet the consecrated and transubstantiated host reserved for administering to the sick or displayed for adoration breeds worms and mold if it isn't disposed of

soon enough. If it were really Christ's body, it could not corrupt.

Tragically, the Mass becomes a cause of condemnation for Catholics, who 'are obliged under penalty of serious [mortal] sin to hear Mass on Sundays and holy days...'[20] According to a recent poll, only 33 percent of American Catholics attend Mass 'on a given Sunday'[21] and far less do so every Sunday as required. Only 12 percent of the Catholics in France (which is 90 percent Catholic) can be found in Mass on any Sunday. This works out to a very high percentage of Catholics who are habitually in mortal sin and thus deprived of 'sanctifying grace' and 'the right to heaven.'[22]

So important is this transubstantiation dogma to Rome that multitudes who could not accept it were burned at the stake. It was for this reason that most of the 288 English martyrs were consigned to the flames during the five-year reign of Bloody Queen Mary, who brought Catholicism back into England after a brief time of tenuous freedom from the papal tyranny.

Many a sincere and devout Roman Catholic desired to save England for beloved Mother Church and rejoiced when the Reformation was turned back. Today it is leading evangelicals who are only too happy to undo the Reformation and thereby deny Christ and His gospel. And in the process, they mock those who did not count their lives dear in order to preserve that gospel for us.[23]

Dave Hunt is right. He is especially on target in describing those in Promise Keepers' leadership when he writes of those "who are only too happy to undo the Reformation and thereby deny Christ and His gospel."

Promise Keepers' open endorsement of the Catholic Church is disgraceful, unchristian and proves once again their full-fledged, unapologetic willingness to defy the Scriptures while giving "lip service" to their commitment to it. No one can accept Catholic doctrine as legitimate and simultaneously confess that he believes the Bible as God's Word. These are diametrically opposed belief systems. Catholicism is but one of the false belief systems recognized by Promise Keepers as legitimate.

Obviously, Promise Keepers does not care what men believe about salvation or their position on the veracity of the Word of God. Otherwise, they could not receive into fellowship the cult of Mormonism, the false religion of Catholicism or the vast array of other perverse belief systems.

And how does Promise Keepers deal with those involved in sodomy, the sinful lifestyle that a humanistic society has been convinced to call homosexuality? God calls homosexuality an *"unseemly, abominable"* and blasphemous activity and describes it as sodomy.

Homo-Bro's in the Promise Keepers Family

There are so many scriptural discrepancies in Promise Keepers' doctrinal positions and their fundamental philosophy of ministry that any discerning and intellectually honest believer who may have made a hasty decision to participate has more than ample reason to reconsider their involvement in this anti-Christian organization. However, one of the most shocking beliefs held by Promise Keepers is their policy and attitude toward those living the perverse life of a homosexual. The Promise Keepers position is their following response to the inquiries of a concerned pastor:

> As to homosexuality, Promise Keepers shares the same historic and biblical stance taken by Evangelicals and Catholics, that sex is a good gift from God—to be enjoyed in the context of heterosexual marriage. Promise Keepers also recognizes that homosexuality is a complex and potentially polarizing issue. There is a great debate surrounding its environmental and genetic origins, yet as an organization, we believe that homosexuals are men who need the support, encouragement and healing we are offering

to all men. While we have clear convictions regarding the issue of homosexuality, we are sensitive to and have compassion for the men who are struggling with these issues. We, therefore, support their being included and welcomed in all events.[24]

This statement is the kind of doublespeak that one might expect from some federal bureaucracy intent upon disguising the true nature of their explanation. Promise Keepers state, "...that they have clear convictions" on the issue of homosexuality, but this gobbledygook is anything but a well-articulated, clearly defined "conviction".

Notice that Promise Keepers puts a tolerant and positive spin on their position statement after they **almost** call sodomy sin before reverting to their usual double-speaking, "avoid-a-conflict", politically correct posture. While assuring the public that Promise Keepers shares the stance of Evangelicals and Catholics "that sex is a good gift from God to be enjoyed in heterosexual marriage," the organization then reverses their tact to echo a humanistic anti-biblical psychoanalysis of the causes of homosexual behavior. This *"fence-straddling"* compromises yet another vital issue confronting the contemporary church. Truthfully, there is no basis for any debate on the morality of homosexuality. The Scriptures leave no question about the fact that homosexuality is considered by God to be a repulsive, perverted and unnatural act (see also Leviticus 20:13, Deuteronomy 23:17, Romans 1:27 and 1 Corinthians 6:9).

Promise Keepers' answer should stun Christians who have even slight biblical insights on this issue. Though the Bible is full of warnings to homosexuals and overflowing with condemnation of this most deviant lifestyle, Promise Keepers' statement does not cite one Scripture, of which there are many, establishing the fact that homosexuality is a grievous sinful abominable activity. Promise Keepers, rather, states that they *"recognize homosexuality is a complex and potentially polarizing issue."* I find this statement deeply disturbing. Again, God's Word is absolute. It is clear. This horrendous sin against nature, humanity and God is vile. The question of whether or not those who practice this sin should be received as *"Christian brothers"* is not an issue open for debate. The Bible condemns the homosexual lifestyle as blatant, willful sin.

In Romans 1, the Apostle Paul goes to great length to establish the previous scripturally stated heart and mind of God on this matter. He walks us through the moral and spiritual scenario of man's sordid sinful and moral declination. At the very bottom of the downward, spiraling cycle that men take in their rebellion against God is the homosexual lifestyle.

In his dynamic declaration to Rome, Paul writes, "Wherefore, God also gave them up to uncleanness through the lusts of their own hearts, to dishonor their own bodies between themselves, who [exchanged] the truth of God for a lie, and worshipped and served the creature more than the Creator, who is blessed forever. Amen" (Romans 1:24-25).

Any casual study of this passage establishes with certainty that the ultimate physical manifestation of man's revolution against God is the sexual perverting of God's created order. Paul says in Romans 1:26-28, "For this cause God gave them up unto vile affections; for even their women did [exchange] the natural use for that which is against nature; and likewise also the men, leaving the natural use of the woman, burned in their lust one toward another, men with men, working that which is unseemly, and receiving in themselves that recompense of their error which was [fitting]. And even as they did not like to retain God in their knowledge, God gave them over to a reprobate mind, to do those things which are not [seemly]."

Contemplating the activities of those involved in this blasphemous sin grieves the spirit and nauseates and repulses the senses of natural men and women. I speak of "natural" here in the same way Paul uses it in Romans Chapter 1 and later in 1 Corinthians Chapter 6 as he identifies the *"unregenerate"* man as "natural" man. Hence, even men who have not been born of the Spirit and remain in a spiritually lost condition by nature understand that homosexuality is a perverse, unnatural act. The only exceptions to this natural revulsion to such horrible perversity are those involved in homosexuality. The Bible teaches us that with their consciences seared against sensing the Holy Spirit's conviction, these people have justified their abominable behavior.

The great Apostle said there comes a moment in time when God *"gives up"* or quits dealing with the hearts of those who have predetermined to live as homosexuals while attempting to justify their sin. These poor individuals arrive at such a state of blasphemous deviance that they become reprobate, meaning that the Spirit of the living God no longer convicts or calls them to repentance. Rather, the Spirit will "give them over" to the filthy activity they so love. God simply calls homosexuality SIN. In spite of Promise Keepers' allusion to the debate on homosexuality being caused by environmental or genetic origins, the homosexual is fully, personally responsible for his actions, as is every sinner. The homosexual cannot escape the absolute and clear Truths of God on this matter; neither can Promise Keepers, despite their attempt to do so with their watered-down subjective posturing.

The homosexual, contrary to Promise Keepers' statement, cannot escape the guilt of his actions any more than Promise Keepers can justify their openness in allowing homosexuals to be included and received into the fellowship by simply saying, "this is a complex issue." Promise Keepers' position statement on homosexuality is a blatant denial of the revelation of the Word of God. Regardless of Promise Keepers' claimed difficulty in understanding the issue, there is nothing at all complex about homosexuality. It is SIN, period!

Promise Keepers' statement that this is a *"potentially polarizing issue"* surrounded by *"great debate"* about the *"environmental and genetic origins"* of homosexuality is not only scientifically unsubstantiated, it is as grievous to the Holy Spirit as is the homosexual act itself. Incidentally, every major statement that God's Word specifically addresses concerning man's sin—whether it is homosexuality, adultery, lying, cheating, stealing and more—is a *"polarizing issue"* to those who refuse to accept God's appraisal of their rebellious nature. Promise Keepers obviously fears that the Truth may intimidate and *"polarize"* a morally bankrupt society if they say anything negative about sin. Such fear of men who have no concept of the liberating nature of God's Word is common among those with an unregenerate mind and heart. Promise Keepers observes that to tell the Truth will *"polarize"*, but Jesus Christ said, "The Truth shall make you free" (John 8:32).

Promise Keepers leadership's suggestion that there is credibility to the ridiculous ongoing secular humanist debate that homosexuality is perhaps rooted in *"genetic"* or *"environmental origins"* is yet another philosophical fist doubled up and thrust in the face of a Holy God and a blatant denial of His Word. The cause and effects of homosexuality are addressed throughout the Scriptures. Homosexuality is not caused by anything other than the demon-energized rebellious nature of man who is defying his Creator with such actions. Every medical study attempting to link homosexuality with genetic malformation or dysfunctional environments has failed to establish even one legitimate, documented, scientifically-proven connection between those factors and homosexual behavior because no such thing exists except in the more fully scripturally developed truth that all sin, homosexuality included, is a result of our inherent genetic heritage, generationally passed down from the bloodline of Adam. Because of the Genesis-recorded fall, each of us comes from a dysfunctional heritage. That, however, exonerates no one from being personally responsible for his or her individual rebellion against God.

The Bible teaches that every man and woman is born with the natural tendency to sin. The fall of Adam, again, did genetically pass on the inherent desire to rebel against God. However, the Bible also teaches that every sinner, though he has an innate potential to sin any kind of sin imaginable, is ultimately, personally responsible for his sin. God, in His grace, has given man a will with which he can choose. Man can opt to persist in rebellion or he can choose to repent. Persistence in rebellion insures that the individual will become increasingly, overtly defiant of God's will, and progressively more committed to that rebellion and more calloused in sensing the call of God's Spirit to repent.

Promise Keepers speaks the deceptive propaganda of a humanistic, antichrist system because of their fear of making distinctions. But God's Word makes distinctions that are absolute and clear on the issue of homosexuality. Clearly, Scripture states that no man who lives in this manner can be a Christian. Note Paul's words in 1 Corinthians 6:9-10: "Do you not know that the wicked will not inherit the kingdom of God? Do not be deceived: Neither the sexually immoral nor idolaters nor adulterers nor male prostitutes nor homosexual offenders nor thieves nor the greedy nor drunkards nor slanderers nor swindlers will inherit the kingdom of God".[25] He readily states that homosexuals, the effeminate and abusers of themselves with mankind will not enter heaven. But some homosexuals were being saved as they repented of such horrendous lifestyles and this gave reason to rejoice, as Paul observes in 1 Corinthians 6:11: "And such were some of you; but ye are washed, but ye are sanctified, but ye are justified in the name of the Lord Jesus, and by the Spirit of our God." Paul said to the sinners of these various groups who **were** living in defiance toward God that some had repented, turned from their sin, been forgiven and were now set apart for God to use.

Promise Keepers states that homosexual men need *"the same support, encouragement and healing"* that the organization makes available to all men. One need only look at the facts about what Promise Keepers "makes available to all" in order to determine what they offer to homosexuals. Promise Keepers offers all men a religious belief system that allows any and all participants to believe and conduct themselves in any way that appeases their natural drives and inclinations without any accountability to the scriptural demands of the Christian lifestyle. What unholy, neo-paganistic religious rebel would not feel comfortable in such a compromised atmosphere that "sanctifies" his godless lifestyle by refusing to confront the sin and sinners? Promise Keepers supports and encourages homosexuals to participate and welcomes them to their events, while at the same time offering them a sanctuary, an atmosphere of acceptance and *tolerance* among those who accept the homosexual's flavor of Jesus. This should so shock astute Christian Bible students that they should overwhelm Promise Keepers with deafening cries of protest.

Homosexual men do not need what Christian men need.

Christian men *have* Christ; homosexual men *need* Christ. Regardless of how loud the homosexuals scream it or how often they repeat it, God's Word says there will be no sexual deviates in heaven unless they have repented of that deviance, ceased living that lifestyle, turned in repentance to the Cross and been changed by the power of a living relationship with Jesus Christ. These people must turn completely from their homosexuality if they are to be truly born again. Homosexuals should feel polarized and separated from fellowship of the church and the fellowship of the justified until they repent of their blasphemous lifestyle and turn to Christ. The church is not a collection of holier-than-thou judgmental Christians; rather, it is a group of repentant sinners who live in a spiritually growing posture and fellowship with others who accept the Word of God and its appraisal of their condition and need.

The non-confrontational relationship that Promise Keepers maintains with homosexuals indicates its spiritually licentious nature and the compromised reasoning that they continue to demonstrate. Every voice of support from pastors and Christian laymen for Promise Keepers Ministry, even of those who are perhaps unaware of Promise Keepers' policies, gives credence to another new and perverse gospel with a freshly concocted Jesus.

The Promise Keepers' joint project with Robert Hicks, *The Masculine Journey, The Six Stages of Manhood* a book that was originally heavily distributed at Promise Keepers rallies, calls our Lord and Savior a *"phallic kind of guy."*[26] Hicks shares with readers that Jesus Christ was tempted with homosexuality himself.[27] A critique of such a sordid, unholy passage would create another book. We have already dealt with the appeal of sin and temptation to Christ in chapter 16. The impeccability of Christ made Him impervious to temptations of any kind, let alone this heinous sin of participating in a homosexual act. I pray it is as repulsive to you as it is to me to even consider this as a possibility of the Son of the Living God. Hicks' reference to the blasphemous movie, *The Last Temptation of Christ,* which was written and produced to be an open, unapologetic assault on Christianity, provides a clear understanding of why his thinking about Jesus and sex is so deviant. Such a low view and demeaning perversion of the deity and holiness of our sinless Lord and Savior, Jesus Christ is disgusting. Of the movie, *The Last Temptation of Christ,* which portrays a Jesus with a "phallic focus" and wandering eye, Hicks says, "I have found this insight to be very helpful for gay men struggling with their sexuality."[28]

To Mr. Hicks I would say two things. First, the use of the word *"gay"* is a misnomer. I have never met a *"gay"* homosexual. These people are not happy. Theirs is a world of dark bondage inundated with inordinately high rates of drug addiction and alcoholism. The suicide rate among homosexual men as a group is appalling when compared to the suicide rate among the general population. Most homosexuals are infected with four or five venereal diseases simultaneously. They have been called by Dr. Paul Cameron *"Typhoid Marys"* because of the numerous diseases that the average homosexual carries from one sexual partner to the next,[29] to say nothing at all about the worldwide AIDS plague which primarily is a homosexual disease in North America. Second, I would say to Mr. Hicks that homosexuals would not have to *"struggle,"* if they would cease their rebellious and perverted lifestyle, repent and find deliverance through the power of an indwelling Holy Spirit as they are born again.

In other parts of the world, the HIV AIDS-causing virus is being spread more widely via heterosexual sex. It is a spiritual constant that when perversion among a minority is tolerated and condoned by the majority, soon the majority will begin to suffer the consequences that come upon the perverse minority.

Why does not this "Christian" ministry, Promise Keepers, simply tell homosexuals the Truth contained in the Word of God? Do they hide the Truth because they consider it to be intolerant, insensitive, discriminating and, according to their statement, *"potentially polarizing"*? The desire of God's heart is that all believers become "polarized," set apart and divided from sinful and destructive lifestyles.

It should stagger the imagination of Christians that Promise Keepers would take such an anti-biblical, humanistic and heartbreaking attitude toward the deceived and spiritually bound people in the homosexual community. To ignore their sin, their plight and their true spiritual condition under the guise of *"loving concern"* anything but demonstrates the love of God.

Sensitivity Course Softens Promise Keepers Men

The list of other groups, sects, cults and lifestyles that Promise Keepers is so tolerant of and open to could fill several more books. One wonders how, while professing to be a Christian ministry, Promise Keepers leadership can overlook so many of their participants' false doctrines of salvation, the antichrist spirit of the cults, and the repulsive lifestyles of the many and various groups they entertain and openly receive as full brothers in Christ. How can this organization claim to be a Christian ministry while maintaining an open-door policy to these vile and wicked groups?

The psychology-based mentoring sessions that Promise Keepers participants attend promotes the central idea that as one "Promise Keeper" develops his relationship with another "Promise Keeper", he should focus on being very "sensitive", especially as "difficult" situations arise. Promise Keepers insist that no one be "judgmental" of the other's doctrine, lifestyle or concepts.

Writing on the topic of *"one anothering,"* Geoff Gorush, co-authoring the Promise Keepers' manual called *"Brothers Calling Men Into Vital Relationship"*, says, "The first job of the men's small group is to learn complete acceptance; no judgment, no 'I told you so' or 'You should have known better.' No hidden agendas! I'm not out to change you and you're not out to change me."[30] Upon reading such mushy-gushy psycho-babble, one wonders why in the world, if men were not desirous for change, they would join Promise Keepers.

God has ordained the local church as a place where Christians are to minister, rebuke, exhort, admonish and correct one another to stimulate spiritual growth. It is impossible to participate in true ministry if those involved in that ministry refuse to release or turn from their sinful lifestyles and reject the fundamental elementary Truth of God's Word. The Scripture tells us in Luke 17:3, "Take heed to yourselves. If thy brother trespass against thee, rebuke him; and if he repent, forgive him." God's Word demands we rebuke, exhort, admonish and reprove "brothers" in Christ. Promise Keepers, on the other hand, flatly rejects God's way as harsh, confrontational and judgmental. The bottom line is that Promise Keepers welcomes all who *say* they are followers of Jesus Christ, regardless of what they truly believe. They desire to avoid conflict, controversy or confrontation.

Nobody enjoys conflict or confrontation, but when those who profess to know Christ believe, preach and practice the doctrines, teachings and lifestyles that contradict the Word of God, then it is incumbent upon true Christians to address that straightforwardly. Jesus, in defining the true nature of God's love, said, "As many as I love I rebuke and chasten; be zealous therefore and repent" (Revelation 3:19).

In the final scriptural analysis, little about Promise Keepers Ministry can be considered true Orthodox Christianity other than its liberal use of the name of Christ and its contextually divorced and illegitimate, occasional use of the Scripture in the feeble effort to support the humanistic, neo-pagan, psychology-based fraternal organization. Little wonder they have a different-flavored *"Jesus"* for each and every kind of man who desires to become, what Promise Keepers calls, a man of "integrity" who keeps his promises, a "real man". But is the finished product at the end of Promise Keepers' process a "real man"? Promise Keepers' process does produce a man, but he is a conviction-neutered, spiritually impotent facsimile of a real man. Promise Keepers produces feminized men with misplaced priorities, ill-spent energies, and a defused focus on God's true call upon him because of a Promise Keepers-induced, double-minded approach to spiritual growth.

How will men ever learn to become what God so desires that they become? What can man do to begin the process of becoming God's ideal, society's strength and a woman's dream come true?

My answer is no more than an echo of the heart of God. In order to be a rock-solid real man, he must run to and be broken by The Solid Rock.

If men would but bend to obey the Word of God and pour their all into doing as the Shepherd commands, the seductive call of man-made, flesh-oriented short cuts to becoming a fully developing and life-filled man would lose its illegitimate appeal.

Once man touches the Glory he can never again be satisfied with anything less than all of **HIM** living through all of him, the man.

"I have made you an assayer and a tester among my people, that you may know and assay their way.

Jeremiah 6:27

CHAPTER 22

The Piggy Backing Promise Keepers

"Stand by the way and see and ask for the ancient paths where the good way is and walk in it and you shall find rest for your souls."

Jeremiah 6:16

For twenty-one chapters we have examined some of the discrepancies in doctrine and the scriptural deficiencies of the Promise Keepers. This examination should provoke the reader to seriously question what is behind the promises of the Promise Keepers. Our investigation of the organization, its leadership's doctrinal beliefs and its philosophy of ministry have led to some conclusions based not upon a subjective interpretation of the facts but rather upon the clear, absolute and irrevocable Truths in the unchanging Word of God. By now, readers should be aware of the hidden agenda and the spiritual danger lurking beneath the surface of the noble-sounding propaganda of Promise Keepers.

Whether the principals involved in such organizations as Promise Keepers are aware of it or not, they are participants in a spiritual war being waged against the Truth of God. In every spiritual and cultural battle, the first target assaulted is always the *truth*. However, *truth,* in and of itself, has many reliable allies; trust, confidence, boldness, integrity, faith, security and stability are unflinchingly loyal to her. The spiritual and cultural war in our nation is proving that when truth is disposed of, her allies leave with her.

Conversely, falsehood, which is the result of compromising truth, is allied with doubt, pseudo-tolerance, weakness and a need for consensus. When non-truth replaces truth, the friends of falsehood will always be present. Such is the case with Promise Keepers' pretentious efforts to fill a role to which it has not been called.

The perception of the Church's failure on the part of society in no way justifies Promise Keepers' ignoble attempt to assume the bridal gown that exclusively belongs to the Bride of Christ. The organization's doctrinal philosophy is so indistinct and ill-defined simply because it raises an illegitimate standard that can be accomplished without supernatural ability and it has no basis in God's absolute Truth.

Augustine said, "When regard for truth has been broken down, or even slightly weakened, all things will remain doubtful".

Promise Keepers is assuming a mission and commission to which they have no legitimate biblical authority or right. This mission and commission have clearly been placed by God upon the Church. Promise Keepers has also presumed to redefine God's call and ministry upon Christian men.

The organization's attractive but illicit and seductive agenda for American Christendom, if accomplished, diminishes the power of the local church's influence upon our society. This ministry, as many before it, is a parasite, piggy-backing and building upon the foundation of the established Body of Christ and drawing men and resources away from the true Church. Promise Keepers' noble-sounding but feeble efforts to appear supportive of the local church and local pastors are not, in reality, what Promise Keepers' program and practice ultimately accomplishes. The condescending *"recognition"* of local churches and pastors by Promise Keepers, while on the surface a kind gesture, fails to honestly acknowledge or promote the absolute all-consuming focus and priority that men should place upon their local church. For those who are serious about becoming true men of God, God has given no way other than through His Church to accomplish this goal. Promise Keepers, in spite of their claims, give the impression that their ministry should rate a higher priority to Christian men than their local church.

Not only is Promise Keepers parasitical in nature, *"sucking"* men's resources and energies away from their local churches, but it is a parasite that is infectious.

The world's largest White Tail deer population inhabits the state of Texas. On many occasions, tens of thousands of these deer as well as other wildlife and livestock have been destroyed by a disease spread by another parasite, a tick which carries *"deer tick fever."* The tick usually remains hidden and it does not irritate the host, thus its presence is irrelevant to that host. But as it buries its powerful straw-like head just beneath the skin and begins withdrawing blood, it transmits the virus of this horrendous disease into its victim's bloodstream. Many outdoorsmen, hikers and hunters take precautions to protect themselves against this innocent-looking but dangerous little creature.

The greatest danger to the Church from ministries such as Promise Keepers is not only the distraction and diversion of its men and resources, but the infectious spiritually-darkened, anti-biblical distorted doctrines and beliefs that Promise Keepers "carries." Men, often subliminally at first, are softened up with scriptural-sounding phraseology, the hyped-up, benign-appearing, fun-filled Promise Keepers rallies and the impressive orations of high-profile popular Christian speakers.

The men who participate in Promise Keepers are slowly but thoroughly convinced and converted to a new "openness" that opens their minds and hearts to the heretical and apostate beliefs and practices that are systemic to Promise Keepers' leadership and mother church, the Vineyard movement. Spiritual cross-contamination is unavoidable. Thousands of the men who attend Promise Keepers functions who hail from solid Bible-believing, Bible-preaching churches, return to those home churches as "carriers" who, without immediate spiritual antidotes, will eventually develop the full-blown manifestation of doctrinal delusions and misplaced priorities. Such men who were either involved in or had the potential to be involved in the life-flow of their local church, where God's plan calls them to focus their full attention, are being diverted from their God-assigned ministries. They are unwittingly being infected by Promise Keepers' poisonous influence. In time, without correction, these men who have been exposed to and contaminated by the Promise Keepers' spiritually diseased doctrine will become "carriers" themselves.

Promise Keepers represents a new version of "replacement theology." Theirs is an attempted unbiblical "takeover" of the God-ordained and God-appointed assignments of the church based upon a popular but erroneous concept that because of the worldwide moral decline, spiritual darkness and societal spiritual decay, the Church has failed to fulfill its God-given mission. This perceived failure precipitates every new but illegitimate effort born in the human heart to fix what is not broken by humanity's search for a way to improve upon God's way and will. The spiritual darkness that provokes men to attempt to help God's reputation which pervades religious societies is a darkness that was seen and foretold by every Old Testament and New Testament prophet. These prophets shared the vision of what the dominant characteristics of the "last days" were to be. The declining moral and spiritual condition that we are witnessing is part and parcel of the prophetic scenario that God has revealed in His Word. One of the major signs that the prophetic events of the "final days" are upon us is the growing effort to consolidate beliefs systems and doctrines into a one-world, unified religious expression. God has not been taken by surprise or out-maneuvered by Satan's *"sleight of hand."* God, through His Word's prophetic statements and by the Spirit of discernment placed within His people, has prepared His Church to recognize and to resist the seductive, deceiving and lying spirits calling for their alliance and allegiance to an unholy unity.

The true Church, represented by only a minority of the total population of all churches, has not and will not fail to fulfill its mission. God will accomplish that which He has begun not only in the life of each of His individual children, but in the life of the Church as well. It was written to believers at Philippi, "He who hath begun a good work in you will perform it until the day of Jesus Christ" (Philippians 1:6).

The Apostle Paul, reinforcing the supernatural gravitation to spiritual maturity innate within our salvation and our participation in the local church, wrote to Ephesus that the purpose of the believer's focused commitment to his local church is for "the perfecting of the saints for the work of the ministry for the edifying of the body of Christ" (Ephesians 4:12).

The *"replacement theology"* of Promise Keepers promotes their attempts to steal the spiritual authority assigned exclusively to the church. It is a bastardly imposition of the most arrogant sort when combined with their openness to fallacious beliefs and cults, and their redefining of manhood, ministry and godliness. Promise Keepers, if for no other reason than that, loses any claim to Christian legitimacy.

So, if Promise Keepers' approach to developing "real men" is false, what is *God's plan* for Christian men to become spiritually mature so that they are able and willing to accept their places of responsibility in the church, society and the home?

I Thought You Would Never Ask

When facing critical needs, the tendency innate within most is to first exhaust all of our strength, plans and personal resources. Only at the point of despair, after we have depleted all of our human resources, do we discover how to believe God and how to experience His moment-by-moment presence in our life.

The popular and contemporary *"seeking"* for physical manifestations as spiritual evidence that God is moving is the result of spiritual shallowness and a preoccupation with the sensual.

We live in an age during which people are under the delusion that if and when they are able to hear God speak, then He must say something that will be pleasant and enjoyable. In fact, few people today have their ears tuned to the Holy Spirit's frequency. So much spiritualistic traffic in the air prevents many Christians from being able to distinguish between the voice of the flesh, that of the world of religious spirits and the true voice of the Holy Spirit.

If this generation is to experience a true revival with the accompanying benefits, we must learn again what it means to be spiritually discerning and we must make that effort among the first priorities in our seeking revival. Christian men and women must tune out all voices that are claiming to speak for God and *"test the spirits"* against the timeless, changeless and true Word of God.

History records numerous instances in which God has, through someone or something, spoken to humanity. Even in those moments when He has been perceived to be silent, His silence has spoken. And often His voice is manifest, as Elijah the prophet discovered, as *"a still small voice."*

In the Old Testament, God speaks to men in visions, and often by suspending natural laws and performing miracles. On occasion in Old Testament times He uses angels as messengers, and He often relays His Word for a people or persons through His prophets.

By the time the Gospels unfold, God's message is personalized in the flesh through His Son Jesus of Nazareth, who, performing miraculous feats, repeatedly proved His deity. He was "a man approved by God among you by miracles and wonders and signs which God did by Him" (Acts 2:22). After the Resurrection and into the birth of the New Testament Age, God's primary agent for communicating to the human heart has been through the person of the Holy Spirit. Through the person of the Holy Spirit, God, in this age of grace, has chosen to draw men to Himself and then to begin the process of sanctification, thereby transforming their lives into the expression of His life. This daily process, born in despair and facilitated by "death to self" and resurrection to His life, changes sinful men and women into godly men and women. Emphasizing this point, the Apostle Paul wrote: "...reckon ye also yourselves to be dead indeed unto sin, but alive unto God through Jesus Christ, our Lord. Let not sin, therefore, reign in your mortal body that ye should obey it in its lusts. Neither yield ye your members as instruments of unrighteousness unto sin but yield yourselves unto God, as those that are alive from the dead, and your members as instruments of righteousness unto God" (Romans 6:11-13).

This is accomplished through obedience to His Word. Hence we realize the faithfulness of God, the patience of the Holy Spirit and the power of Jesus' resurrection life. Paul, reflecting on his own spiritual life, wrote, "Brethren, I count not myself to have apprehended; but this one thing I do, forgetting those things which are behind, and reaching forth unto those things which are before, I press toward the mark for the prize of the high calling of God in Christ Jesus" (Philippians 3:13-14).

As God's people obey His Word as the only Truth, the indwelling Christ begins to exhibit the love and life of God the Father. The glory of God in the life of each believer will match the depth of their obedience to God's Word. We do not experience Christ, live the exchanged life and become all God intends us to be by making promises or vows to one another. Again, we experience this Life by submissive obedience to the living and powerful Word of God.

Spiritual victory over selfishness, greed, pride and lust is not attained by renewed efforts and therapeutic accountability sessions. Paul gave the powerful principle of mastering our destructive tendencies when he wrote, "This I say then, walk in the Spirit and ye shall not fulfill the lust of the flesh" (Galatians 5:16).

What, Paul? No *"promise"* to do better, no keeping of a rule, a law or a vow to *"brothers"?*

To the contrary, Paul states over and over again that the way to experience the outliving of the indwelling Christ is by abandoning our will and yielding to the will, way and Word of God. Contrary to what organizations like Promise Keepers teach, the key to becoming a powerful, exciting and bold man of God is not through the renewed efforts to *"do better," "try again"* or *"work harder"* or have another brother *"keep an eye on you."* The road to discovering how to appropriate and apply His life to our life is also revealed through the Scriptures.

Simply put, the Word of God states, "He (Christ) must increase but I must decrease" (John 3:30).

While God speaks through the Holy Spirit, He uses the believer's intimate fellowship with the Church to strengthen, nourish and mature the believer and to release through him dynamic and supernatural gifts.

Paul defines the Church as the vehicle for this spiritual development. In 1 Corinthians 12 he describes how each believer plays an integral role in the local church. Comparing the church to a body and the believers who are in that local church to parts of the body, Paul writes, "For the body is not one member, but many "(verse 14) and then he emphasizes that every member is vitally important to the success of the whole. In verses 21-22 he wrote, "And the eye cannot say unto the hand, I have no need of thee...nay, much more those members of the body which seem to be more feeble are necessary."

Many American church members are frustrated because they have yet to discover that their full participation in a local church involves far more than simply having their name on the church rolls. The vital relationship that God and His Word have intricately linked between the local church and the believer is undeniable and absolutely necessary if a believer is to walk with God, be filled with His Spirit and to experience all that God has for him. There is no substitute for the local church. There is no alternative or additional way to turn men into real men, and women into real women. The church is God's chosen launching pad for divine operations in the life of every believer.

God's Word focuses on the church in more than 114 references in the New Testament. Over 90 of these refer to the local church. The plan of God to produce godly men and to equip, edify and mature them is uniquely and exclusively relegated to the local church, not to Promise Keepers, even though they lay claim to a *"divine mission"* that began with what they say was the *"call of God."*

The Bride of Christ, the Church, is the body of Christ on this earth for the purpose of demonstrating what God is like to a sinful world. The Church is the recipient of the call of

God to fulfill the true divine mission given by the resurrected Lord Jesus Christ to "...go ye into all the world and preach the Gospel to every creature" (Mark 16:15).

Jesus Christ died on the cross for His Church. He did not die for the Promise Keepers organization, the Masons, the Red Cross or the Sunday Little League. Each of these organizations and others have been able to influence Christians into making commitments to them that far exceed their commitments to the Body of Christ, their local church.

God gave spiritual gifts to men and He gave those men as spiritual gifts to the Church (1 Corinthians 12 and Ephesians 4).

These gifts are *"for the perfecting of the saints"* (Ephesians 4:12). The use of this word *"perfect"* by Paul means full spiritual development and consistent growth into a mature manifestation of godliness. This *"perfecting of the saints"* is one of the primary purposes for which the Church exists. No other organization, group or club can *"perfect"* the people of God. Promise Keepers is not gifted, equipped or commissioned to fulfill this charge. They do, however, pretend to be able to perform it. There are some true believers in Promise Keepers, just as there are in other flesh-based, man-devised organizations, such as the Masons, but that in no way qualifies them to function on this supernatural level.

Continuing in his letter to the Ephesians, Paul writes, "for the perfecting of the saints, for the work of the ministry for the edifying of the body of Christ; till we all come in the unity of the faith, and of the knowledge of the Son of God, unto a perfect man, unto the measure of the statue of the fullness of Christ" (Ephesians 4:12-13).

Volumes could be written without exhausting the glorious expression of *"Christ life"* that the believer discovers by full submission to and participation in their local church. According to Paul, as the church acts like the church, no Christian should ever find it necessary to go outside the body of their local church to find edification, fulfillment or true spiritual satisfaction. The church's interaction between the committed believer in a mutually agreed on ministerial exchange fully meets the need of every believer, as well as the demands of God.

The fraudulent *"unity"* effort that Promise Keepers and other same-minded organizations involved in the current ecumenical effort will not be realized in the unholy alliances that they pursue with men of different religious beliefs. The *"unity of faith"* discovered in the intimate knowing of the Son of God, as the church provokes believers into spiritual maturity and godliness, is not the pseudo-unity expressed in the sensual hype at massive rallies similar to Promise Keepers.

God wants every man to grow up into a fully developed, dynamic spiritual leader, hence, God has put him in His Church. The words of Paul to Ephesians states, "That we henceforth be no more children tossed to and fro and carried about with every wind of doctrine, by the sleight of men and cunning craftiness, by which they lie in wait to deceive" (Ephesians 4:14).

Paul could not have more clearly described today's Christian community in America, who, for the most part concerning their churches, are *"absent without leave"* from the scriptural demand for their participation. It is little wonder that there is so much spiritual immaturity among today's believers and so little spiritual stability. Refusing to cooperate with God's plan for spiritual development by total commitment of the believer's life to serve the Body of Christ in the local church is tantamount to remaining a spiritual midget, to never gain solid, stable, spiritual footing on which to take a stand and to live under the chastening hand of God. To stay away or to be diverted from total commitment to one's local church is high treason and not only deprives the church of that absent believer's gifts and talents, but also robs that Christian who refuses to participate of a deep, joyous and exciting life in the Spirit.

"But You Just Don't Know My Church"

Christians often complain of the spiritual deadness in the church and say things like, "But you just don't know my church." While such a believer has several options when faced with this reality, those options do not include forsaking the assembling of themselves together or dropping out of church.

The writer of Hebrews sounded the standard for every Christian when he wrote: "Let us hold fast the profession of our faith without wavering, (for He is faithful that promised,) and let us consider one another to provoke unto love and to good works, not forsaking the assembling of ourselves together, as the manner of some is, but exhorting one another, and so much the more, as ye see the day approaching" (Hebrews 10:23-25).

It is the local church, with all its discrepancies, failures and shortcomings, through which God has chosen to manifest His glory. Indeed, the average local church that is true to God's Word at first glance is not made up of society's elite.

In truth, God's ways are different than man's. Isaiah prophesied the mind of God when he wrote, "For my thoughts are not your thoughts, neither are your ways My ways, saith the Lord." (Isaiah 55:8). His strengths are best manifest in our weaknesses, hence Paul's word to us which says, "and He said unto me, My grace is sufficient for thee, for My strength is made perfect in weakness" (2 Corinthians 12:9). Very few whom the world considers among the strong, the mighty or the great are in the church of the Living God. The queen of England, at the turn of the century, was said to have been a true follower of the Lord Jesus Christ who constantly bore witness to His power to save. She said on one occasion, "I am grateful for the *"M"* in 1 Corinthians 1:26. I praise Him that it does not say *'not any'* but *'not many* noble are called.'" She was referring to the verse that says, "For ye see your calling, brethren, how that *not many wise* men after the flesh, *not many mighty, not many noble,* are called; but God hath chosen the *foolish things* of the world to confound the wise; and God hath *chosen the weak things* of the world to confound the things which are mighty; and *base things* of the world, and things *which are despised,* hath God chosen, yea, and things *which are not,* to bring to [nothing] things that are, that no flesh should glory in His presence" (1 Corinthians 1:26-29).

The few noble and mighty notwithstanding, God has put in His Church a group of "called out ones" who, if many of us were choosing followers, we would have never chosen. Perhaps our standards would have disqualified ourselves. Yet in God's economy of appraising character that qualifies one to "be called", His standard radically differs from that of men. The Church does not look like she has what it takes to accomplish her God-given task. But therein is God able to will and to do His work. It is required, as every Christian eventually discovers, that men cease all efforts to work for God and allow God to work through them. Paul wrote that he "gloried therefore in his weakness, his infirmity so that the power of Christ" may be brought to bear. He went so far as to say, *"it is when I am weak,"* that I can fully experience His strength (2 Corinthians 12:9-10).

This *"brotherhood"* of the weak, from all appearances, should really never amount to much of anything. But God in His Sovereign grace has separated His Church from the masses and chosen to call them the *"Sons of God."* Through our mutual interactions within the church, exchanging lives and ministering to one another, and learning and obeying the fascinating and deep Truths of God's Word, we become the real men and real women that God desires.

No other organization is granted the power, authority and supernatural intricacies that God has made available to and through this living organism called *"the church."* These Scriptures that address the Christian's need to participate in the Body of Christ, the church, are speaking of the *"church local,"* not some generic universal church.

There are three reasons a person might consider his local church to be so "spiritually dead" that he would rather not attend:

1) The revulsion one senses when attending his church may be because he is not born of the Spirit of God. Unregenerate man should not be comfortable, but rather, convicted when attending the church. Promise Keepers, as well as many ministries and churches today are, however, bending over backward to please, satisfy and comfort attendees. They desire an expression of tolerance over any declaration of truth that may make participants ill-at-ease.

2) The particular local church one feels is such a spiritual

wasteland may have become a social gathering without biblical convictions or commitment to the Word of God. These are churches in *"name"* only.

3) The most likely probability is that many local churches are spiritually dead or dying because of the membership's carnal, loveless, spiritually passionless living. The deadness so obvious in many local churches is a result of the spiritual apathy of most of its members and a result of the people of God who have "left their first love" (Revelation 2:4).

Few believers realize that as they function in their local church it is the exchange of their spiritual gifts with that of others in the same body that builds, develops, matures and makes spiritually dynamic that believer. Such also enlivens the atmosphere at each gathering of the church. Additionally, it is the fresh declaration of the true Gospel and the preaching of the Cross that produces the powerful dynamics of any and every local church. Paul wrote the Church at Rome, "For I am not ashamed of the Gospel of Christ; for it is the power of God unto salvation to everyone that believeth" (Romans 1:16).

Paul, addressing the vitality of the true Church, wrote to the Ephesians, saying "Till we all come in the unity of the faith, and of the knowledge of the Son of God, unto a perfect man, unto the measure of the stature of the fullness of Christ; that we henceforth be no more children, tossed to and fro, and carried about with every wind of doctrine, by the sleight of men, and cunning craftiness, by which they lie in wait to deceive; but, speaking the truth in love, may grow up into Him in all things, who is the head, even Christ; from whom the whole body fitly joined together and compacted by that which every joint supplieth, according to the effectual working in the measure of every part, maketh increase of the body unto the edifying of itself in love" (Ephesians 4:13-16).

Tragically, most Christians, because they misunderstand the doctrine of *"the priesthood of the believer"*, think that they stand alone before God and that they are not accountable to their local church. While each believer indeed does have personal access to God through the Mediator, Jesus Christ, it is the church that God has chosen as His Voice, people and instrument on the earth. God places every member in a local church to accomplish His redemptive purposes through that church and in that individual believer. Each church body is fitted together by God and equipped with spiritual gifts by the Holy Spirit to function as God so desires in that particular body (1 Corinthians 12).

As a Christian I cannot spiritually grow, develop or experience the fullness of the Life of Christ if I refuse to participate 100 percent within my local church or if I divert the energies, gifts and resources that God has entrusted to me to any man-centered, flesh-born organization, no matter how that organization sanctifies its existence.

I recently heard a television preacher yell, *"The Church today is weak, anemic and a wreck."* My response to such an ill-thought statement echoes the heart of God.

If indeed any local church is as this man so describes, it is that way because so many people who are members of that church are weak, anemic and spiritual wrecks. Many local churches are being forced to operate with fewer and fewer people and work with fewer resources because such a large part of their membership is being drawn away by self-appointed prophets leading such ministries as Promise Keepers. However, a living church is a self-contained, self-renewing organism. Not only can it be compared to the anatomical functioning of a physical body, but the church also serves as a repairer of broken lives, much like a body shop repairs wrecked automobiles. If Christian church members would forsake their bitterness, drop their weak excuses for their lack of commitment and discover and employ their spiritual gifts and call, activating themselves in their local church, God would heal their spiritual anemia and replace it with a new vitality and power. God could then infuse their hearts with a vision while taking their wrecked lives and removing the spiritual kinks, dents and blemishes.

The real Church of Jesus Christ is very much alive, well, vibrant, effective and exclusively anointed by God to represent His call, His commission on this Earth. True, there are but few true believers and they are scattered across the land in a few biblically sound, uncompromising churches. But God has never needed a lot of people to accomplish His will. He does need 100 percent of each believer whom He has called and through those few He can and will touch the World.

Jesus said His people are the *"salt of the earth"* (Matthew 5:13). Salt is used as a metaphor by Jesus to illustrate the nature of the true Christian. Salt has many characteristics but among the most poignant is that it is a *"penetrator,"* as Christians are to be in society. Salt gives flavor, unless of course it has lost its savor, or its power to give flavor. Ministries that facilitate Christians losing their *"saltiness"* are those ministries that divert the believer's focus away from their church and onto unnecessary spiritual additives.

Salt is also an agent that has an effect far beyond the proportion used. Very little salt produces the desired effect. God has sprinkled His people around and their effect on the world is far out of proportion with their number. That is the only reason America has not been smitten with the fiery judgment of God. As Isaiah the prophet wrote hundreds of years ago, "Except the Lord of hosts had left unto us a very small remnant, we should have been like Sodom, and we should have been like unto Gomorrah" (Isaiah 1:9).

Conspirators Have Security Leak

Satan is using Promise Keepers Ministries in a myriad of ways in his attempt to hinder the True Church. To suggest, however, that those who lead, participate in and support Promise Keepers are aware of their diabolic alliance and of the harm they are inflicting upon the cause of Christ would be wrong. Such suppositions would presume that the motives of the heart can be correctly judged and I am not qualified to make such judgments. In fact, for the record, I am fully convinced that the vast majority of those at the epicenter of the Promise Keepers phenomenon believe with all their hearts that their efforts are facilitating the accomplishment of God's plan. However, we are warned that many well-intentioned false prophets in these last days will be at work deceiving people because they are deceived. Paul wrote to young Timothy,

"But evil men shall wax worse and worse deceiving and *being deceived"* (2 Timothy 3:13).

Some of my close associates and many of my peers have yet to see the anti-scriptural nature of Promise Keepers. It is not because these men are demon-possessed, false prophets or biblically illiterate. Their receptivity of Promise Keepers, rather, is a result of a failure on their part to scrutinize the fundamental doctrinal flaws and the anti-Christian, unbiblical approach to accomplishing the work of God that is at the core of Promise Keepers philosophy. They have assumed that *"what you see (and hear) is what you get."* Many of these men are not particularly deeply involved in Promise Keepers; instead, they have simply attended rallies at which the organization has gone to great lengths to sanitize and genericize its focus or they have been *"sold"* on Promise Keepers by well-trained *"point men"*.

My stand on this issue has resulted in the loss of a number of close friends and associates who have determined that they have made up their mind on the Promise Keepers issue and do not wish to be confused with the facts.

Aware of the risks presented by writing a book of this nature, I quit writing some three months into the project. The partially finished manuscript sat untouched in the "throw-away" tray on my desk. Every time I saw it, I was smitten with deep conviction that I was in disobedience by not pursuing this project. After spending considerable time praying for confirmation of any kind that I should pursue the project, I received a call the very next day from two major Christian publishers who inquired about the manuscript and expressed an interest in working on the project. Almost 15 months later, I submitted the completed manuscript.

The gentle but constant reminding of the Holy Spirit, the repeated admonitions I received from the Word of God to speak where God has spoken, and such circumstances as the publishers calling when they did, all indicate a desperate need for this kind of work.

The overwhelming urgency, however, that compelled me to finish this book is the fact that after our 25 years in ministry, and after an exposure to the things that are going on behind closed doors of most of this nation's most prominent ministries, I am convinced that the Church must quickly recognize and deal with the pretentious and flesh-fabricated, so-called *"move of the Spirit"* across America.

The power of this false revival to deceive, with its false prophets, false miracles and false gifts, is no more vividly illustrated than in the flamboyant, glitter-covered, infectious, invasive Trojan Horse known as the Promise Keepers. It incorporates every ingredient necessary to work the wiles of the *"wicked one"* to distract and to debilitate men who are hungry for God with a counterfeit experience in the counterfeit ministry of a counterfeit god.

It also contains ingredients necessary to attract and delude pastors and Christian leaders. The propaganda, the sheer masses of men involved and the fascinating array of Christian personalities who lend their time and name to prop up the legitimacy of Promise Keepers are stunningly impressive to the average pastor whose church has less than 100 people in Sunday School on an average Sunday, as do over 80 percent of America's churches.

These men are the primary focus of the Promise Keepers' promotional machine. They are in the spiritual front-line trenches, whose ministries make or break the spiritual backbone of our nation. These are the men who, for better or worse, are the *"voice of God"* to millions of grass-roots American church members. If they can be swayed to receive such overwhelming error and condone such to their people, Promise Keepers has won a great victory. Tragically however, a great victory is also won by those who defy the Word of God, who wish to destroy the doctrinal distinctions of the true Church and who desire to infiltrate local churches with extra-biblical and heretical teachings.

The average pastor in the average church might find it most intimidating to speak out against Promise Keepers' spiritual terrorism. The forces supporting this ill-conceived plot to replace the ministry of the church are powerful, influential and well-financed.

But God still has His remnant and while some of them may be temporarily dazzled by the frenzy and impressed by the glitter, God will not suffer His chosen to long stay under the cloud of deception. He will accomplish, in His way, with His Church, His desires and will move yet again to deliver His people from the *"snare of the fowler"* (Psalm 91:3). He is God and we are His people who belong to His Church in Spirit as well as Name.

I admonish, as did Paul to Timothy, *"Nevertheless the foundation of God standeth sure, having this seal, the Lord knoweth them that are His and let everyone that Nameth the Name of the Lord, depart from iniquity"* (2 Timothy 2:19).

As the church begins again to be the church, the attractions of the false glitter on fool's gold will lose its appeal. Nothing can compare to the glory that is manifested in the Bride of Christ when She walks in full obedience to the Bridegroom.

Speak church, speak in love, but speak against the error, as that is as much a part of your commission as is the speaking of the Gospel.

And thank God that in spite of our often ill-placed allegiances and temporary reluctance to be faithful to His call, *"He remaineth faithful, for He cannot deny Himself"* (2 Timothy 2:13).

Yea, when I break my promises, His covenant stands fixed. He is the only true Promise Keeper who supports with the full authority of His Power, His Person and His Sovereignty, the precious promises of His Word to us, His Beloved, the Church.

The Church of Jesus Christ has not, will not and cannot fail in its mission or in its call. Regardless of the overwhelming numbers, monies, influence and the deceptive powers arrayed against and attempting to replace His Church, *"the gates of hell shall not prevail against it"* (Matthew 16:18b).

Amen, and amen.

Endnotes

Chapter 2

1. *What Makes A Man? Twelve Promises That Will Change Your Life*, (Colorado Springs: NavPress 1992), p. 11.
2. Ibid.
3. Ibid., p. 12.
4. Ibid.
5. Albert James Dager, *Media Spotlight, Promise Keepers, Is What You See What You Get?*, (Redmond, WA: publisher, 1995).
6. *Promise Keepers Fact Sheet*, (May 15, 1995), p. 1.
7. Ibid.
8. Ibid.
9. Ibid., p. 2.
10. *Promise Keepers Fact Sheet*, (September 24, 1996), p. 2.
11. Ibid.
12. Ibid.
13. *Promise Keepers Fact Sheet*, (May 15, 1995), p. 1.

Chapter 4

1. *Promise Keepers' Statement of Faith*, (*Promise Keepers 1996 Magazine*).
2. Ibid.
3. *Promise Keepers' Statement of Faith*, (*Promise Keepers 1996 Magazine*), p 5.
4. Ibid.

Chapter 5

1. *Promise Keepers' Statement of Faith*, (*Promise Keepers 1996 Magazine*).
2. Ibid.

3. Ibid.
4. Ibid.

Chapter 6

1. Randy Phillips, *Seven Promises of A Promise Keeper*, (Colorado Springs: Focus on the Family, 1994).
2. Ibid. p. 8.

Chapter 7

1. Ibid.
2. Ibid.
3. *Vines Expository Dictionary of Biblical Words*, ("Time and/or Times and Seasons")(Editors W.E. Vine, Merrill Unger, William White, Jr., Camden, New York, Nashville: Thomas Nelson, 1984), p. 633.
4. Ibid.

Chapter 8

1. Nancy Justice, *Women Charge Paulk with Abuse*, (*Charisma*, Feb. 1993), p. 54-55.
2. *Seven Promises of a Promise Keeper*, p. 98.

Chapter 9

1. C.S. Lewis, *Mere Christianity*, (New York: Macmillan, 1952), p. 112.
2. *The Seven Promises of a Promise Keeper*, (*Promise Keepers 1996 Magazine, Men of Integrity*), p. 6.
3. *Vines Expository Dictionary of Biblical Words*, (Editors W.E. Vine, Merrill Unger, William White, Jr., Camden, New York, Nashville: Thomas Nelson, 1984) p. 554, 683-684.
4. *Seven Promises of A Promise Keeper*.
5. Ibid.
6. *New Webster's Dictionary of the English Language* (Danbury, CT: Lexicon Publications, 1993).
7. *Seven Promises of a Promise Keeper*.

Chapter 10

1. Anton Szandor LaVey, *Satanic Bible*, (New York: Avon, 1969).

Chapter 11

1. C.S. Lewis, *Mere Christianity*, (New York: Macmillan, 1952).
2. *Seven Promises of a Promise Keeper.*
3. *Seven Promises of a Promise Keeper*, p. 19.
4. Dave Hunt, *A Woman Rides the Beast*, (Eugene, OR: Harvest House, 1994).
5. *The Story of Civilization*, Vol. 4, (New York: Simon & Shuster, 1950), p. 784.
6. Ibid.
7. Dave Hunt, *A Woman Rides the Beast*, (Eugene, OR: Harvest House, 1994).
8. *A Woman Rides the Beast*, Dave Hunt quoting Austin Flannery, O.P. Gen Ed. Vatican Council II: *The Conciliar and Post Conciliar Documents*, rev. ed. (Costello, 1988, Vol. 1, pp. 104-107-109).

Chapter 12

1. *Seven Promises of a Promise Keeper.*
2. Ibid.

Chapter 13

1. Ibid.
2. Ibid.
3. Pastor Bill Randles, *An Open Letter to Bill McCartney*, (Believers Grace Fellowship Church, 3336 Prairie Dr. NE, Cedar Rapids, IA 52402, August 15, 1995).
4. Ibid.
5. Ibid.

Chapter 14

1. *Seven Promises of a Promise Keeper.*

2. *Vines Expository Dictionary of Biblical Words*, p. 446.
3. *Matthew Henry Commentary on the Whole Bible*, Vol. V, (Fleming H. Revell Co., Old Tappan, NJ) p. 1164.
4. Ibid.
5. Ibid.
6. *The New International Dictionary of the Bible - Pictorial Edition,* (General Editor Merrile C. Tenny, Grand Rapids, MI: Zondervan, 1984) p. 237-238.
7. *What is a Promise Keeper?, Promise Keepers' Statement of Faith, (Promise Keepers 1996 Magazine)*, p. 5.
8. *Seven Promises of a Promise Keeper.*

Chapter 15

1. Paul Clayton, *Psychology as Religion: The Cult of Self-Worship*, (Vitz, Endmanns, 1977), p. 10.
2. *Promise Keepers'* inquiry response to *The Masculine Journey, Understanding the Six Stages of Man* by Robert Hicks, *(*Promise Keepers National Office, PO Box 103001, Denver, CO 80250, May 10, 1996*)*.
3. *Psychoheresy Awareness Ministries*, (4137 Prima Vera Rd., Santa Barbara, CA 98110).
4. *Promise Keepers'* endorsement statement to *The Masculine Journey, Understanding the Six Stages of Man* by Robert Hicks, *(*Promise Keepers National Office, PO Box 103001, Denver, CO 80250, May 10, 1996*)*.
5. Dr. Gary Collins, *Can You Trust Psychology?* (Downers Grove: Inter-Varsity Press, 1988).
6. Don Matzat, *Christ Esteem, Where The Search for Self-Esteem Ends,* (Eugene, OR: Harvest House, 1990) p. 28-29.
7. Ibid.

Chapter 16

1. Robert Hicks, *The Masculine Journey, Understanding the Six Stages of Man*, (Colorado Springs, CO: NavPress, 1993) p. 9
2. Daniel Levinson, *The Seasons of a Man's Life* (New York: Ballantine Books, 1978).

3. Martin & Deidre Bobgan, *Psychoheresy Awareness Ministry*, (4137 Prima Vera Rd, Santa Barbara, CA 93110).

4. Daniel Levinson, *The Seasons of a Man's Life*, p. 16.

5. Ibid. p. 17.

6. Viktor Frankle, *The Unheard Cry for Meaning*, (Simon & Shuster. New York, 1978)

7. Bruce Narramore & John D. Carter, *The Integration of Psychology and Theology, Grand Rapids, MI* (Zondervan), p. 11.

8. Dr. Gary Collins, *Can You Trust Psychology?* (Downers Grove: Inter-Varsity Press, 1988), p. 85.

9. Robert Hicks, *The Masculine Journey, Understanding the Six Stages of Man*, p. 324.

10. Ibid. p. 24.

11. Ibid.

12. Ibid. p. 26.

13. Ibid. p. 56.

14. Ibid. p. 31.

15. Ibid. p. 33.

16. Ibid.

17. *Study Guide to the Masculine Journey - Exploring the Issues with Other Men*, p. 21.

18. Hicks op. Cit. p. 177.

Chapter 17

1. *Promise Keepers Biblical Discernment Ministries*, (Vol. 3 #2, 1994).

2. Ibid.

3. Promise Keepers Fax, *James Ryle's Comments On The Beatles* (Promise Keepers Public Relations, May 1996).

4. John F. MacArthur, Jr., *Charismatic Chaos* (Grand Rapids, MI: Zondervan, 1992), pp. 66-73.

5. Pastor James Ryle, conclusion of *"Sons of Thunder,"* (Denver, CO: Harvest Conference, November 1990).

6. Carl Widrig, Jr., *The Promise Keepers Fax Scandal*, (The Christian Conscience, September 1996).

Chapter 18

1. Robert Dean, *Don't Be Caught Dead in the Undertow of the Third Wave Biblical Perspectives*, (May-June 1990).

2. C. Peter Wagner, *The Third Wave of the Holy Spirit*, (Ann Arbor, Vine, 1988), p. 112.

3. John Wimber, *Power Evangelism*, (San Francisco, CA. Harper & Row, 1986), p. 122.

4. Andrew Shead, *Spiritual Warfare: The Critical Moment, The Briefing*, (April 24, 1990), p. 7.

5. Philip Seldan, *Spiritual Warfare: Medical Reflections - The Briefing*, (April 24, 1990), p. 9.

6. Ibid. p. 20.

7. John MacArthur, *The Charismatics*, p. 134.

8. Peter Jennings, *In The Name of God* (ABC News Special, March 16, 1995).

9. John Wimber, *Power Evangelism*, p. 89.

10. John Wimber, *Healing Seminar* (3 tapes) 1981 Edition (unpublished), Tape 1.

Chapter 19

1. *Praise The Lord program*, (TBN, Oct. 17,1989 hosted by Paul and Jan Crouch whose guests were two Catholic priests, Father John Hamster and Father Herbert DeSoza).

2. *Los Angeles Herald Examiner*, (*Religion Page*, Sept. 19, 1987).

3. *What is a Promise Keeper?*, (*Promise Keepers 1996, Breakdown the Walls, Magazine*), p. 5.

4. Al Dager interview with Randy Philips, (*Media Spotlight*, 1994, Redmond, WA 98073-0290), p. 11.

5. Elliott Mulla and Robert M. Bowman, Jr. *The Vineyard*, (*Christian Research Institute* paper, 1989).

6. John MacArthur, *Charismatic Chaos*, p. 148.

7. *What is a Promise Keeper?*, (*Promise Keepers 1996, Breakdown the Walls, Magazine*), p. 5.

8. *Promise Keepers Workbook*, (*Seize the Moment Men's Conference*, Portland, OR, June 18, 1994).

Chapter 20

1. James Hewitt, Editor, *Illustrations Unlimited*, (Wheaton, IL: Tyndale House, 1988).
2. *Promise Keepers Magazine, What is a Promise Keeper?*, p. 5.

Chapter 21

1. Jon Dart, *Promise Keepers, A Message to Los Angeles Men*, (*Los Angeles Times*, May 6, 1995).
2. Craig Branch, *Culting of Christianity* (Promise Keepers *New Man* magazine, October 1996 edition).
3. Ibid.
4. Ibid.
5. Roman Catholic Catechism, (London, England: Catholic Truth Society, Geiermann, 1985), p. 101-103.
6. Craig Branch, *Culting of Christianity* (Promise Keepers *New Man* magazine, October 1996 edition).
7. Mike Nelson, *Promise Keepers, Promises Spiritual Renewal for Man*, (*The Tidings*, 1995), p. 98.
8. *Promise Keepers' Statement of Faith*, (*Promise Keepers 1996 Magazine*), p. 5.
9. Pope John Paul II, *Crossing the Threshold of Hope.*
10 *Pope Yields on Evolution*, (www.catholic.net/cgi-bin/HyperNews/get/evolution/9.html, October 24, 1996, 12:04:45 GMT).
11. Ibid.
12. Dr. Michael Denton, *Evolution—a Theory in Crisis*, (Bethesda, MD: Adler & Adler, 1986).
13. Chuck Colson, *Promise Keepers Rally - June 21-22*, (Charlotte, NC, aired October 19, 1996 on *Promise Keepers - This Week* radio program).
14. Ibid.
15. Chuck Colson & Father Richard Neuhaus, Evangelicals and Catholics Together, (First Things, New York: Institute on Religion and Public Life, May 1994)
16. Richard D. Land & Larry L. Lewis, *Statement Regarding Evangelicals and Catholics Together* (Atlanta, GA: Home Mission Board, SBC, April 6, 1995)

17. John MacArthur, *Masterpiece Magazine*, (Winter 1988).

18. Chuck Colson, *Promise Keepers Rally - June 21-22*, (Charlotte, NC, aired October 19, 1996 on *Promise Keepers - This Week* radio program).

19. Dave Hunt, *A Woman Rides the Beast*, (Eugene, OR: Harvest House, 1994).

20. Dave Hunt, *A Woman Rides the Beast*, John A. Hardon, S.J., *Pocket Catholic Dictionary* (Doubleday, 1966), p. 248.

21. Dave Hunt, *A Woman Rides the Beast*, Catholic World Report, April 1994, p. 38.

22. Dave Hunt, *A Woman Rides the Beast*, (Hardon, op. Cit.), p. 271.

23. Dave Hunt, *A Woman Rides the Beast*, (Eugene, OR: Harvest House, 1994), p. 387.

24. *FAX from Promise Keepers to Gregg Dixon*, Pastor of Indianapolis Baptist Temple, (December 8, 1993).

25. *Holy Bible, New International Version.*

26. Robert Hicks, *The Masculine Journey.*

27. Ibid. p. 181.

28. Ibid. p. 6

29. Dr. Paul Cameron, *Chairman, Family Research Institute, Inc.*, (PO Box 2091, Wash. DC 20013).

30. Geoff Gorush with Dan Stephen, *Brothers Calling Men Into Vital Relationship*,(op. Cit.), p. 50.

Appendix A

The Promise Keepers FAX Scandal
by Carl Widrig, Jr.

Were the Beatles "anointed" by God? Did they reject this anointing? A candid look at the controversial statements of PK leader, Pastor James Ryle.

> It looked like a Sergeant Peppers Hearts Club jacket... it looked like a military jacket, and it started floating back and I knew that that represented the anointing, the mantle, the covering that was coming to the 'Sons of Thunder.' And not long ago, the Lord said, 'I'm giving you the permission to pass the jacket out.'

> —Pastor James Ryle, conclusion of "Sons of Thunder," Harvest Conference, Denver, CO, November 1990.

Suns of Thunder

During the latter half of 1989, at the height of the "Kansas City Prophets" nationwide tour of Vineyard Christian Fellowship, Vineyard pastor James Ryle had three dreams involving the Beatles which God allegedly interpreted for Ryle after he woke up from each dream. By February 1990, Ryle was sharing the contents of his Beatles "anointing" dreams, and the alledged God-given interpretation thereof, with other Christians—a "revelation" concerning a musical "anointing" that God gave exclusively to the Beatles to usher in a worldwide revival, and then took away from them in 1970 to be reserved for Christian musicians ("The Sons of Thunder") in the 1990's, for the purpose of ushering in a worldwide revival.[1]

On July 1, 1990, at the local Vineyard he pastors, and also in November 1990, at the "Harvest Conference" held in Denver, Colorado with "K.C. Prophet" Rick Joyner, Ryle, in a message entitled, "Sons of Thunder," shared the details of his Beatles' "anointing" dreams and their interpretation. The latter message (especially) has since been accessed via audio tape by multitudes and become the subject of much controversy.

By 1994, Promise Keepers was becoming very popular in the evangelical church in America. In February 1994, James Ryle, who by this time was a rising star Director of Promise Keepers, wrote a piece for *Charisma* magazine (published by the same publisher as the PK organ, *New Man*) titled "The New Sound of Music," wherein he toned down quite a bit what he had emphasized on earlier occasions about the Beatles' exclusive "anointing." Instead he attributed their success to the "social climate" of the time, not unlike contemporary 1990's culture. Thus in the name of "history repeats itself" he claimed that

> we will see musicians who are anointed by God and gifted with even greater ability than The Beatles...these musicians will not fail to glorify God and therein will be the secret of their success. (Charisma, 2/94, p.14).

This was a much more reasonable-sounding-to-evangelicals rendition of his original "Beatles were anointed by God" "revelations" circa 1989-90.

Later, in 1995, Bill Randles, a Pentecostal pastor in Cedar Rapids, Iowa, wrote what has become one of the most well-known critical pieces on Promise Keepers, "An Open Letter to Bill McCartney," wherein Randles voiced numerous concerns (many of which PK has responded to via fax), including one

---

[1] The part of Ryle's "revelation" about God giving Christian musicians in the 1990's revival-ushering musical "anointing" was nothing new at the time—such was commonly "prophesied" by the "K.C. Prophets" who were circulating around the Vineyard at the time. I was an eyewitness to these events, and the object of one such "prophecy" on March 7, 1990, by the assistant prophet to Larry Randolph, a man named Howard Jones, who "prophesied" that God would place an "anointing" on me and I would play "a new song" with my guitar at beaches and in parks and people would gather around and God would "manifest" his presence and the people would get saved.

about Ryle and his Beatles dream interpretation (specifically Ryle's aforementioned "Sons of Thunder" message at the Nov. 1990 Harvest Conference).

Then on January 11, 1996, Steve Chavis, National Spokesman for Promise Keepers and co-host of the "Promise Keepers This Week" radio program, appeared on a local Denver/ Boulder radio program called, "The Grant Connection", claiming that, "It's not true" that "James Ryle said, 'The Beatles were anointed by God.'"

In more recent months, Promise Keepers released a fax titled, "JAMES RYLE'S COMMENTS ON THE BEATLES," that specifically refers to Ryle's 1990 "Sons of Thunder" conference message as the sole subject of their fax. This fax they have been distributing to their Ambassadors, this time admitting to the word "anointing" in Ryle's Beatles' revelation, but spinning what Ryle said into this:

> Ryle referred to that gift [the Beatles had] as an "anointing" indicating only that the gift was from God.

As the reader who considers the historical record to be further elaborated on might notice, James Ryle and Promise Keepers seem to be making a unified and concerted effort to tone down and "spin-doctor" what Ryle actually said God showed him earlier in the decade about an alleged musical anointing that God gave exclusively to the Beatles and then took away from them in 1970 to be reserved for Christian Musicians ("The Suns of Thunder") in the 1990's. Coincidentally (?), the toning down and spin-doctoring has taken place alongside the growing popularity of Promise Keepers which Ryle is a Director of, and of which Bill McCartney and Randy Phillips (who both call James Ryle their "pastor") are the Founder and President respectively.

Lack of Integrity

My own examination of the evidence has yielded several items of interest. I compared what Ryle was actually saying circa

1990 with what PK has been saying of late via Steve Chavis and this PK fax. I have come to the conclusion that this PK fax is a blatantly skewed portrayal of the historical facts. It's as if they didn't think those who read the fax would ever become privy to the facts via listening to the audio tape recording of Ryle's "Sons of Thunder" message—the most interesting part of which (having to do with Ryle's three dreams) was also virtually transcribed verbatim in Rick Joyner's *Morning Star Prophetic Newsletter*. The whole thing has to leave one wondering why PK has suffered such a lapse in the integrity department.

1. Important Contextual Information

The background provided in the PK fax, regarding the context in which Pastor James Ryle's comments about the Beatles were made, is unbelievably misstated, so much so that they must have thought that the reader would never actually hear the "context" with their own ears.

In 1990, Pastor Ryle spoke at a conference and gave a message entitled, "The Sons of Thunder" containing three main points: 1) God wants the entire world to be evangelized (John 3:16); 2) God wants us to become all things to all men, that by all means men might be saved (1 Cor. 9:22); 3) God provides gifts to all of us through which we can reach out to the lost. Pastor Ryle went on to elaborate on the third point, stating that all gifts are a blessing from God—doctors are gifted with healing, teachers with the ability to communicate information, judges with wisdom, and musicians with music, etc.

What the PK fax doesn't tell the reader is that moments before Ryle gave his "Sons of Thunder" talk, Rick Joyner spent many, many minutes setting up the crowd to be open to "weird revelations" (having to do with "new music") they were about to hear about from James Ryle. Joyner even went to the point of emphasizing that Ryle's prophetic message was particularly for Colorado at that particular time. Ryle's own message contained the same effort to set up the crowd to find what he was about to share to be reasonable, based on the theme of "evangelism" (as if "evangelism" would make whatever he was about to share legitimate). The set-up concluded with these words:

Now, all that so I can tell you these three things [his three dreams]. I just had to set that as a framework as to the burden of the Lord and the passion of the Lord towards evangelism.

"Framework" is a long way from the PK fax's "three main points." There is no way even a casual listener of Ryle's message could think that Ryle was merely "elaborating" when he finally brought up the Beatles "gift." Nor did Ryle even mention *a single word* about "doctors," "teacher," "judges" or "musicians" as historical examples of those who have "gifts" like the Beatles had – that suggestion by the author of PK fax is a blatant attempt to completely revamp the message Ryle actually spoke in history.

2. The Result of Dreams

Ryle's "Beatles" thing came about from dreams Ryle, after much careful deliberation, claimed God personally explained to him and appointed him to "report":

Isaiah 21:6 is a verse that the Lord quickened to me at the outset of this year, and this is what it says: "This is what the Lord says to me: 'Go post a lookout and have him report what he sees.'" And what I'm going to tell you right now is three separate dreams that the Lord gave me over a period of several months. And I say that up front because I want you to realize that what you're about to hear is not the fruit of zealous immaturity. This is something that has been thought out, it's been prayed over, it's been examined, it's been investigated, scrutinized, and laid before the Lord and shared with others who are certainly more esteemed than I am in these types of seeings and it has, to this point, stood the test. And so I am confident in saying this much, that the Lord, to a degree, has appointed me as a lookout and has shown me some things and I want to show you and tell you what he showed me. (James Ryle, Harvest Conference, Nov. 1990)

One would hardly know about this context upon reading PK's recent fax on the issue which makes it seem as if James Ryle simply picked the Beatles on a whim, as a mere "example" to make the unobjectionable-to-any-evangelical-ear point that the Beatles had a God-given plain-Jane musical "gifting" that could have been used for honorable evangelistic purposes, which "gifting" God later took away. The problem with this spin is that the gifts of God are irrevocable (Rom. 11:29), and we all know that John, Paul, and George didn't suddenly lose their musical gifting in 1970 (assuming Ringo never had it in the first place).

3. Ushering In A Worldwide Revival

The Beatles "anointing" that Christians were hearing Ryle talk about in 1990 was supposedly so special and powerful that it could have ushered in a worldwide revival—an anointing that God allegedly held back for over 20 years and soon planned to "release" to the Church. That anointing is quite a different animal than Ryle's 1994, "greatly gifted by God", and PK's recent fax, "gift as an 'anointing' indicating only that the gift was from God." Following this line of thought, if Ryle's 1990 "anointing" was really just a plain-Jane musical "gifting" that has been held back for over 20 years now, that would also logically imply that no one has had this plain-Jane musical gift since 1970!

4. Gifting the Rebellious?

Ryle misquotes Psalm 68:18 which actually reads (NKJV, NASB, NIV),

> When you ascended on high, you led captivity captive, *you RECEIVED gifts FROM men, even AMONG the REBELLIOUS, that God may dwell in our midst.*

Ryle, in both his Nov. 1990 Harvest Conference

presentation, and in the *Morning Star Prophetic Newsletter*, misquotes Psalm 68:18 as saying,

> *When you ascended on high, you led captivity captive, and you GAVE gifts TO men, even TO the REBELLIOUS, that God may dwell in our midst.*

Ryle needs Psalm 68:18 to say "gave" to justify his teaching that God really could have given the Beatles this special "gift"/ "anointing". Ephesians 4:8 (which Ryle never acknowledges) quotes a portion of Psalm 68:18 and then reads, "and gave gifts to men", but in context this is clearly referring to grace given to each one in the Body of Christ (cf. Eph. 4:7), and the passage omits any mention of "the rebellious."

This leads to an important point: It is not in accord with God's Word that God would clumsily and unknowingly give a special, worldwide, revival-ushering anointing to unbelievers like the Beatles, who would then pull a fast one on God and use it for the devil's purposes (preaching a false message accompanying the anointing) while God just sits there and lets it go on until 1970 (!) before taking it away from them. Using this logic, Ryle's "God" could just as well give this type of anointing to end-times false prophets and the antichrist to work lying signs and wonders to deceive, if possible, even the elect (Matt. 24:24)!

5. Strange Gospel for Evangelism

The fact that the PK fax gives the impression that PK finds no trouble with the content of Ryle's "Sons of Thunder" message is itself a witness against the discernment of PK. For example, the PK fax highlights that Ryle's message was all about "evangelism." But the evangelism Ryle speaks of is not your typical "preach the gospel that Jesus died for your sins and rose again and is coming back unto salvation, and then those whom God has appointed to salvation are regenerated and believe and are saved."

As Rick Joyner was prepping the audience to receive Ryle's

"intense" prophetic message at the 1990 Harvest Conference, he stated, "We've had a lot of our concepts about evangelism, and I think the Lord is going to change some of them." Minutes later, Ryle was saying the following which makes evangelism seem more like a Vineyard healing service than the evangelism we know of per the Bible:

> ...a light shines from above and there's a woman standing in the midst of the church, and she stands up and she begins singing this song under the anointing of the Holy Spirit. And the song had one sentence that she kept singing over and over. And the song was this: "In the name of Jesus Christ the Lord we say unto you: Be saved!" And she would just start singing that, she would sing it up to that part of the balcony, and I started watching, and it was like wind blowing on a wheat field. The people in that whole section just began to swoon under the presence of the Holy Spirit, and many of them would collapse into their seats, sobbing, proclaiming, "Jesus is Lord."

> And then she would sing it over here, "In the name of Jesus Christ the Lord we say unto you: Be saved!", and salvation was spontaneously and sovereignly happening all over that place. And that was the end of the dream.

> [After waking up] the Lord showed me some things, and I submit these to you for your prayer and consideration and discussion. But this is the thing that he showed me.

Ryle's "gospel" as per his "Sons of Thunder" article in the *Morning Star Prophetic Newsletter* is likewise troubling:

> The Lord said, "Say this to the church: 'Stand in the light. Lift up your voice and sing in the streets. Sing the simple message of the gospel—In the Name of Jesus Christ the Lord, be saved. Lift up your voice as a witness to Christ and the Spirit of God will cause people to be converted.'" (Ryle, "Sons of Thunder", *The Morning Star Prophetic Newsletter*, Vol. 1, No. 4. (Winter 1991), pp. 23-29.)

This cross/resurrection/hope-absent "evangelism" and "gospel" of James Ryle doesn't seem to trouble PK according to their fax. Instead, one would think based on the PK fax that Ryle had spoken a wonderful Scriptural message on evangelism that no genuine Christian could have any trouble with, and therefore must have "misunderstood."

6. A Straw Man

The PK fax presents a "straw man" of the objections that have been raised by Christians who judged Ryle's Beatles prophetic dreams as false:

> Pastor Ryle regrets that his comment was misunderstood by believers who thought he was endorsing the message and lifestyle of the Beatles. He only intended to convey his understanding of the power of music and that it is a gift from God. Pastor Ryle did not mean to imply that he believed the Beatles were used by God, only that their gift was from God and it could have been used for the glory of God.

Again, here the PK fax is bypassing the fact that the things that Ryle actually said – rather than being Ryle's mere "comments" and "his understanding" – were emphasized by Ryle himself in 1990 (the time period under consideration in PK's fax) to be prophetic dreams interpreted by God Himself, thus implicating GOD (!) in "endorsing the message and lifestyle of the Beatles" via His unique "gift" to the Beatles of a worldwide-revival-ushering "anointing."

Any student of the Bible knows that God doesn't give decade-long, worldwide-revival-ushering anointings to unbelievers or false teachers, since such an anointing would obviously tend to give credibility and/or added impact to the message accompanying the anointing. Would God endorse the Beatles' message?! Read the sidebars! One would think from Ryle's "revelations", however, that God's priority is an "at-least-something-is-happening" anointing, while meanwhile God can be quite tolerant (for a decade, at least) with a false message accompanying His worldwide-revival-ushering musical anointing.

The PK fax also conveniently avoids specifying exactly who had thought that Ryle was "endorsing the message and lifestyle of the Beatles" and "believed the Beatles were used by God," so that the reader can't confirm the claim. It gives the reader the impression that these are the *only* two possible "misunderstandings" known to Promise Keepers, and thus Ryle is easily cleared of all charges laid against him. Such is not the case, however.

For example, perhaps the most well-known voice objecting to Ryle and his Beatles dreams is Pentecostal pastor Bill Randles, who wrote, "An Open Letter to Bill McCartney," which focused particularly on this "anointing" issue that Chavis and the PK fax seems so focused on themselves to deny or spin-doctor. Sometime in 1995, Randles wrote,

> Frankly, Mr. McCartney, another huge reservation that I am having with P.K. is the fact that James Ryle, a man who claims that God told him the Beatles were anointed to bring forth a worldwide revival and "usher in my (God's) spirit," is your pastor and mentor. According to Ryle, it wasn't until 1970 that God removed His anointing from the Beatles (*Sgt. Pepper's Lonely Hearts Club Band* was anointed by God? 1970 was the year the Beatles broke up!). I am leery of a "prophet" who discerns the demonic as anointed.

The details of Randles' objections here are based on what Ryle actually said—Randles had listened to the audio tape and is judging Ryles' Beatles dream interpretation as Ryle himself instructs his readers to do in his two books on dreams (cf. May '96 CC). But PK doesn't appear to be the least bit interested in even acknowledging the existence of what Ryle actually said, since it is so obviously unbiblical and indefensible—thus they have propped up a straw man of the criticisms to give the appearance of having dealt with the situation when in fact they have not.

No Repentance

Ryle's circa 1990 "revelations" about the Beatles' potential worldwide-revival-ushering musical "anointing", that God then waited until 1970 to take away from them to be reserved for and "imminently" distributed to Christians in the 1990's doesn't at all sound like something the God who inspired the Scriptures would do and say. Ryle's "revelations" rather cast some dark shadows on God's holy character. Does PK know this? It appears they are going out of their way to equip their Ambassadors with misrepresentations, both regarding what Ryle actually said and wrote in 1990 and what the critics have been saying since.

Ryle himself hasn't repented of his 1989-1990 Beatles "revelations" either (why would he need to repent if he was simply "misunderstood" as the PK fax would like us to think?) – such a repentance would entail him publicly admitting that he lied or was otherwise massively deceived when he, Director of Promise Keepers, "Pastor" of the founder and President of PK and the rest of those who attend the Boulder Valley Vineyard, and author of two books on the subject of "revelatory" dreams (cf. May '96 CC), in true "humility" (defined according to Ryle at the 1990 Harvest Conference as, "agreeing with what God says about you"), went around claiming to multitudes of people, many of whom "went up to the front" and embraced this "word" to their own spiritual deception, that God has appointed James Ryle as a lookout to both "report" about and "pass out" this worldwide-revival-ushering Beatles "anointing" to 1990's Christian musicians.

Ryle does seem to have toned down in the last few years his extravagant claims and reporting of "what God showed" him, as evidenced by what he had to say in his one-page Feb. 1994 Charisma piece. But such doesn't change the historical facts, that PK has seen fit to "spin-doctor" in a public relations fax what Ryle was openly emphasizing earlier in this decade.

We are obviously asking James Ryle and Promise Keepers to face up to, and respond with an exemplary display of integrity whatever the cost, to what James Ryle was actually saying and writing in 1990 on this Beatles "anointing" issue. No more lies, no more spin-doctoring, no more straw men – we want the truth; the Ambassadors of PK, and those the Ambassadors are currently funneling misinformation to, deserve the truth and nothing but the truth.

In the meantime, and even if Promise Keepers was to actually repent and begin to behave with integrity on this matter, the take-home message of this whole incident has got to be something like this: PK is more than willing to play fast and loose with the truth, even to the point of equipping their own Ambassadors with false information, in order to cover the errors of their leadership who are guilty of misleading Christians with their false doctrines and false prophecies.

ADDENDUM: (*Transcribed Text & Documentation*)

RYLE, "Sons of Thunder", Harvest Conference, 11/90:

Psalm 68:18 says, "When you ascended on high, you led captivity captive, and you gave gifts to men, even to the rebellious, that God may dwell in our midst." The Lord spoke to me and said, "What you saw in the Beatles – the gifting and that sound that they had – was from me. It did not belong to them, it belonged to me. And it was my purpose to bring forth through music a world-wide revival that would usher in the move of my spirit in bringing men and women to Christ."

And I want to tell you those four lads, the fab four, they aborted something. They took what did not belong to them and used it in a way that it was not intended by God to be used. It did bring a revival of music – but it brought it on the other side of the fence if you know what I'm sayin'. And the Lord spoke to me and He said, "In 1970 I lifted that anointing off of them. And it has been held in my hand ever since." And the Lord said, "The reason you saw it in the equipment room of that church is because that anointing belongs to the church." It is part of our equipment. It doesn't belong to the world. It belongs to the Lord Jesus.

And the Lord said, "Now I'm looking for those who I can place that anointing back upon. And as surely as I place it upon 'em, they will come forth with a sound that is distinctive, that will turn heads of men and women and capture their hearts."

And in response to me asking, "What's it doing here?", suddenly the Lord stood me in the midst of a church and he showed me the woman who was the church herself standing in the midst of the world singing under the anointing of the Holy Spirit in a simple but powerful word, "In the name of Jesus Christ the Lord we say unto you: Be saved!"

RYLE, "Sons of Thunder", *The Morning Star Prophetic Newsletter*, Vol 1, No. 4. (Winter 1991), pp. 23-29.:

Here's the provocative thing that the Lord said that day as I prayed and sought for an understanding on this dream- the Lord said that he had called those "four lads from Liverpool" to himself. There was a call from God on their lives, they were gifted by his hand, and it was He who anointed them. The Lord had a purpose for them and it was to usher in the charismatic renewal with musical revival around the world. But He said that the four lads from Liverpool went AWOL and did not serve in his army. They served their own purposes and gave the gift to the other side. In a sense, the Beatles were like the first man, Adam, who was called to rule the earth but fell to rebellion and rejected his call. But the purpose of God will be fulfilled through "the last Adam," Christ. The purpose of God in bringing forth a music that helps to prepare for the coming harvest will likewise be fulfilled by others.

RYLE, *Charisma* magazine, 2/94, p. 14:

Lest I be mistaken for commending The Beatles, let me quickly add that their spiritual, moral and social failures disqualified them from having any message for us other than, "Don't do what we did." Yet despite their shortcomings, no one can doubt that John, Paul, George and Ringo were greatly gifted by God. It is clear, however, that they did not honor God with their gifts and therein lies the reason for their downfall.

CHAVIS, "The Grant Connection" radio program, 1/11/96:

One great unfounded rumor is that he [Ryle] taught and teaches the Beatles were sent by God and their music was anointed by God. Interesting rumor but not based on much in the way of fact. The message he taught at that time was about the gift of music and how God gifts man with creativity. Whether that gift is used for the Lord or not makes a big difference and the Beatles are one example of a group that was incredibly creative and talented yet their gift wasn't used for the Lord's purposes. And what a disappointment that was to the Lord. What a shame it was, that their gift wasn't used for the Lord's purposes. That particular message has blessed many, many musicians and brought many, many musicians with questions about their own faith into the family of God and that's the kind of fruit from that particular message. But it comes out as James Ryle said, "The Beatles were anointed by God." It's not true.

PK FAX, mid-1996: JAMES RYLE'S COMMENTS ON THE BEATLES:

Promise Keepers would like to provide some background of the context in which Pastor Ryle's comments about the Beatles were made.

In 1990, Pastor Ryle spoke at a conference and gave a message entitled, "The Sons of Thunder" containing three main points: 1). God wants the entire world to be evangelized (John 3:16); 2). God wants us to become all things to all men that by all means men might be saved (1 Cor. 9:22); 3). God provides gifts to all of us through which we can reach out to the lost. Pastor Ryle went on to elaborate on the third point, stating that all gifts are a blessing from God—doctors are gifted with healing, teachers with the ability to communicate information, judges with wisdom, and musicians with music, etc.

Pastor Ryle's message focused on the power of the gift of music. He stated that music is a universal language and it speaks to the heart of men like no other medium. All musicians have received the gift of music from God, whether they are

Christians or not. Pastor Ryle used the Beatles as a stellar example of the power of music. These musicians influenced an entire generation and people followed them into drugs, sex and eastern mysticism. Pastor Ryle asked his audience to imagine the tremendous influence that the Beatles could have had if they had been Christians; if they had used their gift to glorify God and to impact His kingdom. In fact, this message has led numerous musicians (including some prominent secular names) to write to Pastor Ryle saying things like, "at last I know why I was born with the gift of music."

In his reference to the Beatles' gift of music, Ryle referred to that gift as an "anointing", indicating only that the gift was from God. Pastor Ryle regrets that his comment was misunderstood by believers who thought that he was endorsing the message and lifestyle of the Beatles. He only intended to convey his understanding of the power of music and that it is a gift from God. Pastor Ryle did not mean to imply that he believed that the Beatles were used by God, only that their gift was from God and it could have been used for the glory of God.

Appendix B

August 15, 1995

AN OPEN LETTER TO BILL McCARTNEY

From: Pastor Bill Randles
Believers in Grace Fellowship Church
3336 Prairie Drive NE
Cedar Rapids, IA 52402

Dear Mr. McCartney:

My name is Bill Randles and I am the pastor of Believers in Grace Fellowship Church that I founded in 1982. I am writing to express certain reservations and concerns I have about Promise Keepers. The reason this is an open letter is because there are probably thousands of other pastors who have similar reservations. You know this also because you referred to this at a meeting in Detroit on April 29, 1995. In fact, I have listened to that message carefully, and heard you make some very emphatic statements about the reluctance on the part of pastors to ally themselves with Promise Keepers. You actually went so far as to say that any clergyman who isn't planning to go to your February 1996 Pastors Gathering in Atlanta "needs to be able to tell us why he doesn't want to go."

Mr. McCartney, this is my response to your brotherly challenge. I agree that I need to tell you what my reservations and concerns about P.K. actually are. First of all, however, in the interest of clarity, let me transcribe for you that portion of your speech which promoted the writing of this letter. You said in Detroit:

> "We have a great army that we are assembling. They're the Christian men of this nation. However, our leadership, our clergy are not uniform. Our clergy are divided. Division is many visions. There's no unity of command...there is tremendous division in our clergy. We have to assume that responsibility. We have to say, 'Are we impacting our clergy in a way that's going to take them and make them all that they have to be in order to lead this army because the shepherds are the ones God's chosen to lead us out of here.' We are not to go out of here and lead ourselves. We're to go out of here and to go back to our bodies, our church bodies, and be led by our shepherd. God has hand-picked them. He's gifted them, He's trained them, He's invested in them, He's nurtured them...
>
> "Now, I think many of you are in touch with the fact that we're having a pastor's gathering in Atlanta on February 12th, 13th and 14th. This gathering in Atlanta should exceed 100,000 clergymen. Why? Because we have many more than that, and every single one of them ought to be there. We can't have anybody pass up that meeting. If a guy says that he doesn't want to go, he needs to be able to tell us why he doesn't want to go. 'Why wouldn't you want to be a part of what God wants to do with His hand-picked leaders?' We need to understand that our clergymen, many of them, are reluctant to go. Many of you come from churches and your clergymen have never been to a Promise Keepers gathering because they're keeping a distance from us. You need to go back and tell them: Promise Keepers wants to come along side you and be everything you need by encouraging [your] men and giving resources.
>
> "Now listen to me, men. February 12th, 13th and 14th to me is not a coincidence that it comes over Valentines Day. I think we're going to have another St. Valentine's Day massacre. I think Almighty God is going to rip open

the hearts of our leaders. I think He's going to tear them open. And I think He's going to put them back together again as one. One leadership. We've got to have one leadership, one leadership only." (Promise Keepers, Detroit Silver Dome, April 29, 1995)

ONE LEADERSHIP

Mr. McCartney, my response to that is a simple question. What do you mean when you call for the clergy to become one leadership? In fact, minutes after, you made another statement about the things that we could do "if we are in control, if we come together, if our unity of command responds." You said we can accomplish things like "pay off the national debt, and feed the poor...we can dissolve gangs,...and be an impact in the inner city."

These kinds of statements underscore my initial reservations. I am very cautious when the call is made for "One Leadership" and "Unity of Command". On the other hand, I am troubled by this because in actual reality, the church already is under one leadership. Jesus Christ is Himself the Head of the Church! If you and I each submit to His headship through obedience to His Word, we are already in unity and don't need to manufacture it. Evidently what you are calling for is one [human] leadership and one unity of [human] command. Mr. McCartney there already is an organization claiming that kind of leadership and command: The Roman Catholic Church under the headship of the Pope. Because of this "One human leadership and command," almost a billion people are locked in spiritual bondage.

The call for clergy to become one leadership and unity of command reminds me of the shepherding movement in the 1970's and 80's, which sprang out of the Word of God charismatic community in Ann Arbor, Michigan, and was nurtured by the Fort Lauderdale five: Bob Mumford, Derek Prince, Don Bashum, Charles Simpson and Ernie Baxter. You mention in *Ashes to Glory*, that you enjoyed fellowship with the Word of God Community. Have you perhaps been influenced by that particular vision of church government?

I have a threefold problem with humanly centralized church leadership, and unity of command: (1) it has to be a man-made unity; and it denies the reality of the unity of the Spirit that all Christians currently partake of; (2) another problem I have is that it concentrates a tremendous amount of influence into the hands of well-meaning but sinful men; (3) finally, where there is a centralized, carnally unified command, it makes it easier for deception and manipulation of the Church of Satan. Look at the dark ages under the Papacy! I am glad that the church doesn't have that kind of unity today (yet). Ours is a spiritual unity based on devotion to Jesus, not a political unity based on "Shepherding" principles. The way things are now, Satan has to deceive the Christians one church at a time, but under a "unified command", all he has to do is deceive the leadership.

ECUMENISM

Mr. McCartney, a second but closely related concern I have is with the ecumenical unity promoted by P.K. Of course, I believe in the true ecumenism: the communion of the saints everywhere on earth, based on the truth of the Gospel. But I am extremely wary of the "unity-at-the-expense-of-truth" movement. People are being encouraged to de-emphasize doctrines so they can come together as though doctrine is a meaningless detail. What is doctrine, but the body of truth entrusted to the saints once and for all?

Doctrine divides because truth divides. There are many denominational barriers that should be kept in place. The basis for unity of the faith (truth), a faith which has a content and makes specific demands of people. Any other basis for unity, such as maleness, politics, social concerns, etc., will only prove to be a house built on sand.

Mr. McCartney, do you believe the following statement made by the Pope? "On this universal level, if victory comes, it will be brought by Mary. Christ will conquer through her, because He wants the church's victories, now and in the future, to be linked to her" (From *Crossing the Threshold of Hope* by 'His Holiness' John Paul II). How am I to find common ground with anyone who believes this way? Scripture commands us not to fellowship or even wish Godspeed to those who deny the doctrine of Christ. Another example would be this statement from the 1994 Catechism of the Catholic Church, page 128, section 460:

> "The Word became flesh to make us partakers of the divine nature...For the Son of God became man so that we might become God. The only begotten Son of God, wanting to make us sharers in His divinity, assumed our nature so that He, made man, might make men Gods."

Mr. McCartney, we are to refute such heresies! How am I to find spiritual unity with people who worship Mary or believe they will become gods? While I can find all sorts of commonality on the basis of being a human being, or the desire that a man be a better father, husband, have integrity, purity, etc., I would hardly mistake those things for Christian Revival. If P.K. is supposed to be a great move of God, doesn't truth and discernment count for anything? What is to stop the Mormons or the Jehovah's Witnesses from starting P.K. chapters in their denominations? Why not? They can make identical promises.

JAY GARY AND THE STAR OF 2000

Mr. McCartney, is Promise Keepers going to be used to mobilize worldwide support for a bimillenial celebration of Jesus' 2000th birthday and Jubilee? The reason I ask is because of the favorable review in the July/August 1995 *New Man* Magazine (the official P.K. magazine) of Jay Gary's book, *The Star of 2000*. Gary's self-published book advocates such celebration.

Are you aware, Mr. McCartney, that in a recent Spiritual Counterfeits Project article entitled, "Sign of the Times: Evangelicals and New Agers Together", Mr. Gary is the subject of much concern. Our particular concern is his recent association with ex-secretary general of the U.N. and well-known New Age author, Robert Muller, who wrote *New Genesis: Shaping a Global Spirituality*. This book amounts to a call to all religions to find common ground and work together for a one world religion.

This S.C.P. article, which I am enclosing should sober anyone who is taking Mr. Gary and his plans for a bimillenial birth celebration for Jesus seriously. The article states that Gary invited Robert Muller to be key adviser for his B.E.G.I.N. (Bimillenial Global Interactive Network). In Gary's book, *The Star 2000*, he recommends a book by Muller called First Lady of the World in which Muller attempts to detail suggestions on how the UN should prepare for the bimillenial celebration. In a March/April 1992 publication of Gary's *Bimillenial Research Report*, another of Muller's books, *The Birth of a Global Civilization*, is recommended. Gary describes it as an "inspiring look at an emerging global system, including new global human rights, global networking, global core curriculum and global celebrations culminating in the year 2000." Just a paragraph at the end of this recommended book will give you an idea where Muller comes from:

> "And God saw that all nations of the earth, black and white, poor and rich, from North and South, from East and West and of all creeds were sending their emissaries to a tall glass house on the shores of the river of the rising sun on the island of Manhattan, to study together, to think together, and to care for the world and all its people. And God said that is good. And *it was the first day of the New Age of the earth"* (Robert Muller, The Birth of a Global Civilization, p. 134).

Mr. McCartney, all I have to go by is what P.K. actually says or promotes. As far as I know, when *New Man*, the official voice of P.K. promotes Jay Gary, they probably agree with him. Again I ask, is P.K. going to be used to mobilize world wide support for a bimellenial celebration of Jesus' Birthday in the year 2000, a celebration already contaminated by the New Age movement?

ROBERT HICKS' MASCULINE JOURNEY

I would like to know why, Mr. McCartney, when you had 50,000 turned on, pumped up spiritually hungry men, of all the books you could have chosen to offer for spiritual growth you chose *The Masculine Journey* by Robert Hicks? It is my understanding that 50,000 of these books were distributed at Boulder in 1993. The book actually has the P.K. imprimatur on it. Do you honestly subscribe to Hicks' concept of the Phallic male? Doesn't it bother you that Hicks quotes New Age authors Sam Keen and Robert Bly without any warning? Hicks sets off his chapter entitled "The Phallic Male" with a quote from Keen's New Age bestseller *Fire in the Belly*. The quote is, "The lions are the place of judgment" (p.47).

Are you trying yet to implement Hicks' statement on page 51? "We are called to worship God as phallic kinds of guys, not as some sort of androgynous, neutered non-males, or the feminized males so popular in many feminist enlightened churches. We are told by God to worship Him in accordance to what we are—phallic men."

This is growth for men? When did the apostles even remotely encourage anything like this? I could give you countless other examples of this kind out of Hicks' book, but I don't need to.

What were you thinking this book would offer when you promoted it? Was there some particular emphasis in this book that you thought would help men spiritually? Maybe you see the need for initiation rites as Hicks advocates in his accompanying workbook under the section, "Exploring the Issues with other Men":

> "Our culture has presented many initiation rites or passages to manhood that are associated with the phallus. Which ones have you experienced? Do you have a story to share with other men about one such event?"

Do you lament, as Hicks does, that the church doesn't offer any alternative initiation rites, such as circumcision? In his *Masculine Journey* which P.K. promotes, Hicks teaches us that somehow or the other we should celebrate the different passages of a young man's life—such as his first drunk or sexual experience (p. 177): "I'm sure many would balk at my thought of celebrating the experience of sin. I'm not sure how we could do it. But I do know we need to do it. For example, we usually give the teenagers in our churches such a massive dose of condemnation regarding their first experiences with sin that I sometimes wonder how any of them recover. Maybe we could take a different approach. Instead of jumping all over them when they have their first experience with sex or drugs, we could look upon this as a teachable moment and a rite of passage. Is this putting a benediction on sin? Of course not, but perhaps at this point, the true elders could come forward and confess their own adolescent sins and congratulate the next generation for being human. Then they could move on to all the important issues of forgiveness and restoration, but this time on common ground, with the young person as a fellow sinner!"

Mr. McCartney, do you believe in this kind of celebration? If not, why promote it? At the end of the *Masculine Journey* there's a P.K. promotion that states, "P.K. wants to provide men's materials (like this book)." And you wonder why pastors are reluctant to let you "help them"?

JAMES RYLE AND THE VINEYARD

Frankly, Mr. McCartney, another huge reservation that I am having with P.K. is the fact that James Ryle, a man who claims that God told him the Beatles were anointed to bring forth a worldwide revival and "usher in my (God's) spirit," is your pastor and mentor. According to Ryle, it wasn't until 1970 that God removed his anointing from them. (Sgt. Pepper's Lonely Hearts Club Band was anointed by God? 1970 was the year The Beatles broke up!) I am leery of a 'prophet' who discerns the demonic as anointed.

Let's face it; although P.K. is rapidly growing and attracting an increasingly diverse portion of the Church, it is primarily led by Vineyardites. The "Prophet" Ryle is on the Board of Directors, Randy Phillips is the President and you go to Ryle's church (you told us to explain why I won't attend the Saint

Valentine's Day Massacre). I need to tell you I have a great reservation about the Vineyard movement. Your Pastor and mentor is one example, with his unscriptural prophecies. It is not my intention to paint every Vineyard church with a broad brush. I believe there are, no doubt, many fine Christians in the movement that want nothing more than fulfillment of the Great Commission. But we have to remember that it was the Vineyard movement who by and large promoted the Kansas City prophets and kept them in circulation to this day. The mystical "Toronto Blessing" is primarily a Vineyard pheno-menon although there are many Vineyard congregations who do not claim it. What makes P.K. different from the other Vineyard ventures? Mr. McCartney, do you believe in the validity of this "Laughing Revival"? Can a fountain bring forth both sweet and bitter water?

WHY NOT MEN OF DISCERNMENT?

I applaud your many charges for men to become "men of integrity," family men, "men of purity" and so forth, but I notice that there isn't much of a call for men to be men of discernment. If you truly want to know where many of us pastors are coming from, I'll tell you. A lot of us don't see the lack of physical unity, nor lack of social action, nor lack of signs and wonders, as the true challenge of the last days church. According to II Thessalonians 2, the ultimate issue facing us is "will we love the truth, more than the lie, in the face of a false 'revival' of lying signs and wonders?" This is why many of us are seeing truth as the ultimate issue, not tolerance.

Of course, I love all Catholics, Mormons and Jehovah's Witnesses.

All of these "name the name of Jesus!" But almost all of them worship a different Jesus. I can't claim most of the above as brothers in Christ. If a Mormon keeps all seven of your promises, that could well make him a moral person, but that moral Mormon will go right to Hell. Why? Because in spite of his morality, unity, good father skills, marital fidelity, he is still doomed because he doesn't believe the testimony

God gave of His Son.

What I'm saying is this: What a person believes shouldn't be downplayed as insignificant. We should rather preach the Word of God without compromise, no matter how much it divides.

SEEMS LIKE BROADWAY
"Broad is the road that leads to destruction."

Finally Mr. McCartney, I am wary of P.K. because it seems to be such a broad, inclusive way; Catholics, Mormons, and even homosexuals are encouraged to be "included and welcomed in all our events." There are common denominators that anyone can stress that almost every human being can admit to. But when the true God-ordained organization, the Church, upholds the Word of God, it divides people either onto the broad way that leads to destruction or the narrow way that leads to life. A telltale sign that there is something wrong is the press being given to Promise Keepers by the worldly media. Why is the world promoting your organization when Jesus said the world would hate us as it hated Him? God has an organization already, the Church of the Living God, the pillar and ground of the truth, and the world rejects it. God's work is not based on being male or female, Jew nor Greek, bond nor free. Whosoever will, may come.

May the Lord inspire a healthy dialogue on the subject.

Pastor Bill Randles

P.S. Thank you, Mr. McCartney, for speaking out for the unborn!

Appendix C

PROMISE KEEPERS UPDATE

MORMONS, CATHOLICS LAUD MEN'S MOVEMENT

MEDIA SPOTLIGHT
Biblical Analysis of Religious and Secular Media
Volume 16, No. 1

by Albert James Dager

Since our initial report on Promise Keepers some significant events have transpired which have borne out some of our concerns. This is especially true in the area of ecumenism.

Due to Promise Keepers' non-committal stance on doctrine, there is a growing acceptance of Promise Keepers among Roman Catholic and Mormon leaders, at least in the Los Angeles area. Christian Van Liefde, pastor of St. Hilary Catholic Church in Pico Rivera, California, is quoted in the Saturday, May 6 Los Angeles *Times* extolling the virtues of Promise Keepers:

> Promise Keepers places a very strong emphasis on returning to your own church congregation or parish and becoming an active laymen.[1]

According to Liefde, Cardinal Roger M. Mahony, Archbishop of Los Angeles, urged him to determine whether Promise Keepers programs would be appropriate for Catholic parishes. One parish—St. John Eudes in Chatsworth, California—has held a Promise Keepers seminar featuring Roman Catholic priests as speakers.

The official newspaper for the Los Angeles Archdiocese, *The Tidings*, dedicated a full-page article in its March 31 issue endorsing Promise Keepers, and encouraging Catholic men to attend the past May 5 and 6 conference at the Los Angeles Coliseum. Mike Nelson, staff writer for *The Tidings*, states:

> Promise Keepers is a basic program of evangelization for men of faith, begun among more fundamentalist and evangelical Christian communities, but now being expanded to include Catholic congregations.[2]

Van Liefde is quoted in the *Tidings* article as well:

> There is no attempt at proselytizing or drawing men away from their faith to another church. The primary message of the weekend is turning your life over to Jesus Christ and standing tall as a man of faith.[3]

Van Liefde is optimistic that Promise Keepers can grow at the parish level without adversely impacting existing parish programs or finances.

> "Rather, the opposite is true," he asserts. "One of the primary promises of the program is to return to one's local church and become a force for good in the local community. Another is the commitment in financial support of one's local church. The men are challenged to give generously of their time, treasure and talent to their local church."[4]

> Nelson points out that Promise Keepers is making local parish presentations in addition to its large-scale conferences held in various cities. Among those in the Catholic community endorsing Promise Keepers is Captain Steve Ruda of the Los Angeles Fire Department, a former seminarian and parishioner at St. John Eudes Church. Ruda attended the

Promise Keepers conference in Anaheim, California, in 1994, and claims that it was an event that changed his life. "I believe that the men of America are looking for answers, and they are looking toward Jesus to provide them," says Ruda. "And at this weekend, something happened there of great importance – 54,000 men gathered to lift up their voices in a spirit of unity and began to glorify God."[5]

After the conference, Ruda brought Promise Keepers into his Catholic community, and conducted a Promise Keepers seminar for 100 men with presentations by local priests.

In a letter to Ruda dated July 14, 1994, Cardinal Mahony stated that he was impressed with Promise Keepers at the 1994 Anaheim seminar. Says Mahony:

> I would be very interested to know how the Archdiocese of Los Angeles and I could be of assistance in the fuller promotion of Promise Keepers, and how we might be able to work closely together to encourage this deeper level of discipleship for our Catholic men throughout the Archdiocese.

> I would be open to any suggestions that you, Father Joe Shea, or Father Chris Van Leifde might have on moving forward with an expansion of the Promise Keeper concept among our Catholic men. It seems to me that there are many options available to us, and I would surely be interested in exploring these with all of you.

Mahoney continues:

> This seems to me to be a wonderful way to prepare for the Third Millennium of Christianity which begins in the year 2000.

The Catholic charismatic magazine, *New Covenant,* featured Promise Keepers on the front cover of its April 1995, edition. In his article, "Bands of Brothers," writer Bob Harvey cites Promise Keepers as a hope for bringing men back into the churches. He rightly points out that Promise Keepers is a backlash against the feminist influences in our society, and focuses on male bonding as a means to restore men's identities as members of a warrior class.

There is an issue involved here that I believe escapes most people both for and against involvement with Promise Keepers. It centers on the fact that Promise Keepers founder, Bill McCartney is an ex-Roman Catholic.

There seem to be emerging within non-Catholic Christian circles a number of ex-Catholics who relate a fondness for their former church. Throughout my Christian experience, those ex-Catholics I've encountered have been vociferously anti-Catholic. Not in the sense of hating Catholics, but in their rejection of the institution itself as a valid expression of the true Faith. While maintaining that Catholics may have a faith which is largely hindered by the unbiblical teachings of their church, yet love the Lord, most ex-Catholics offer no such grace to the hierarchy. Many Roman Catholics do not necessarily believe all the doctrines of their church; many do not understand the implication of those doctrines.

Knowing Roman Catholic doctrine, and the political machinations of the Vatican, we ex-Catholics are understandably suspicious of someone who would leave Roman Catholicism, which is extremely possessive of its members, and still seek unity with its hierarchy.

We are also suspicious of any Roman Catholic prelate who endorses a movement founded by an ex-Catholic. To the Roman Catholic hierarchy, those who leave their church are considered anathema—eternally damned, without hope unless they return in contrition to "Holy Mother Church." They are, in fact, excommunicated and fellowship with them is forbidden.

Knowing these things, we are not out of line to ask what's going on with McCartney, the Archbishop of Los Angeles, and the Promise Keepers' ecumenical stance. The Roman Catholic counter-reformation attempt exceeds in secrecy even the expertise of the CIA. Is it possible that there is a fifth column among us? Vatican II has stated that all Roman Catholic involvement in ecumenism must be for the benefit of the Catholic Church. It seems reasonable to assume that there are men posing as ex-Catholics to convince non-Catholics that the devil behind the mask of Roman Catholic piety is really the Holy Spirit encouraging "Christian unity."

My question to them is, "If Roman Catholicism is acceptable to you, why did you leave it and risk eternal damnation? Or did you ever really leave it?"

Mormon Endorsement

As is the Catholic Church, the Church of Jesus Christ of Latter-day Saints is just beginning to become aware of the potential of Promise Keepers to enhance their church's outreach to its men. Because of Promise Keepers' ecumenical, interdenominational approach, Mormon leaders of the Palos Verdes, California, Stake (group of congregations) are urging members to participate in Promise Keepers. The Los Angeles *Times* quotes Mormon stake president Chip Rawlings:

> "The movement's 'Seven Promises' are like something straight out of the men's priesthood manual for the church," states Mormon attorney Chip Rawlings, who indicated that several Mormon leaders would be attending the Los Angeles Promise Keepers convention.[6]

Promise Keepers, while claiming to lead men to Christ at their conferences, preaches a non-doctrinal gospel—one which finds acceptance even among Mormon leaders, whose theology and Christology are aberrant, and Roman Catholic clergy, who, while espousing belief in salvation by grace alone, insist that true salvation rests in the sacraments of the Church.

In our analyses of Promise Keepers study guides and other materials we have found the organization to be largely non-committal in affirming the tenets of the Faith. Emphasis is placed upon the person of Jesus, but the question arises, "Which Jesus?" Evidently it may be a Jesus with whom the Mormons identify: Satan's brother, the product of the Father's physical intercourse with Mary—a man who attained godhood as did His Father.

Or it may be the Jesus of the papacy—God incarnate whose sacrifice on the cross was insufficient to pay the full penalty for our sins, necessitating the Church's intervention through the sacraments. Most notably the sacraments of the mass and penance as well as time spent in Purgatory are essential elements of the Roman Catholic Church's salvation. (See our special report, "Six Roman Catholic Doctrines that Nullify Salvation by Grace.")

God's flock is being devoured by this wolf of ecumenical deception, and the hireling shepherds are leading them to the slaughter. These shepherds refuse correction from those who attempt to point out their error. Especially for those who are unschooled in the mechanics of seminary training.

They can run circles around us with their theological discourses and milk-quality teachings that never really go beyond the basics of the Faith. But they haven't the discernment to recognize error and deception even when pointed out to them by the "common folk" who suffer from seeing their beloved pastors succumb to the mob mentality.

In spite of the loose attitudes toward sound doctrine, Promise Keepers continues to grow by leaps and bounds, thanks in large part to naïve pastors who believe that a few hours in a stadium can impart some spiritual life into the men under their care. Desperate for men who don't present too many problems to have to deal with, many pastors are looking to Promise Keepers to provide the "discipling" environment that the pastors and elders of the local churches are unable or unwilling to provide themselves. They take little thought of the adverse effects of lending credibility to those among the eclectic mix of speakers for Promise Keepers.

While there are some good speakers at the conferences, there are several who are not worthy of attention by godly men. But, as I stated in our special report on Promise Keepers, the conference messages focus primarily on the seven promises of a Promise Keeper in a cursory manner. The true objective of the conference is to recruit Promise Keepers Ambassadors and Point Men. These men are needed to take the Promise Keepers agenda and teachings into the churches—any churches. Dale Schlafer, Vice President of Pastoral Ministries for Promise Keepers, bears this out in the April 1995 *Men of Action* magazine:

A Promise Keepers conference is simply a piece to a much larger puzzle of building men's ministry in your church. It is designed to be a catalytic event. Men will become excited by their relationship with Jesus Christ; some will accept Jesus Christ as their Savior, while others will want to get involved in their church or begin meeting as a small men's group. You can facilitate this process by thinking ahead and having a plan in place following a conference.[7]

This agenda does not center on true biblical discipleship of the men, but rather psychology-based, male-bonding encounter groups.

The effectiveness of Promise Keepers in meeting that objective is nothing short of amazing. Glowing reports abound of how Promise Keepers men are more committed to their families and to their churches as a result of their involvement in the conferences.

Based on the testimonies of wives as to the changed attitudes of their husbands after becoming involved with Promise Keepers, more and more men are being encouraged by their wives and friends to get involved. Those who decline or waver are looked at askance. Yet one thing is certain: they will not be built up in sound doctrine. And the long-term results of their involvement in the small men's group encounter sessions will not be apparent for awhile.

No one can argue that men should not be strong leaders at home and in their churches. But are they becoming stronger leaders or are they becoming more compliant mates and members? And in which direction are they leading if, in fact, they are leading at all?

No doubt there are some genuine conversions involved. Some men may be taking a stronger leadership role in their marriage and/or in their church. Sometimes that results in happier wives and pastors. Sometimes it results in less happy wives and pastors.

Many women want their men to be strong leaders provided they lead in the direction that their wives want to go. Glowing reports of wives in response to Gary Smalley's male-emasculating teachings abound. That they want husbands who think and act more like women (i.e., more "in touch with their feelings") reveals that those wives don't really want strong male leadership. They want husbands who are compliant with their wife's "needs."

Many pastors want their men to be strong leaders provided they lead in the direction the pastor wants them to go. They rejoice in Promise Keepers founder Bill McCartney's insistence that we need our pastors to rightly divide the Word of Truth for us because we can't do it ourselves.

It takes a strong commitment to God's Word to lead in the direction God wants to go. Often that direction is contrary to that of wives or pastors.

It is highly unlikely that an organization that waffles on doctrinal integrity will inspire men to truly be men of God. Strength of leadership honors God only when it is in compliance with God's written Word. To ignore doctrinal integrity nullifies any other claims to integrity. And that is eventually borne out by the actions of those Promise Keepers who are less than honest in their attacks against their detractors.

SOME PERSONAL EXPERIENCES

The repercussions to our Promise Keepers report have come in waves. Many of our readers have written or called to express thanks for putting in their hands the information that they needed to inform their pastors who want to get involved with Promise Keepers.

My personal experience with some pastors would be frustrating were it not for the realization that my responsibility ends at warning them; they must undertake to do what is right according to God's Word.

The Reformers were divisive—over sound doctrine. And, yes, we are divisive—over sound doctrine

Those with whom we have faced off think we are deficient in our hermeneutics, our exegesis and our logic because we don't see things their way. They see nothing wrong with integrating psychological theory into their Sunday school teaching or pulpit ministry. Nor do they think that the issues we've raised over Promise Keepers are of any great concern.

One pastor informed me that I had erred in my assertion that Promise Keepers promotes heresy through Robert Hicks' writings, one of which is used as a study guide in their small men's groups. Given the task of checking out our Promise Keepers report for his church, he called Doug Engburg, the Washington state director for Promise Keepers, and asked him about Hicks' *The Masculine Journey.* He was told that Promise Keepers just grew so fast that they couldn't keep up with everything, and it was just a mistake that they endorsed the book. On that basis, the pastor felt that the other issues weren't of any great concern and he recommended that the church promote Promise Keepers.

I informed him that I had a copy of a seven-page letter from Promise Keepers defending their use of Hicks' book. I also reminded him that Promise Keepers didn't make a mistake; they co-published the book with the Navigators and gave away over 50,000 copies to the men who attended the Boulder conference in 1993, and they still continue to sell the book.

Because he didn't trust me, he wrote to Promise Keepers himself. Now, he has found out that I was right all along. But to this date he's still behind his church's involvement.

It was my understanding that the reason he initially decided it was okay to go with Promise Keepers was that I was wrong in my assertion that *The Masculine Journey* is used extensively by Promise Keepers. Evidently I was wrong; his decision was already made and nothing I could say was going to change his mind.

I have repeatedly asked people why they would want to give credibility to men they don't agree with; why they would encourage the men in their church to become involved in an obviously ecumenical endeavor; why they would promote something that is so doctrinally unsound. The results have not been dissimilar to those I encountered when I was approached by a Moonie several years ago. When I confronted him with the truth of the Gospel I could literally see a glaze come over his eyes; not wishing to be proven wrong he remained entrenched in his error. I have found this same glaze come over pastors' eyes when I ask them point-blank about why they would lend credibility to Promise Keepers in spite of all the problems which they *agree* exist.

The answer some give is that they will only encourage the men to attend the conference at the stadium, but they won't bring Promise Keepers into the church.

Okay. But what will happen when their men hear some false teacher who sounds good at the conference, and then buy his books or tapes, based on the trust in their pastor who sent them to listen to him?

What will happen when the men come back all charged up and, as point men, ask the pastor to implement the Promise Keepers program in the church? Will the pastor tell them, "Well, I don't agree with Promise Keepers, so I don't think we should do that"? If he does, he'll get hit with, "Well, if you don't agree with them, why did you promote them in our church?"

No amount of waffling on this will convince the men that the pastor may not be so trustworthy after all, regardless of whether or not they approve of Promise Keepers themselves.

A Radio Response

On May 11, I was interviewed for the radio program, *Issues, Etc.*, hosted by Chuck Spomer on KFUO radio in St. Louis, Missouri. The subject was Promise Keepers. In the last twenty minutes of the one-hour format Chuck opened the lines to callers. All of the callers took exception with my position. One woman was distressed that I would question this wonderful movement that is bringing men closer to God and to each other. Seeing that I was getting nowhere with her on the specific issues of ecumenism, psychology, and unbiblical teachings, I asked her, "How would you feel if you knew your husband was sharing his most intimate secrets regarding your relationship with him?"

She didn't think Promise Keepers would promote such a thing, and insisted that I was off base.

I told her that they do indeed promote such a thing, and I asked again how she would feel about it. She weakly said, "Well, if it's with one other man."

To this I responded, "No, with a whole group." She still

wouldn't believe that Promise Keepers would do this. I explained that Promise Keepers is not a biblical discipleship program, but a male-bonding encounter group, and that they do encourage men to share their most intimate sexual secrets and fantasies with one another.

I don't think I was able to convince her of this, and I didn't have my copy of the study guide for *The Masculine Journey* on hand, having loaned it to someone else. So I'll offer a few things from the study guide here that I didn't have room for in our original report.

One method of breaking the ice in the men's group is to play a game called "People Bingo." In this game the men review categories pertaining to certain trait and experiences, and mark a box that contains those elements. They go from man to man asking about those traits and experiences. The first person to complete five in a row in any direction within a set time wins. The traits and experiences are based upon Robert Hicks' book, *The Masculine Journey*, and many center on the men's sexuality. I call it spiritual voyeurism.

Some of the questions regarding traits and experiences ask if they have been arrested at least once; if they are wearing boxer shorts or bikini briefs; if they were neglected or abused by their father; if they have emotional battle scars from a recent family feud; if they have had a circumcision, vasectomy or prostate operation.

In the chapter dealing with the phallic male, the group leader is told how to get the men to open up about their deepest sexual experiences including their sexual fantasies:

> **Note to the leader:** If the men in your group are likely to have difficulty talking vulnerably and emphatically with each other about their sex lives, then stop and talk about why you are having that difficulty.[8]

One question designed to get the men to open up is found under the section, "Exploring the Issues with Other Men:"

> 3. Our culture has presented many initiation rites, or passages to manhood, that are associated with the phallus. Which ones have you experienced? Do you have a story to

share with other men about one such event?

☐ When I was potty trained and stopped wetting the bed.

☐ Pubic hair and growth

☐ An unfortunate experience with pornography

☐ My first dating experience

☐ My first really embarrassing moment with a girl

☐ The wedding night

☐ Conceiving my first child

☐ Other:[9]

How many wives who are supportive of Promise Keepers would really want their husbands to answer some of these questions, especially pertaining to the conception of their first child or their wedding night?

The manual asks what creative alternatives to these might the church offer as a rite of passage. Further on it suggests that the children's sins might be celebrated as rites of passage in the following manner:

> Instead of jumping all over teenagers when they have their first experience with the police, alcohol, sex, or drugs, we could look on this as a teachable moment and a rite of passage. Perhaps the true elders could come forward and confess their own adolescent sins, and congratulate the next generation for being human. Then they could move on to the all-important issues of forgiveness and restoration, but on common ground with the young person, as a fellow sinner![10]

What does Scripture say?

But fornication, and all uncleanness, or covetousness, let it not be once named among you, as becometh saints;

Neither filthiness, nor foolish talking, nor jesting, which are not convenient: but rather giving of thanks.

For this ye know, that no whoremonger, nor unclean

person, nor covetous man, who is an idolater, hath any inheritance in the kingdom of Christ and of God.

Let no man deceive you with vain words: for because of these things cometh the wrath of God upon the children of disobedience.

Be not ye therefore partakers with them.

For ye were sometimes darkness, but now are ye light in the Lord: walk as children of light:

(For the fruit of the Spirit is in all goodness and righteousness and truth;) proving what is acceptable unto the Lord.

And have no fellowship with the unfruitful works of darkness, but rather reprove them.

For it is a shame even to speak of those things which are done of them in secret.

But all things that are reproved are made manifest by the light: for whatsoever doth make manifest is light.

Wherefore he saith, Awake thou that sleepest, and arise from the dead, and Christ shall give thee light.

See then that ye walk circumspectly, not as fools, but as wise,

Redeeming the time, because the days are evil. (Ephesians 5:3-16)

Promise Keepers begs the question by stating in response to this Scripture:

The key to understanding these passages lies in what he means by having these things "named."

Paul is encouraging the church of Ephesus to not let these sins be found in their lives. He is not placing a prohibition upon even talking or mentioning such sins, because he himself does so on numerous occasions...Paul, it seems, wrote about these subjects so that the church would have proper insight on what it means to live as Christians.[11]

This is only half true. Yes, Paul spoke of these sins as things to be avoided in practice. But he did not sanction speaking of them as a means to male-bonding. Further, he certainly didn't suggest that we should dwell on these things and indiscriminately share them in groups. If a man is having difficulty in avoiding sexual sin or any sin, he should seek ministry from his elders, not from a group of the guys.

Also, where in Scripture are we ever told to "celebrate" our sins as a rite passage? Or to congratulate someone for being human (i.e., sinful)? For the elders to get suckered into this would only denigrate them in the eyes of the youth; it would further justify the young men's sins in their own eyes.

Naïve pastors who think Promise Keepers is going to somehow enhance their standing in the eyes of their congregants might be interested in the following psychological mumbo jumbo:

> 11. For men to survive their wounding, they need to feel safety among fellow sufferers. How can you improve the dynamics in groups of men so that men would feel that safety and start sharing their pain?
>
> ☐ Have the pastor model his own woundedness from the pulpit.
>
> ☐ Have other men in power ("bully pulpits") share their heart wounds.
>
> ☐ Create a Christian fellowship of soldiers, athletes, or businessmen whose ticket for admission is the admission of wounds (as in "AA").
>
> ☐ Sponsor more AA-type recovery groups for the man in the pew.
>
> ☐ Create "Purple Heart Awards" for broken spirits, not just war wounds.
>
> ☐ Other:[12]

Okay, pastor, get up there and open yourself up to your congregation; tell us all about your woundedness—especially the times your wife rejected your sexual advances, or your father abused you, or share with us your innermost struggle with sexual sin.

These guys are playing with some dangerous stuff here. This is group therapy with no holds barred. And this is just the tip of the iceberg. Space doesn't allow for the full gamut of unbiblical and ungodly psychological manipulation at the hands of amateur therapists who think they want to lead these men's groups.

You think women can be gossips? We've already heard about how men are gossiping about the things they hear in these groups.

The marriage bed is sacred; it isn't up to men to share with other men in a group therapy session the intimacies of their relationship with their wives. Nor are we to dwell on past hurts and learn to feel our pain and the pain of others all over again.

Brethren, I count not myself to have apprehended: but this one thing I do, forgetting those things which are behind, and reaching forth unto those things which are before,

I press toward the mark for the prize of the high calling of God in Christ Jesus.

Let us therefore, as many as be perfect, be thus minded: and if in any thing ye be otherwise minded, God shall reveal even this unto you.

Nevertheless, whereto we have already attained, let us walk by the same rule, let us mind the same thing.

Brethren, be followers together of me, and mark them which walk so as ye have us for an example.

(For many walk, of whom I have told you often, and now tell you even weeping, that they are the enemies of the cross of Christ:

Whose end is destruction, whose God is their belly, and whose glory is in their shame, who mind earthly things.)

For our conversation is in heaven; from whence also we look for the Savior, the Lord Jesus Christ:

> *Who shall change our vile body, that it may be fashioned
> like unto His glorious body, according to the working whereby
> He is able even to subdue all things unto Himself. (Philippians
> 3:13-21)*

Promise Keepers, while claiming to be an instrument to
draw men closer to Jesus Christ, is in reality minding earthly
things. Their god may not be their belly, but it certainly appears
to be their loins.

Did I Lie?

In April of this year I received a phone call from Dr.
Martin Bobgan, whose booklet, *Promise Keepers &
PsychoHeresy*, is among the materials we offer. He wanted
me to know that he had received a letter from a lady in Canada
who was concerned about a report she had received from a
pastor in the States. This pastor's parents, who attend her
church, stated that I admitted to this pastor that I had lied in
my report on Promise Keepers. Dr. Bobgan wanted to know
how he should respond to her.

I suggested that if she would arrange a three-way conference
call between herself, this pastor and myself, I would be happy
to have him explain in my presence just where I had admitted
to him that I had lied in my report.

After hearing from Dr. Bobgan she called me personally
to express some concern about the pastor who is involved in
Promise Keepers. It seems she asked his parents to query him
on the exact nature of my lies and to report back to her after
their trip to see him. When they returned and she asked them
about it, they did not wish to discuss it. She wanted me to
know that, as far as she was concerned, his claim was unfounded.

That such a case would arise is somewhat ludicrous when
one thinks about it. Having spoken about Promise Keepers
with many people over the past few months, I can't recall
who this pastor may be. But his claim that I admitted to him
of having lied in my report on Promise Keepers is false.

So much for that Promise Keeper being a man of integrity.

Taken To Task In The Media

Another instance involves L.J. Popovich, Pastor of Rapid City Church of the Nazarene and head of the local chapter of Promise Keepers International. In a letter to the Rapid City *Journal* on Saturday, April 22, Pastor Popovich took me to task, as well as John Beardsley, who had written a critique on Promise Keepers in the April 8 *Journal*. He accused us of publishing distortions and half-truths, and lacking Christian clarity and tolerance toward those with whom we disagree.

This is the standard lament of our detractors. Because we insist upon purity of doctrine as a criterion for fellowship we are labeled as bigots and full of hate.

Popovich implies that I am a racist because I "find fault in McCartney's commitment to embracing all ethnic groups into the Promise Keepers movement." He disagrees with my statement that "We should not embrace a man because he is of the same or different race, but because he is of the same belief." He states, "if you don't believe exactly as Dager or Beardsley, they apparently want nothing to do with you!"

This is not true, or course. I was speaking of embracing others as brethren in Christ, not as friends or acquaintances. And our brethren need not believe exactly as we do; but serious departures from biblical truth preclude fellowship.

We are also accused of not wanting men to become better fathers, husbands and disciples of Jesus:

It is hard to conceive that anyone would have a problem with Christian men striving to become better disciples of Jesus, better fathers and better husbands. Apparently Beardsley and Dager do!

I wouldn't even make that claim against Hitler. No one has a problem with these things (I'm speaking in hyperbole; Hitler may have). But evidently Popovich can't read past his own biases. Our 16-page report dissected the seven promises and demonstrated how, while little can be argued against them as stated, in practice they are not met by Promise Keepers in the biblical sense.

As do so many, Popovich cites the phenomenal growth of

Promise Keepers to argue that "Promise Keepers is the best hope for a Holy Ghost revival in America."

It amazes me how some people will claim the Holy Spirit's blessings upon movements that disregard sound doctrine. Unable to defend their ecumenical and unscriptural position, they resort to playing the numbers game. We hear constantly how many hundreds of thousands of men are in Promise Keepers. But if we want numbers let's look at Islam, Buddhism or even Roman Catholicism. This is an appeal to the arm of flesh, not to the Spirit of God.

The Navigator's Position

Many choose to focus on the things that unify rather than the things that separate. One of our readers sent our Promise Keepers report, among other things, to Terry Taylor, president of the Navigators, asking how he could justify publishing *The Masculine Journey* and Bob Beltz's *Daily Disciplines for the Christian Man.* He also asked how the Navigators could feature Renovaré's Richard Foster at their August 2-6, 1995 Family Conference. In his response Taylor states:

> By the way, what I don't see prominently stated in the publication you sent me is a clear acknowledgment of the overwhelming positive influence Promise Keepers is having on men in our society—a society in which marriage and fatherhood have never been in deeper trouble. That oversight is disturbing. The positives far outweigh the negatives in what is truly a remarkable work of God in our time.

Why should we dwell on the so-called positive aspects of a movement that is fast-becoming an idol in itself? Promise Keepers' P.R. work is excellent; they don't need our endorsement. Their literature is full of self-congratulatory remarks. Besides, our focus isn't on the benefits to society, but rather on the detriment to the Body of Christ that the Promise Keepers' ecumenical fervor poses. Those who reject the Word of God in favor of ecumenical emotionalism are as good as dead themselves.

CONCLUSION

These experiences convince me all the more that we are involved in a great spiritual deception. There is occurring a great separation of the true brethren from out of the establishment churches. More and more people are writing and calling us asking where they can find strong biblical fellowship. Their churches are steeped in psychological prattle and ecumenical fervor; people are falling under the spell of strange, mystical behavior that runs contrary to sound doctrine and practice.

While there are some fine pastors who truly desire to adhere to God's Word without admixture of human wisdom (as has been attested to by those from whom we hear), the vast majority today seem to be caught up in the deception. As products of seminaries and Bible schools that require psychology courses, their world view has been tainted, and they don't realize it. As a result, their flocks are wandering without proper direction. Confusion is reigning in the churches as it did in Israel when the Lord came to earth.

But when he saw the multitudes, he was moved with compassion on them, because they fainted, and were scattered abroad, as sheep having no shepherd.
(Matthew 9:36)

Those complacent shepherds that do not watch out for the Lord's people, but rather, in the name of unity or out of love for man's wisdom, lead them in the way of spiritual error, should take heed to God's Word:

Son of man, prophesy against the shepherds of Israel, prophesy, and say unto them, Thus saith the Lord GOD unto the shepherds; Woe be to the shepherds of Israel that do feed themselves! Should not the shepherds feed the flocks?

Ye eat the fat and ye clothe you with the wool, ye kill them that are fed: but ye feed not the flock.

The diseased have ye not strengthened, neither have ye

healed that which was sick, neither have ye bound up that which was broken, neither have ye brought again that which was driven away, neither have ye sought that which was lost; but with force and with cruelty have ye ruled them.

And they were scattered, because there is no shepherd: and they became meat to all the beasts of the field, when they were scattered.

My sheep wandered through all the mountains, and upon every high hill: yea, my flock was scattered upon all the face of the earth, and none did search or seek after them.

Therefore, ye shepherds, hear the word of the LORD;

As I live, saith the Lord GOD, surely because my flock became a prey, and my flock became meat to every beast of the field, because there was no shepherd, neither did my shepherds search for my flock, but the shepherds fed themselves, and fed not my flock;

Therefore, O ye shepherds, hear the word of the LORD;

Thus saith the Lord GOD; Behold, I am against the shepherds; and I will require my flock at their hand, and cause them to cease from feeding the flock; neither shall the shepherds feed themselves any more; for I will deliver my flock from their mouth, that they may not be meat for them. (Ezekiel 34:2-10)

Because so many pastors are willing to overlook doctrine for the perceived benefit of a male bonding ministry in their churches, they are being confronted by those who recognize the spirit of Esau who sold his birthright for a mess of pottage. He didn't wish to suffer what it would take to remain true to his calling; he took the quick and easy way out.

Those who will not take that route refuse to compromise their birthright as sons of God; Scripture is the sole authority in their lives. As a result, Promise Keepers is developing into an issue of divisiveness.

But brethren, take heart. These things must come to pass. And worse things yet:

> These things have I spoken unto you, that ye should not be offended.
>
> They shall put you out of the synagogues: yea, the time cometh, that whosoever killeth you will think that he doeth God service.
>
> *And these things will they do unto you, because they have not known the Father, nor me.* (John 16:1-3)

Religious men believe in their hearts that they are standing for the truth; they are not always conscious of their error. They even hold sound doctrine themselves, as did the Pharisees whom Paul pitted against the Sadducees in Acts 23. They will teach sound doctrine from the pulpit and insist upon sound practices in the church. But they will compromise that doctrine if the popular movement of the day suggests that fellowship may be extended beyond sound doctrine. They will, in fact, persecute to one degree or another those who insist upon purity of doctrine in relation to fellowship. That, in itself, is false doctrine as testified to in Romans 16:17-18.

> *Now I beseech you, brethren, mark them which cause divisions and offences contrary to the doctrine which ye have learned; and avoid them.*
>
> *For they that are such serve not our Lord Jesus Christ, but their own belly; and by good words and fair speeches deceive the hearts of the simple.* (Romans 16:17-18)

Interestingly, it is we who are accused of being divisive. Yet we are the ones insisting on having nothing to do with those whose doctrine is not sound. Notice that Paul tells us not to have anything to do with those who cause division and offenses contrary to the doctrine which we have learned from him (God's Word).

Promise Keepers, headed by Vineyard adherents, is worming its way into thousands of churches in the same manner the

Vineyard movement does: offering seminars and help to the local churches, while maintaining an agenda of influencing those churches with their philosophy. This will result in many splits, as has happened with those churches that succumbed to the Vineyard deception. Those pastors who resist will be dismissed. Those pastors who go along with the program will cause many members who see the deception either to leave or be disfellowshipped. Over what? Insistence upon sound doctrine and practice? No, upon the basis that they won't get with the program—the Promise Keepers program. And it will be those who resist the deception who will be accused of being divisive. One need only ask the question, however, "Which side is insisting on sound doctrine as a basis for fellowship?"

Answer that question honestly, and you will know which direction to take.

I can see the "Jesus" of Promise Keepers: There he is, standing on the mountainside, exhorting his listeners:

"I want you all to go back to your homes, your synagogues, your pagan temples, and don't forget Pilate's Praetorium! I want you to take leadership roles in all those arenas and proclaim to your hearers that you are men of integrity who have learned how to be sensitive and in touch with your feelings! But be careful not to judge others on what they believe. If they practice sin, remind them that they can escape it if they just follow my example. This should especially be your sensitive approach to homosexuals; remind them that I was tempted with homosexuality myself, but I managed to abstain."

This is not the genuine Jesus, of course; it is the "Jesus" of the Promise Keepers. It isn't so hard these days for those who refuse to separate Jesus from His Word (sound doctrine) to identify with Paul's lament:

Would to God ye could bear with me a little in my folly: and indeed bear with me.

For I am jealous over you with godly jealousy: for I have espoused you to one husband, that I may present you as a chaste virgin to Christ.

But I fear, lest by any means, as the serpent beguiled Eve through his subtlety, so your minds should be corrupted from the simplicity that is in Christ.

For if he that cometh preacheth another Jesus, whom we have not preached, or if ye receive another spirit, which ye have not received, or another gospel, which ye have not accepted, ye might well bear with him. (II Corinthians 11:1-4)

Those who do not accept just any "Jesus" are rebuked with sentiments similar to that stated by Pastor Popovich: "They need to get on board or get out of the way!"

Let's see...

Isn't that what the Pope said about the Reformers?

NOTES

1 John Dart, "Promise Keepers, a Message to L.A. Men" Los Angeles Times, May 6, 1995, p. B4.

2 Mike Nelson, "Promise Keepers' Promises Spiritual Renewal for Men," The Tidings, March 31, 1995, p. 3.

3 Ibid.

4 Ibid.

5 Ibid.

6 John Dart, op.cit.

7 Dale Schlafer, "Clergy: Think Strategically!" Men of Action, (Promise Keepers, April, 1995), p. 11

8 Robert Hicks with Dietrich Gruen, Study Guide, The Masculine Journey (Colorado Springs: NavPress Publishing Group, 1993), p. 32

9 Ibid., p. 33.

10 Ibid., p. 81

11 Pete Richardson, Promise Keepers letter to Al Dager, April 7, 1995, p. 6.

12 Hicks, op. Cit., pp. 57-58.

Appendix D

PROMISE KEEPERS STATEMENT
on
The Masculine Journey

Letter to
Al Dager of Media Spotlight
from
Promise Keepers Pete Richardson
April 7, 1995

Thank you for voicing your concerns to Promise Keepers regarding the book *The Masculine Journey*, by Dr. Robert Hicks. Since April, several other individuals have also expressed concern about this book, as well as Promise Keepers endorsement and distribution of the book at Promise Keepers '93 and in our resource listings.

We are committed to honor Jesus Christ in responding to concerns of this nature. We desire to facilitate true biblical unity in the body of Christ, not the division that results from unnecessary and dishonoring debate. With this posture of heart, we have compiled the questions about *The Masculine Journey* and our responses.

1. Who is Promise Keepers, and why did you endorse the book *The Masculine Journey?*

Our Purpose Statement: Promise Keepers is a Christ-centered ministry dedicated to uniting men through vital relationships to become godly influences in their world.

Our Statement of Faith:

1. We believe that there is one God, eternally existing in three persons: the Father, the Son, and the Holy Spirit.
2. We believe that the Bible is God's written revelation to man, and that it is verbally inspired, authoritative, and without error in the original manuscripts.
3. We believe in the deity of Jesus Christ, His virgin birth, sinless life, miracles, death on the cross to provide for our redemption, bodily resurrection, and ascension into heaven, present ministry of intercession for us, and His return to earth in power and glory.
4. We believe in the personality and deity of the Holy Spirit, that He performs the miracle of the new birth in an unbeliever and indwells believers, enabling them to live a godly life.
5. We believe that man was created in the image of God, but because of sin, was alienated from God. That alienation can be removed only by accepting through faith God's gift of salvation which was made possible by Christ's death.

The following Seven Promises encapsulate our values as a ministry and raise the standard for what it means to be a godly man.

1. A Promise Keeper is committed to honor Jesus Christ through worship, prayer, and obedience to God's Word in the power of the Holy Spirit.
2. A Promise Keeper is committed to pursue vital relationships with a few other men, understanding that he needs brothers to help him keep his promises.
3. A Promise Keeper is committed to practice spiritual, moral, ethical, and sexual purity.
4. A Promise Keeper is committed to build strong marriages and families through love, protection, and biblical values.
5. A Promise Keeper is committed to support the mission of his church by honoring and praying for his pastor and by actively giving his time and resources.
6. A Promise Keeper is committed to reach beyond any

racial and denominational barriers to demonstrate the power of biblical unity.

7. A Promise Keeper is committed to influence his world, being obedient to the Great Commandment (Mark 12:30-31) and the Great Commission (Matthew 28:19-20).

We believe that Christian growth starts by making some promises—promises we intend to keep. The Seven Promises are not stated to enforce a new list of commandments. Rather, they are meant to guide us toward the life of Christ, so that He might transform us from the inside out.

We understand that this kind of change is a process, and that we need the grace and strength of the Holy Spirit. Only then will we be in the process of becoming more like His Son, Jesus Christ, and be godly influences in our relationships and world.

Promise Keepers desires to lead men into God's Word and to lift Jesus Christ up as our model through the resources that we develop or sponsor. In 1992, Dr. Hick's manuscript for *The Masculine Journey* was presented to NavPress and Promise Keepers as a candidate for inclusion in the(sic) our line of books. What we discovered was a biblically-centered, frank and honest account of a man's journey with God. We were convinced that it would help men pursue Jesus Christ amidst the challenges of the twentieth century.

The book was not designed, nor was it written, to be an inclusive statement of the values and distinctives of the ministry of Promise Keepers. We endorsed it because we believed that it would be a book that challenged men to grow in Christlikeness, to become *zaken*—or "wise men of God"—as Hicks writes.

Since then, we have received reports from men who, after studying the book, were relieved to discover that all men go through similar struggles. In other words, by understanding the biblical words that describe the growth process of a godly man, men are experiencing less isolation and a new and more intimate relationship with Jesus Christ and their brothers in the Lord.

Dr. Hicks is certainly qualified to write about men's issues. He is a Professor of Pastoral Theology at the Seminary of the East in Dresher, Pennsylvania. He serves as Senior Chaplain for a fighter group in the Air National Guard, holding a rank of Lieutenant Colonel. He is the author of numerous books including the critically acclaimed *Uneasy Manhood* (Nelson, 1990). He holds the Th. M and D. Min. degrees from Dallas Theological Seminary where he has served as Assistant Professor of Christian Education.

Through his ministry to men, he is known as a compassionate listener and biblical counselor. He is the founder of a professional Christian counseling center and through his own family counseling practice has personally ministered to the needs of hundreds of men, women, and families. In brief, he is an able helper of men, a man whose passion is to live for Christ and honor God's Word.

2. Why did Dr. Hicks choose the six Hebrew words for man to describe the male journey? Isn't he just superimposing psychological categories on the Bible?

It is logical to return to the language in which the Old Testament was originally written to find the natural meanings for the word *man* as it appears in the Bible. Some have commented that there are a few more words in Hebrew that are used for *man*, but Dr. Hicks' research shows that those terms are not "common to all men." For example, the Hebrew word *rosh* means "chief," and refers to a male, but not all men are or will be "chiefs." Dr. Hicks chose to emphasize the six Hebrew terms that do have potential universal application to men.

If these common Hebrew terms for men happen to correspond to something that a non-Christian writer or psychologist has written, this alignment does not condemn the biblical terms or their application for men today. For example, Dr. Hicks referred to Levinson's chart to show that many thinkers in our culture are thinking hard about the stages of life. Levinson happened to be the first to articulate these different seasons for a male adult. But the stages that *Dr. Hicks* discusses are qualitatively different from Levinson because they are rooted in the God-inspired vocabulary of the Bible.

Robert Hicks consistently refers to the poor attempts of leaders in the secular men's movement to find a definition of manhood, leaders like Robert Bly and Sam Keen. He states, "...the Jungian definition of manhood doesn't work for me," and he writes about the differentiation and individualization that employs much of psychotherapy today. Dr. Hicks is clearly choosing God's Word to describe maleness.

3. **Is Promise Keepers becoming a "psycho spiritual" movement? After all, along with Dr. Hicks and his book, don't other psychologists like Dr. James Dobson, Gary Smalley, Dr. Gary Oliver and Dr. John Trent speak at your conferences?**

We in the body of Christ believe that any association with psychology will taint a person's spiritual life. For example, in an April issue of *The Berean Call*, the author attacked *The Masculine Journey* and Promise Keepers over what he calls the "psycho spiritual" approach. The leadership of Promise Keepers is committed to listen to criticisms of this nature and to prayerfully take them to heart. As mentioned under question one, we desire to provide Christ-centered, biblically-rooted principles and resources for men.

The spiritual life is centered around the transformation of the human soul from darkness to light. Only the Holy Spirit can lead a human soul to Jesus Christ, bringing him or her out of darkness and into light (Colossians 1:13-14). The Greek word in Scripture for the word "soul" is *psuche* from which we derive the term "psyche" and from which derives "the study of the human soul" and the behaviors that result, i.e., "psychology."

Promise Keepers believe that the psychologist who does not allow the Word of God to govern and direct his/her studies and conclusions is misdirected and deceived. The goal of every follower of Jesus Christ, as the Apostle Paul states, is to "consider everything a loss compared to the surpassing greatness of knowing Christ Jesus my Lord" (Philippians 3:8), not to validate every aspect of theology or psychology. Promise Keepers is committed to unite men based upon what we have in common—our love for Jesus Christ and our rebirth by the Spirit of God.

Dr. Dallas Willard has written:

> There is a deep longing among Christians and non-Christians alike for the personal purity and power to live as our hearts tell us we should. What we need is a deeper insight into our practical relationship with God in redemption. We need an understanding that can guide us into constant interaction with the Kingdom of God as a real part of our daily lives, an *ongoing spiritual presence* that is at the same time a *psychological reality*. In other words, we must develop a psychologically sound theology of the spiritual life and of its disciplines to guide us. (*The Spirit of Disciplines*, p. 34)

"The Sermon on the Mount," says Oswald Chambers, "is not a set of principles to be obeyed apart from identification with Christ. The Sermon on the Mount is a statement of the life we live when the Holy Spirit is getting his way with us" (*The Psychology of Redemption*, p. 34). John Calvin, the great Reformer, in writing his famous compendium of theology, *The Institutes of the Christian Religion*, began the very first page with these words: "In order to know God, one must know himself. In order to know himself, one must know God. I'm not sure which comes first." Historically, many of the great protestant and evangelical theologians did not ignore the value of biblically-grounded conclusions regarding the study of the human soul, or psychology.

Certainly, there is a great deal of commendable and understandable concern in the body of Christ over the issue of how and where psychology fits in the Christian life. Some very clear humanistic ideas not only conflict with Christian values, but flatly contradict biblical teaching. But those are not the values nor the teachings that we find in the writings of Dr. Hicks, Dr. James Dobson, Gary Smalley, Dr. John Trent, and Dr. Gary Oliver. Nor do we find it in the teachings of the founder of Promise Keepers, Bill McCartney. All these men seek to understand the human soul and the behaviors that are born out of the human soul from a biblical perspective. Their ultimate goal is to help others follow Jesus Christ in a way that glorifies God. It is not their desire, nor the desire of Promise Keepers, to ever make the Bible subservient to psychology.

A recent review in *The Calvary Baptist Theological Journal* had this to say about *The Masculine Journey*: "Unlike other books on practical Christian living which this researcher has read, Hicks' book does not presuppose principles founded in the world of business or sports or politics as its basis of content and structure ... Perhaps the factor that struck me the most about the book is its biblical basis both for structure and for content."

Something is wrong here. Perhaps the book reviewed by *The Berean Call* and the book reviewed by *The Calvary Baptist Theological Journal* are different books. Or perhaps one reviewer is reading carefully to find something wrong. Or perhaps there is a third option: that is, that the problem is in the way that the book is read. Simply stated, the problem may be this: Looking for prescriptions where the author is simply being descriptive. The reviewer in *The Calvary Baptist Theological Journal* writes: "Hicks contends that 'Manhood is reflected differently throughout the adult life cycle. There exist certain predictable eras in the male life cycle' (p. 19). His aim in detailing these six stages is not to be prescriptive but descriptive; this is not the only way to look at the male journey but is one way of looking at the masculine journey

(p. 20)." We believe that this reviewer has correctly identified the problem.

4. **In places in *The Masculine Journey*, Dr. Hicks quotes favorably from certain secular psychologists and in other places he clearly disagrees with these same writers. Isn't he being inconsistent? Worse yet, isn't it an accommodation to liberal thinking and a sell-out to man's so-called wisdom?**

This issue really has to do with one's theology and how one conceives truth. Evangelical scholar Francis Schaeffer said that when the Marxist says the system is corrupt, we should agree with him on the basis of our biblical and personal experience; when he says, we should destroy the system with guns, we disagree on the basis of the revealed truth of God. In other words, when even our non-Christian enemies may speak the truth (however they got it), we should agree with them because we know it to be true on the basis of Scripture. When they speak falsehood, the only way we know it is false is again on the basis of Scripture. This seems to be the long-standing way of viewing truth for evangelicals and the way proper theology has always been done. John Calvin often quotes Augustine (who in turn quotes Greek philosophers Plato and Aristotle), sometimes agreeing with him, sometimes disagreeing. The basis for agreement or disagreement is always the same – Scripture.

Even with the Scripture itself, the Apostle Paul quotes pagan poets (Acts 17:28) and a Cretan poet (Titus 1:12). Certainly, Paul was not accommodating pagan thinking by quoting these writers. He quoted them because they agreed with the point of revealed truth he was trying to make. If this methodology is found both within the Scripture and throughout the history of theology, then Dr. Hicks' approach in quoting relevant outside material (when they agree with the biblical point he is trying to make) is in keeping with serious evangelical scholarship.

5. Isn't Dr. Hicks too frank and graphic in his portrayal of the "Phallic Man" in Chapter 3? Doesn't the Bible ask us to be silent on such things?

This question is usually raised on the basis of Ephesians 4:29 and 5:3-4. These passages say, "Let no unwholesome word proceed from your mouth," and "do not let immorality or any impurity or greed even be named among you." It is important to understand the context of these specific verses and how sexual subjects are talked about in the Bible.

First, Paul is admonishing the Ephesian church to have all the conversation be such that it will build up in accordance with the needs of the moment and will give grace to those who hear it. The passage does not specify what builds up or tears down, but just establishes the principle of grace-oriented speech. In the second passage, he does get more specific. Here, Paul says, there are some things that should not be "named" among the believers in the church at Ephesus. He lists, "immorality, impurity, greed, filthiness, silly talk, and coarse jesting" (5:3-4). The key to understanding these passages lies in what he means by having these things "named."

Paul is encouraging the church of Ephesus to not let these sins be found in their lives. He is not placing a prohibition upon even talking or mentioning such sins, because he himself does so on numerous occasions (Romans 1:24-27; 1 Corinthians 5:1; 6:16-20; 7:1-5; 8:1-6; 2 Corinthians 7:1; 12:21; Galatians 5:19; Ephesians 4:19; Colossians 3:5; 1 Thessalonians 4:3-6; 1 Timothy 1:8-11, 5:11; 2 Timothy 2:22, 3:4). Paul, it seems, wrote about these subjects so that the church would have proper insight on what it means to live as Christians.

God also warned the nation of Israel about sexual sins (Exodus 20:14; Leviticus 15:2-18, 18:6-30; Proverbs 1-23; Song of Solomon; Ecclesiastes 2:8; Isaiah 3:1-10). In both prohibitions and instructions, God makes it very clear how men are to live sexually—a life-long devotion to the bride of their youth if they are married and sexual abstinence if they are not married.

Any deviation from a man's commitment and sexual faithfulness to his wife was punishable, sometimes by death. But God Himself names these perverted practices in order to provide instruction about how His people should live.

6. **Dr. Hicks has been quoted as saying that men should worship Jesus with their phallus. Isn't this a blasphemous statement? Why would someone associate Jesus with sexuality?**

This raises two issues. First, the nature of worship, and second, the issue of associating Jesus with sexuality. The idea of worshipping Jesus with one's sexuality grows out of Dr. Hicks' understanding of the nature of the book of Leviticus.

This Old Testament book is essentially a book about worship, or as Dr. Bruce Waltke has said, "To enjoy His (God's) fellowship, His people and priests must be holy in all particulars in contrast to their pagan neighbors" (*Zondervan Encyclopedia of the Bible*, p. 917). Since Israel's pagan neighbors had fused their religion with sexual practices, God makes it very clear to His people how they are to worship Him, even in the sexual area. As mentioned above, God seeks to regulate the worship of His people by establishing how they can worship Him as a clean vessel. Leviticus 15-18 gives very detailed explanations about how one can become cleansed from even normal sexual relations, let alone perverted ones. Many of the pagan and Canaanite sexual practices are prohibited. Thus, Dr. Hicks concludes, "every time he (the Hebrew) used his penis, he was making a spiritual statement about who he was (a circumcised Hebrew) and whom he worshipped (by keeping the commandments of his God) and why" (p. 52, parenthesis added). As a redeemed Hebrew, he was to glorify God even in his sexual practices.

This seems to be the argument in the New Testament as well. As Christians, we must regulate our sexual life according to the parameters given to us by God's Word (2 Corinthians 7:1). The rationale is that we are a redeemed people who must learn to honor Jesus in every area of our lives. Just as the Apostle Paul had much to say about regulating sexuality under the motivation of wanting to please Christ, we as Christian men must learn to honor Jesus Christ with our sexuality. We must choose either to honor the God-ordained institution of the marital bed (Hebrews 13:4), or worship a false god of sexuality by rejecting God's way and gravitating to other perverted sexual expressions (Romans 1:24-26; 1 Corinthians 6:15; and Matthew 19:9). We end up worshipping Almighty God if we pursue His way. We worship a false god if we don't.

The second issue is more difficult. Can Jesus be associated with sexuality? This leads to the long-standing discussion about the mystery of the two-natures of Christ. If Christ was *fully divine*, then He can have no personal association with evil or be tempted to sin (James 1:13). But if Christ is *equally human*, He must be human in every way, thus suffering the full range of human emotion, passion, and temptation (Hebrews 4:15). The doctrine of the full humanity of Christ is not a settled issue in evangelicalism. There is room for disagreement.

However, for Christ not to be fully sexual (capability alone) and to have normal sexual desires would make Christ not quite human and thus only *seem* to be human. Holding such a view would cause one to fall into the ancient heresy of docetism, which diminished the full humanity of Christ. Dr. Hicks merely asserts his understanding of the full humanity of Christ (without sin!) which qualifies Jesus to be our high priest (Hebrews 4:15).

Without this understanding, one falls into the tendency of Platonic and Gnostic thinking, whereby Christ's human nature is divided into parts: Christ was tempted in certain areas, but not others. It's important to understand that Scripture does not teach that temptation is sinful. It's how a man *responds* to the temptation that determines whether he sins or not. Once a man yields to an evil desire, he has transgressed from temptation to sin (James 1:13-15).

Consequently, Scripture is clear that sexual desire itself is not sinful but amoral, since God ordained it before sin entered the world (Genesis 1:28). However, when a man sexually desires a woman other than his own wife, Scripture also clearly calls this adultery (as in Matthew 5:27). Therefore, it is not improper or unbiblical to associate Jesus with sexuality. As our high priest in heaven, He may have been *tempted* sexually, but He never *sinned* sexually. We can be assured that the magnitude of His temptation was far beyond anything that we can comprehend and much more powerful. This knowledge helps us realize that Jesus understands the intensity of our struggle with temptation, even sexual temptation; and He offers us hope because He overcame all temptation to sin.

In a recent poll by the National Center for Fathering, 33% of Christian men polled reported looking regularly at sexually oriented material which would include videos and magazines, and 74% stated that their sexual thoughts are a concern to them. Yet only 32% have someone who can hold them accountable for their sexual thoughts and behaviors. What are these men telling us?

They are telling us that Christian men are struggling with sexual sin in their lives. We understand that historically and in our day and age it is all too easy to worship the false god of sexuality. Our sexuality, and specifically the act of sex, is very important to God! Why? Because He wants us to live our lives so "That in all things God may be glorified through Jesus Christ" (1 Peter 4:11). We praise God that his only Son, Jesus Christ, is our hope and salvation and that through Him we can live a sexually pure life that brings honor to God.

At Promise Keepers we recognize that our responsibility is great when we endorse any resource. We also realize that by endorsing a resource not fully created by Promise Keepers, the resource will not communicate a comprehensive definition of the ministry. In conclusion, we feel that *The Masculine Journey* is a valid resource for men to grow in Christ, but it does not encompass all of the values and distinctives of Promise Keepers.

Thank you again for your expression of concern for Promise Keepers. We appreciate the prayers and encouragement that we receive as a result of the great work God is accomplishing in men's hearts. May Jesus be lifted up!

Appendix E

Promise
K e e p e r s
Men of Integrity

Statement on *The Masculine Journey*
(For information contact:
Steve Chavis, Manager of Public Relations, 303-964-7759)

Promise Keepers no longer distributes the book *The Masculine Journey* by Robert Hicks, published in 1993 by NavPress. *The Masculine Journey* was distributed to the men who attended our 1993 conference in Boulder, CO and at one time was included in the Promise Keepers resource catalog.

The theological foundation for the ministry of Promise Keepers is found in our Statement of Faith. Our Mission Statement and "Seven Promises" serve as our guiding objectives.

# # #

Source: Promise Keepers Fax, May 10, 1996

Appendix F

Archdiocese of Los Angeles
Los Angeles, California 90015-1194

July 14, 1994

Mr. Steve Ruda
10001 Wilbur Ave.
Northridge, CA 91324

Dear Steve:

Thank you so very much for your letter of June 26, concerning the group called "Promise Keepers."

I was very impressed with the group at the meeting in Anaheim, and I am very intrigued by the whole concept. After all, it is the bringing of our discipleship with Jesus Christ into our daily lives that is at the very heart and soul of our spirituality.

It is obvious that the Promise Keepers have advanced this practical discipleship in a very substantial and affirming manner for men, and I commend all of you who are involved in this superb effort.

I would be very interested to know how the Archdiocese of Los Angeles and I could be of assistance in the fuller promotion of Promise Keepers, and how we might be able to work closely together to encourage this deeper level of discipleship for our Catholic men throughout the Archdiocese.

I would be open to any suggestions that you, Father Joe Shea, or Father Chris Van Liefde might have on moving forward with an expansion of the Promise Keeper concept among our Catholic men. It seems to me that there are many options available to us, and I would surely be interested in exploring those with all of you.

Thanking you for the witness of your own life of faith in Christ, and looking forward to pursuing this possibility even more fully, I am

Fraternally yours in Christ,

Cardinal Roger Mahony
Archbishop of Los Angeles

cc: Father Joseph Shea
    Father Christian Van Liefde

P.S. This seems to me to be a wonderful way to prepare for the Third Millennium of Christianity which begins in the year 2000.

Bibliography

Adams, Jay E. *A Call to Discernment: Distinguishing Truth from Error in Today's Church*. Eugene, OR: Harvest House, 1987.

de Semlyen, Michael. *All Roads Lead to Rome?* The Ecumenical Movement. Bucks, England: Dorchester House, 1993.

Hunt, Dave. *A Woman Rides The Beast*. Eugene, OR: Harvest House, 1994.

Hunt, Dave and McMahon, T.A. *The Seduction of Christianity*. Eugene, OR: Harvest House, 1986.

Lewis, C.S. *Mere Christianity*. New York: Macmillan, 1952.

MacArthur, John F., Jr. *Charismatic CHAOS*. Grand Rapids, MI: Zondervan, 1992.

MacArthur, John, Jr., *Our Sufficiency in Christ*. Dallas, TX: Word, 1991.

Matzat, Don. *Christ Esteem: Where the Search For Self-Esteem Ends*. Eugene, OR: Harvest House, 1990.

Matzat, Don. *Inner Healing: Deliverance or Deception?* Eugene, OR: Harvest House, 1987.

Randles, Bill. *Making War in the Heavenlies: A Different Look*. Cedar Rapids, IA

About the Author

Phil Arms, pastor of Houston Church, in Houston, Texas for over ten years, also leads a nationally known television and radio ministry.

Pastor Arms spent fifteen years as a Southern Baptist Evangelist preaching revivals, conferences and city-wide crusades across America before beginning his pastorate. He has spoken to hundreds of thousands of students on high school, middle school and college campuses addressing the moral, cultural and political issues of the day from a spiritual perspective.

In 1972, Phil Arms accepted Christ while on the streets of Houston. His search for fulfillment in the no-holds-barred lifestyles of the late '60's and early '70's left him empty and searching. Though the son of a Baptist preacher and in spite of being raised in a Christian home, Phil turned his back on his heritage and became disillusioned with "religion" while he was still a teenager. In college, his frustrations only increased and drove him to search for meaning in the social extremes of the day.

Finally, at twenty-three years of age, he knelt on a street and surrendered his life to Jesus Christ. The prodigal had returned. His search was over. He was compelled to begin immediately sharing this new reality and life-changing experience with others.

As God began to open doors and word of his conversion and his ability to communicate spread, invitations came to share his message.

The fast-paced growth of this new ministry and the blessings God was obviously manifesting upon it caused unusually rapid opportunities to come to Phil Arms. Within twenty months of his conversion, a new radio and television program were born under his direction which would soon span the nation and then the North American Continent. *Phil Arms Presents*, the weekly television program is now heard weekly in over twelve hundred cities and towns across the USA.

Phil is probably best known for his straightforward, no-nonsense approach in the presentation of an uncompromised message God has called him to deliver.

His knowledge on a wide range of topics, such as prophecy, political events in the Middle East, (where he has traveled on thirty-four occasions) and the cultural breakdown now occurring in America has made him a sought-after guest in the secular, as well as Christian media.

Phil has authored two books on the principles of living a victorious Christian life, *"Wet Flies Can't Fly"* and *"The Winner in You."* He co-authored a number of other books dealing with biblical prophecy, among them *"The Triumphant Return of Christ"* and *"Earth's Final Days."* Other nationally known authors who participated in these books with him include Dave Breese, Chuck Missler, John Wesley White and William T. James.

Suzanne, Phil's wife, is an accomplished pianist, soloist and author. She has recorded two albums and has authored the book *"Raising Children to Honor Christ."* Her deep love for and knowledge of the Word of God have blessed women at women's retreats and conferences for years.

Phil and Suzanne have been married for twenty-two years and have three children. They are Brittany, who is sixteen years of age, Lindsey, now twelve years old and Philip William, six years of age.

Phil Arms Ministries has a deep and abiding burden for those without Christ and longs for a sweeping revival in the Church of America. Every effort stemming from this ministry is initiated by that dual burden and a full knowledge that God's Truth, though desperately needed within and without the Church, is not always popular. Yet, the focus of this unique ministry continues to have as its goal the reaching of vast cross sections of this nation's populace with a clarion call for a return to the scriptural values and spiritual principles upon which this great nation was built.

Resources

For other resources available through this ministry, catalogues are available. To order, call 1-800-829-9673 or write: Phil Arms Ministries, PO Box 770, Alief, TX 77411.

Items of Interest

Videos or Audio

Prophecy, The Last Generation	12 Parts
Future Tense	4 Parts
Countdown to Meltdown	4 Parts
Promise Keepers	3 Parts
How To Be A Man Of God	4 Parts (Audio only)
A True Road To Recovery	8 Parts
How To Win Against The Odds	4 Parts (Audio only)
Building A Spiritual Hedge	3 Parts (Audio only)
Islam: What They Don't Want You To Know	4 Parts
The Nation Of Islam & Louis Farrakhan	1 Part (Video & Audio)

Books

Wet Flies Can't Fly by Phil Arms

The Winner In You by Phil Arms

The Triumphant Return of Christ co-authored by Phil Arms

Earth's Final Days co-authored by Phil Arms

Raising Children To Honor Christ by Suzanne Arms

By Our Friends

The Dorie Story - Video of Dorie Van Stone

Panorama of Creation - Book by Dr. Carl Baugh

New Age Cults and Religions - Book by Texe Marrs

The Battle: Creation vs Evolution - Video/Audio
   by Dr. Carl Baugh

The Real Jurassic Park - Video/Audio by Dr. Carl Baugh

Big Sister is Watching You - Book by Texe Marrs

A Palace For The Antichrist - Book by Dr. Joseph Chambers